PRESENTED TO:

_____

FROM:

_____

DATE:

_____

SIMPLE PURSUIT

A HEART AFTER JESUS

THOMAS NELSON
Since 1798

Published in Nashville, Tennessee, by Thomas Nelson. Thomas Nelson is a registered trademark of HarperCollins Christian Publishing, Inc.

Thomas Nelson titles may be purchased in bulk for educational, business, fund-raising, or sales promotional use. For information, please e-mail SpecialMarkets@ThomasNelson.com.

Unless otherwise noted, Scripture quotations are taken from the Holy Bible, New International Version®, NIV®. Copyright © 1973, 1978, 1984, 2011 by Biblica, Inc.® Used by permission of Zondervan. All rights reserved worldwide. www.zondervan.com. The "NIV" and "New International Version" are trademarks registered in the United States Patent and Trademark Office by Biblica, Inc.®

Scripture quotations marked ESV are taken from the ESV® Bible (The Holy Bible, English Standard Version®). Copyright © 2001 by Crossway, a publishing ministry of Good News Publishers. Used by permission. All rights reserved.

Scripture quotations marked HCSB are taken from the Holman Christian Standard Bible®. Copyright © 1999, 2000, 2002, 2003, 2009 by Holman Bible Publishers. Used by permission. HCSB® is a federally registered trademarks of Holman Bible Publishers.

Scripture quotations marked NASB are taken from the New American Standard Bible®. Copyright © 1960, 1962, 1963, 1968, 1971, 1972, 1973, 1975, 1977, 1995 by The Lockman Foundation. Used by permission. (www.Lockman.org)

Scriptures marked THE MESSAGE are taken from *The Message*. Copyright © by Eugene H. Peterson 1993, 1994, 1995, 1996, 2000, 2001, 2002. Used by permission of Tyndale House Publishers, Inc.

Scripture quotations marked NLT are taken from the *Holy Bible*, New Living Translation. © 1996, 2004, 2007, 2013 by Tyndale House Foundation. Used by permission of Tyndale House Publishers, Inc., Carol Stream, Illinois 60188. All rights reserved.

All uses of Isaiah 26:8 are paraphrased. Emphasis in scripture verses is added by the authors.

ISBN-13: 9780718087623

Printed in China

16 17 18 19 20 TIMS 6 5 4 3 2 1

CONTENTS

CONTENTS

INTRODUCTION

As we walked toward the open meadow, I was about to hyperventilate. I was trying to play it cool, yet I had been imagining this day for months. I was a twenty-one-year-old student at Georgia State University, an urban campus some 2,500 miles away from where I stood.

We had entered the national park mid-afternoon, made the drive up the mountain, and parked at Paradise Visitors Center, nine thousand feet below the summit of this giant in the Cascade Range.

I thought I knew what was coming.

Having meticulously studied this mountain in my GSU Geography 201 lab, I knew what to expect and was prepared to impress my traveling companion with my intricate knowledge of its shape, scope, and features. He had no idea he was traveling with an expert on Mount Rainier!

We started following a narrow trail through the trees, and soon the path opened to a field of blooming wildflowers skirted with a thin layer of snow. We stopped on a ridge above a precipitous drop, with only the split-rail fence separating us from a stunning view of the snow-draped volcanic cone that is the top of Mount Rainier.

Grateful for a rare, clear day, I thought I knew what was coming.

But what I saw was far more majestic than I could have dreamed, especially given that my study was based on squiggly-lined topographical maps, not high-definition reality. In a time before the personal computer (crazy, I know), I really didn't have a clue what Rainier even looked like.

Looking up, I was stunned.

Have you ever been there? No, not to Mount Rainer, per se, but have you ever become an expert about something or someone on paper, yet never seen it in real life?

I wasn't prepared for what happened next. As the grandeur of the mountain started to sink in, I couldn't contain the beauty. Within a moment, tears were streaming down my face, and though I tried to avert it, I started to sob.

Understand, this did not create the most comfortable moment for two young guys standing in a flowery meadow on a mountainside, especially given that my friend had no clue why I was so emotional.

I never gave my Rainier Expert speech that day.

The lesson from Mount Rainier became clear to me: *there's a huge difference between knowing a lot about something and truly knowing something.*

That night, staring up at the inside of a tent in Coos Bay, Oregon, I decided: I didn't want to spend my life just knowing *about* God, I wanted to *know Him.*

That moment of revelation and conviction changed the direction and complexion of my entire life. Today, the same invitation is extended to you.

The amazing thing about God (a self-sufficient, always-existing, in-need-of-nothing God) is that He wants to be known by you. He invites you to come, to explore, to taste, and to see.

And, incredibly, you can come as high up on the mountain as you wish.

This invitation is central to everything the Passion Movement is about. From the start, we have wanted to see a generation stand in awe of Jesus: to fall in love with the wonder and majesty of who He is. And we have sought to inspire them to reflect that glory to their world.

But how does this happen? It is the by-product of a daily pursuit of Jesus, a steady climb into the knowledge of God that ultimately impacts every dimension of our lives. Our heartbeat has been rooted in the confession of the prophet of old:

> Yes, LORD, walking in the way of your truth, we wait eagerly for you; for your name and your renown are the desire of our souls. (Isaiah 26:8)

Flowing out of this verse we shaped the 268 Declaration, five statements that describe what it looks like to walk out this proclamation as we seek to spread the fame of Jesus far and wide.

The world changes when we change. The nations will stand amazed at Jesus when we walk amazed by Him wherever our paths may take us. So allow your peers (the college-aged generation Passion has sought to serve) who have penned these daily entries to spur you on as you dive into His Word and come to know Him day by day.

He is waiting to be known by all who seek His face.

—LOUIE GIGLIO

268 DECLARATION

Yes, Lord, walking in the way of your truth, we wait eagerly for you; for your name and renown are the desire of our souls.
ISAIAH 26:8

During the early days of Passion, God connected our story to the confession found in Isaiah 26:8, specifically the last phrase that says, "for your name and renown are the desire of our souls."

The heart of Passion is God's glory, and God is most glorified in us when we live lives that are fully satisfied in Him. In an effort to flesh out this desire, the 268 Declaration was crafted around the following five statements and prayers:

1. **A PASSION TO KNOW GOD ABOVE ALL THINGS.** Because I was created by God and for His glory, I desire to make knowing and enjoying God the passionate pursuit of my life.

God, give me a desire to know You more.

2. **LOVE FOR THE LOCAL EXPRESSION OF HIS CHURCH.** Because Christ established the church for God's glory, I will invest the gifts He has given me in the life and mission of my local church.

God, give me a greater love for Your church, the body of Christ.

3. **UNITY AMONG BELIEVERS THAT AMPLIFIES HIS NAME.** Because God's fame is amplified when believers love each other, I will strive for unity among all Christians on my campus.

God, give me a desire to lift up Your name above all other names.

4. **A DESIRE TO SEE CHRIST CELEBRATED WHERE I LIVE.** Because many around me are separated from God, I will share the story of Jesus where I live.

God, cause my life to be an unmistakable source of grace and hope to those around me.

5. **WILLINGNESS TO SHINE THE GOSPEL TO ALL PEOPLE.** Because God is seeking worshipers of all peoples, I will spread His fame among the nations, fully participating in His global purposes and engaging poverty and injustice in Jesus' name.

God, kindle in me the desire to go anywhere, at any time, at any cost, to do anything to proclaim the gospel of Jesus Christ.

A PASSION TO KNOW GOD ABOVE ALL THINGS

Because I was created by God and for His glory, I desire to make knowing and enjoying God the passionate pursuit of my life.

I was a teenager when I first started to think about *knowing* God. I began my journey of faith a little earlier than that, and to be clear, I knew quite a few things *about* God. But in my teenage years I started to understand that it was possible to go beyond just knowing about God and actually *know* Him.

I think it started in the Psalms. I was fascinated by so much of the language in this songbook found right at the heart of the Bible. Sometimes the psalmist's angst shocked me—it felt so undiluted, raw, and real. But the thing that got my attention in these ancient songs was how these songwriters would talk about their hunger for God. They had such a passion to know Him:

> One thing I ask from the LORD,
>   this only do I seek:
> that I may dwell in the house of the LORD
>   all the days of my life,
> to gaze on the beauty of the LORD
>   and to seek him in his temple. (Psalm 27:4)

And then I came across the apostle Paul saying something so similar in his writings:

Yes, everything else is worthless when compared with the infinite value of knowing Christ Jesus my Lord. For his sake I have discarded everything else, counting it all as garbage, so that I could gain Christ. (Philippians 3:8 NLT)

These are such strong and compelling words. Paul is saying that there's nothing better in the whole of this life than to know Christ; next to that, everything else just seems dull and uninspiring. Over the years I began to realize that knowing Christ is the most privileged and powerful pursuit a soul can ever set out on in this life.

One of the best signs of how much someone really *knows* God is what level of reverence for Him they convey through their lives. Some claim to know God well, but when they speak about Him, they make Him out to be a tame, domesticated version of Himself. Yet when we truly draw near and *know* God, we will find Him to be more holy than we ever imagined—and more awesome than our hearts and souls can ever come to grips with. As we draw near to Him, our sense of His majesty always increases and never decreases.

You and I are caught up in an unfathomable mystery. We can draw near to almighty, holy God, and He will draw near to us. We can know Him who logic tells us should be unknowable. It is a miracle of grace. May our defining passion in life be to know this Jesus.

—MATT REDMAN

WHO NEEDS A FIVE-YEAR PLAN?

"I know the plans I have for you," declares the LORD, "plans to prosper
you and not to harm you, plans to give you hope and a future. Then
you will call on me and come and pray to me, and I will listen to you.
You will seek me and find me when you seek me with all your heart."

JEREMIAH 29:11–13

Where do you see yourself in five years? How are you going to get there?

You've probably heard these questions a time or two. Society seems to expect young adults to know exactly what we'll do for the rest of our lives. And, actually, knowing what our future has in store is also one of the deepest desires of our hearts. We all want purpose—to live for something greater. We try to plan each tiny detail of our lives, and we want them to play out according to our timing.

Despite our best-laid plans, God has some ideas of His own for our lives. And when we focus less on figuring out our own five-year plans and more on knowing and enjoying God, we begin to see the future He has in store for us—His perfect plan—unfold.

God's promise is clear—He'll lead us to a place of prosperity and hope. This promise doesn't include a blueprint or an answer to every question. It doesn't include a specific date to expect restoration. He just said, "I promise."

When your future is flooded with uncertainty, rest in God's promise, knowing He is directing every step you take.

Father, create in me the passion to seek Your presence above
all things and to trust You with the unknown.

BETTER THAN LIFE

Because your love is better than life, my lips will glorify you.
I will praise you as long as I live, and in your name I will
lift up my hands. I will be fully satisfied as with the richest
of foods; with singing lips my mouth will praise you.

PSALM 63:3–5

What satisfies your soul? You may be familiar with the cravings of your belly—but what about the cravings of your soul? And which is more important? The psalmist's answer is clear: God's love satisfies and permeates the soul deeper than the greatest promises of the world.

The word *life* in today's passage refers to earthly abundance. Even on a mountaintop of success and satisfaction, where you could not imagine life getting any better, God's love *is still better*. It's greater than any career, any relationship, and even life itself. In fact, the key to living an abundant life is only found in the freedom, confidence, and joy that come from God's love.

It's easy to say, but do you believe His love is better than life? If you say you believe, do you prove your belief with your actions? Dwell on the Lord, and let your joy overflow into praise as you delight in His incomparable love.

Lord, change my perspective when I don't believe that You and Your love are the best things in my life. May I only seek to be satisfied by You.

GOD'S COMFORTING GREATNESS

Oh, how great are God's riches and wisdom and knowledge! How impossible it is for us to understand his decisions and his ways! For who can know the LORD's thoughts? Who knows enough to give him advice? And who has given him so much that he needs to pay it back? For everything comes from him and exists by his power and is intended for his glory.

ROMANS 11:33–36 NLT

How often do we find ourselves thinking we know exactly what's best for us? Probably more often than we'd like to admit. Romans 11 speaks to our pride and foolish tendency to think we can figure things out on our own. It proclaims that God's greatness, wisdom, and ways are far above our own. There is no greater wisdom or knowledge than that of the Lord, and everything on earth shows us this truth.

Understanding God's greatness exposes our frailty and fickleness. When we humble ourselves by proclaiming His greatness, we set aside our pride and make space to learn from Him. When we declare that God is sovereign above all things, we can easily see His glory and grace. The more we realize that God is in control, the more readily we shift our trust in ourselves to trust in God—which provides far more comfort than trusting ourselves ever could.

We'll never have all the answers, but we know the One who does. So we can walk confidently and joyfully through whatever comes our way.

Lord, remind me today of Your greatness. Humble me, help me, and teach me to trust in Your truth.

THE VINE AND THE BRANCHES

"I am the vine; you are the branches. If you remain in me and I in
you, you will bear much fruit; apart from me you can do nothing."
JOHN 15:5

What is the first thing you do in the morning? Do you jam to
music so loud that your ears ring for the rest of the day? Do you
scroll through your social media feeds to see what you missed
while you slept? Do you read tweets about celebrities, gossip, current events, and sports?

Most of the time, we wake up and walk into another day with
the world at the front of our minds, only thinking about our own
agendas. When we crawl into bed at night, it shouldn't surprise us
that we can't seem to *feel* where God was during our day when we
seek ourselves instead of Him.

Let's wake up! We can't sustain ourselves with our world's
media, music, and empty promises. Today's verse reminds us that
we aren't the vine; Jesus is. We are the branches. We have to be
connected to the vine—Jesus—so we can bear fruit, be fulfilled,
and live abundantly. When we turn our focus from our Twitter-,
Instagram-, Facebook-, and Pinterest-saturated lives, we can see
that apart from Him we "can do nothing."

Father, please keep me from allowing the world to consume
me today. Let my heart yearn for Your truth, my ears listen to
Your Spirit, and my eyes seek Your face.

THE DWELLING PLACE

One thing I ask from the LORD, this only do I seek: that I may dwell in the house of the LORD all the days of my life, to gaze on the beauty of the LORD and to seek him in his temple.

PSALM 27:4

What do you desire above all else? What does your heart long for?

David longed to live in the tabernacle, the dwelling place of God's presence, and to be surrounded every day by the beauty, glory, and wondrous mystery of almighty God. This insatiable ache to meet Him daily, to know Him and His character personally, could only be satisfied by time in God's presence.

According to Psalm 27:4, God created in us a desire to seek the "one thing" that satisfies: to commune with the Lord. When we gaze upon His beauty and behold His glory, we begin to live as God designed us to. The desire of our hearts is fulfilled.

David found a place for himself where he could know and enjoy God. Where is that space for you? Find your tabernacle today. Passionately pursue that dwelling. When you make that "one thing" the ultimate goal of your days, you will have no room to forget how good, great, sovereign, and beautiful our Lord is.

Jesus, I want to know You more. Help me passionately pursue communion with You today.

LIKE FATHER, LIKE SON

Jesus answered, "I am the way and the truth and the life. No one comes to the Father except through me. If you really know me, you will know my Father as well. From now on, you do know him and have seen him."

JOHN 14:6–7

Do you struggle with understanding who God really is?

Actually, God gave us a pretty direct way to get to know Him: He gave us His Son. In fact, Jesus says so Himself. In John 14, He explained to His disciples that He was going to heaven before them to prepare a place for them there, and not to worry once He departed this world. The disciples immediately asked Jesus how to get to heaven, and Jesus replied that the way was through Jesus *Himself.* God sent Jesus into the world as a model demonstrating how believers should treat others. This is how we inherit the kingdom of God.

So by knowing Jesus, we can lay aside all our worries—about careers, about assignments, or about anything else in this life—because we know that He has prepared a place for us. We get the fullness of God Himself when we know Jesus, which is far more life-giving than anything we could ever imagine.

Lord, help me seek Your Son to know You more today.

PAST, PRESENT, AND FUTURE

For you did not receive the spirit of slavery to fall back into fear, but you have received the Spirit of adoption as sons, by whom we cry, "Abba! Father!" The Spirit himself bears witness with our spirit that we are children of God, and if children, then heirs—heirs of God and fellow heirs with Christ, provided we suffer with him in order that we may also be glorified with him.

ROMANS 8:15–17 ESV

The gospel is the thread that connects our past, present, and future. Look at it this way: we *were* slaves to this world, but now we *are* adopted children with an assured hope that we *will* spend eternity in heaven.

In Romans 8, Paul broke down how the gospel alters our state of being. When Paul said we believers are not supposed to "fall back into fear," he was referring to our former state as slaves in fear of death and the penalty of the law. Instead, through the Spirit, we are adopted into and become part of God's family.

As God's children, all ties to past sins are severed and forgotten. Now, we can look forward to a future filled with an unshakeable hope and a shared inheritance of Christ's glory.

Since we are freed from our past, cared for in our present, and assured of our future, let's live our faith boldly, love sacrificially, and treasure Christ greatly.

> Father, thank You for the gift of adoption into Your family. I trust You with my past, present, and future!

OUR REFUGE

"Because he loves me," says the LORD, *"I will rescue him; I will protect him, for he acknowledges my name. He will call on me, and I will answer him; I will be with him in trouble, I will deliver him and honor him. With long life I will satisfy him and show him my salvation."*

PSALM 91:14–16

We've all been caught in a rainstorm. The rain comes out of nowhere, leaving us with only two options: either stick it out or run for cover.

Life is the same way sometimes. Everything can be going great, and suddenly our world shifts in an instant: a break-up, a car accident, the death of a close friend. We aren't promised a life without trouble, but we have a good Father in whom we can take refuge. Like an umbrella in the rain, the Lord promises to cover and protect us when we call on His name.

God is described as our shelter, refuge, and fortress throughout Psalm 91. We make the Lord our refuge by loving Him and acknowledging His name. God is sovereign over every circumstance of our lives, and if we fix our eyes on His unchanging sovereignty, we can find shelter from the fiercest storms.

Ask the Lord to reveal how you can dwell in His shelter. He is faithful to walk through every season of life with us, and when we love Him for who He is and what He's done for us, we enter into the safest place of all—His presence.

Jesus, thank You for always being my refuge. Help me find peace in You and Your protection over my life.

IN HIS JOY

"The kingdom of heaven is like treasure hidden in a field,
which a man found and covered up. Then in his joy he
goes and sells all that he has and buys that field."

Matthew 13:44 esv

Leading into the parable of the hidden treasure, Jesus had given His audience pictures of what the kingdom of heaven is like. In this particular parable, the "treasure hidden in a field" represents salvation. In order to get the treasure, the man in the parable has to sell everything he has. Notice the man doesn't buy salvation with a set price; he buys it with a yielding of his heart. Following Jesus means surrendering everything, yet it's a struggle. Surrender goes against every fiber of our beings. But, actually, joy is found in the surrender.

As you read today's verse, don't miss the words used to describe the way the man sells everything he has: "in his joy." We cheat ourselves of all Jesus has to offer when we don't surrender everything, because we cheat ourselves of joy! The surrender is beautiful, freeing, and overflowing with gifts. The man in the parable has joy because he knows the value of salvation in his life.

We have a choice to make: will we choose to fully surrender daily and inherit true riches, or will we hold back and pursue our own agendas?

> Father, help me surrender to You daily. When faced with Your majesty, love, and mercy, let my response be to joyfully let go and let You fill every aspect of my life.

11

BE ON GUARD

Dear friends, since you have been forewarned, be on your guard so that
you may not be carried away by the error of the lawless and fall from
your secure position. But grow in the grace and knowledge of our Lord
and Savior Jesus Christ. To him be glory both now and forever! Amen.

2 PETER 3:17–18

In today's scripture, we hear a warning and a command. We are warned to be on guard so that we are not carried away by the "error of the lawless." Earlier in 2 Peter 3, Peter described "the lawless" as scoffers who followed their evil desires (v. 3). And because the lawless rejected the law of the Lord, they could not know the joy of living for Him.

It's imperative that we stay on guard so we can protect our secure position. The "lawless," the scoffers, and the self-interested will try to distract us from Jesus and make us doubt our faith. But He has the power to keep us safe. We must dive into the Scriptures to grow in Christ. We must swim in His grace to learn more about who He is and to remind ourselves of who we are in Him. The more we know Him, the more we will become like Him. The more we grow in His grace, the more we will glorify Him!

Father, knowing You is my one great desire. May the distractions and the scoffers of this world fade away as I contemplate Your beauty and majesty.

CALL TO HIM

While Jeremiah was still confined in the courtyard of the guard,
the word of the LORD came to him a second time: "This is what the
LORD says, he who made the earth, the LORD who formed it and
established it—the LORD is his name: 'Call to me and I will answer
you and tell you great and unsearchable things you do not know.'"

JEREMIAH 33:1–3

While Jerusalem was under the brutal siege of a foreign king, Jeremiah was imprisoned for prophesying the nation's coming destruction if they did not obey the Lord. It was in his desperation, with this dark cloud of destruction lurking overhead, that Jeremiah heard from the Lord.

God is the Covenant Maker and Covenant Keeper. Though He told Jeremiah of the death that was to come, God assured Jeremiah of His faithfulness. Despite His people's disobedience, God said He would still heal, restore, and bless His people in abundance. And if God's people called to Him, He would answer them.

Maybe you feel your world is crumbling around you, that you're trapped with no way out, or that life is out of control. Take heart, because God's promises are for you too. He has not abandoned you and will never break His promises to you, even if you break your promises to Him. Turn from what holds you back, call to Him, and He will answer you! Rest today in God's unending faithfulness.

> Lord, give me courage to call to You and grace to hear and believe what You say.

THE STREAM OF LIFE

*Blessed is the one who does not walk in step with the wicked or stand in the
way that sinners take or sit in the company of mockers, but whose delight
is in the law of the LORD, and who meditates on his law day and night.
That person is like a tree planted by streams of water, which yields its fruit
in season and whose leaf does not wither—whatever they do prospers.*

PSALM 1:1–3

Sometimes we're misled to believe that other paths are "better"
or "more exciting" than walking with God. Temptation may lead
us away from God toward paths of sin, but if we continue to walk
down temptation's path, its mirage will inevitably fade. Our vices
won't satisfy us, and we will find ourselves deep in the desert, far
from the stream of life, where God wants us to be.

More than anything, God wants us to live according to His
will and follow the paths He lays before us. He knows we find life
only in Him, and David knew it too when he wrote Psalm 16:11:
"You make known to me the path of life; you will fill me with joy
in your presence, with eternal pleasures at your right hand."

As sinners, we're all prone to wander from God's paths. But
know this: no matter where we are, our Father calls us back with
open arms. Trust that following His path is the best way to go.
Remain in His love, and be the tree planted by streams of water,
yielding fruit for His glory in season, in His perfect timing.

Father, give us the faith to follow the paths You lay before us.

PERFECT COMMUNION

"Father, I want those you have given me to be with me where I am, and to see my glory, the glory you have given me because you loved me before the creation of the world. Righteous Father, though the world does not know you, I know you, and they know that you have sent me. I have made you known to them, and will continue to make you known in order that the love you have for me may be in them and that I myself may be in them."

John 17:24–26

Since the beginning, Christ has lived in perfect unity and communion with God and the Holy Spirit. And while He was on earth, Jesus showed the world, in human form, who God is.

Ultimately, Jesus came to earth so He could invite us into the perfect communion He had with God. His prayer for us in today's passage is startling: He asks the Father "that the love you have for me may be in them and that I myself may be in them." In other words, Jesus prayed that God's eternal love, the same kind of love He had for Jesus, also be given to us, and that Jesus Himself might exist in us. This passage is a deep mystery, yet at the center of it is this truth: Jesus is the way into the perfect intimacy of the Holy Spirit and love of the Father. So let us draw close to Jesus, for He has drawn close to us and made the Father known to us.

Father, thank You for Your Son Jesus, who has made a way for us to You.

OUR RIGHT HAND

I keep the LORD in mind always. Because He is at my right hand, I will not be shaken. Therefore my heart is glad and my spirit rejoices; my body also rests securely. For You will not abandon me to Sheol; You will not allow Your Faithful One to see decay. You reveal the path of life to me; in Your presence is abundant joy; in Your right hand are eternal pleasures.

PSALM 16:8–11 HCSB

Amazing confidence comes from knowing the all-powerful and fully loving God. Why? Because our dependence and trust in Him will not come to nothing; He is perfectly good and faithful in everything He does.

David faced many trials in his life, and often it seemed he would be overtaken by his enemies. Yet David always kept the Lord in his sight and resolved not to put his hope in any other god or person. He knew that because God was at his right hand—a place of authority, power, and defense—he would not be defeated or given over to death. David was so elated by this promise that his innermost soul rejoiced! But today's passage is more than a helpful reminder from David; it is a foretelling of God's ultimate faithfulness: to reconcile us to Him through the death and resurrection of Jesus.

We too can have confidence that God is for us and that He offers us eternal life. Through faith, repentance, and trust in Jesus, we have access to abundant grace that covers our debts. We can rest securely and rejoice!

> Father, help me put all my faith and confidence in You, for You alone are the path to life.

16

HIS WAYS ARE GREATER

"For my thoughts are not your thoughts, neither are your ways my ways,"
declares the LORD. *"As the heavens are higher than the earth, so are my*
ways higher than your ways and my thoughts than your thoughts."

ISAIAH 55:8–9

Take a moment to think about how vast and complex the earth is—everything so beautiful, unique, and perfectly created. God set *everything* into motion. Can you wrap your mind around that? There's no way we can fully comprehend who God is and what He's done. Yet somehow, He wants to know us personally and enter into a relationship with us, and He has crafted a beautiful plan for our lives that allows us each to play a small role in His big story.

Isaiah spoke of an invitation to know the Lord: the only One who can satisfy, the only One whose faithfulness is never failing. He's the only One who loves us unconditionally. We can be confident that God has a purpose for each of our lives, even when we can't fully see it. Through trials and tribulations, God holds the master plan, and it is far greater than ours.

Often it is hard to understand why things turn out a certain way. Today's verse reminds us that His ways and plans for our lives are more perfect than we could imagine.

Father, help me relinquish control of my own plans so I can know Yours better.

BOAST IN HIM

This is what the Lord says: "Let not the wise boast of their wisdom or the strong boast of their strength or the rich boast of their riches, but let the one who boasts boast about this: that they have the understanding to know me, that I am the Lord, who exercises kindness, justice and righteousness on earth, for in these I delight," declares the Lord.

JEREMIAH 9:23–24

With social media always at our fingertips, it is hard not to boast about how great our day is, how awesome the food we are eating is, or how we aced our last test. As humans, we love to brag about our achievements and possessions. But as believers, we have something far more compelling to talk about.

We know and are known by the Creator of the universe—the One who calls us by name, who comforts us in our darkest times, encourages us to move forward, and loves us despite all the wrong we've done.

Let's change what we brag about. Since we know God, we should also boast in the things that He cares about. We can talk about justice for the captives in slavery, stories of people coming to know Jesus, and believers who do good things in His name. What God delights in, we should too.

Take a second to focus on the things He cares about today—and blast it all over Facebook!

> Jesus, we want people to know Your name. Show us good things to boast about in You.

18

ASK "WHO," NOT "WHY"

Then Job replied to the LORD: "I know that you can do all things;
no purpose of yours can be thwarted. You asked, 'Who is this that
obscures my plans without knowledge?' Surely I spoke of things I
did not understand, things too wonderful for me to know. You said,
'Listen now, and I will speak; I will question you, and you shall answer
me.' My ears had heard of you but now my eyes have seen you."

JOB 42:1–5

In difficult seasons, followers of Jesus can shift their focus from asking *why* something is happening to asking *Who* is sovereign over our lives.

Job was well acquainted with hopelessness. He faced an extremely difficult season filled with death, sickness, and loss. At first, like most of us would, he felt entitled to know *why* he was experiencing so much pain. Yet Job shifted to a posture of humility as he saw *who* God was. When he encountered the living God, he could not help but stand in awe as his perception of God transformed from someone he had heard about to One he saw and experienced himself.

Like Job, we have an invitation to ask "Who?" and to come to know the God who so intimately wants to know us, and we can experience the joy of trusting in God Almighty.

Father, open my eyes to see who You truly are. In the midst of joys and struggles, make it my heart's deepest desire for You to be glorified.

19

HE KNOWS YOU

You have searched me, LORD, and you know me. You know when I
sit and when I rise; you perceive my thoughts from afar. You discern
my going out and my lying down; you are familiar with all my ways.
Before a word is on my tongue you, LORD, know it completely.

PSALM 139:1–4

Do you feel abandoned? Insecure? Afraid? God sees you. Are your memories haunted with shame? Regret? Trauma? He knows. Have you been betrayed? Have you made mistakes? Are you trapped in silence? He is still there. God knit you together inside your mother's womb, and never for a moment has He taken His eyes off you. God, the Almighty, knows you.

The same One who knows absolutely everything about you is the One who loves you with an all-enduring, all-powerful heavenly love. Inescapable, God's presence is a bright light revealing the secrets of every dark crevice. But God is not fazed by your history, and He will not run away. He will love you perfectly and endlessly because you are His creation. His promise is to stay.

This knowledge is too grand for us to fathom. But believe it, and rest. God is pursuing you, so stop trying to hide. Let yourself be known to God because you are completely known and completely loved, and there is nothing you can do to change it.

> Jesus, thank You for knowing me, loving me, and never leaving me. Help me believe this, even when my days are dark.

FOR THE JOY OF THE SABBATH

"If you keep your feet from breaking the Sabbath . . . then you will find
your joy in the LORD, and I will cause you to ride in triumph on the
heights of the land and to feast on the inheritance of your father Jacob."

ISAIAH 58:13–14

For many of us, going to church sums up our entire practice of the Sabbath. While there is nothing wrong with this, routine and our busy schedules can distract us from the point of the Sabbath: rest, trust, and worship.

For Israel, keeping the Sabbath meant taking a break from work and trusting in God's provision. In today's verse, we see that God's people had forgotten the point of the Sabbath; they were working and not trusting God to meet their needs. God challenged them to delight in the Sabbath and trust Him. And if they did so, He promised joy and provision.

While believers today don't face the same strict practices in observance of the Sabbath (Colossians 2:16), we can still apply its principles. But it's easy to miss the point, just as the Israelites did. Don't let Sabbath practices become an inconvenience or routine—something that you just *do*. If you practice the Sabbath, God wants your heart to be in it. As you go to church this Sunday, and throughout the rest of the day, look at the time as a delight, and ask God to fill you with His joy as you worship.

> God, help me delight in practicing the Sabbath, even through my routines and busy schedule. May I find rest in Your joy.

BUILDING CHARACTER

"LORD, who may dwell in your sacred tent? . . . The one whose walk is blameless, who does what is righteous, who speaks the truth from their heart; whose tongue utters no slander, who does no wrong to a neighbor, and casts no slur on others; who despises a vile person but honors those who fear the LORD . . . Whoever does these things will never be shaken.

PSALM 15:1–5

Character is important to God. In this psalm, David described the character of those who dwell in the Lord's "sacred tent." These are not requirements we need to fulfill in order to earn God's love. Rather, they are encouragements that show how God intends His people to live.

In Psalm 14, David wrote about the fallen nature of humanity and the longed-for deliverance of God. Given the Israelites' sordid history, David was likely witnessing widespread rebellion. In reflection, he logically asked, "Lord, who may dwell in your sanctuary?" What follows is a plea to remember the good design for which God created us.

When we live as God intended, His character is reflected through us, and we bring Him glory. This is a gradual process, but as we grow to know Him and His salvation, we are molded into people who reflect God to a broken world. Will you dwell in God's presence today and carry His goodness with you?

Lord, on my own, I have no ability to be a person of character. Mold me into someone who lives as You desire and reflects You to others.

FREE NOURISHMENT

"Come, all you who are thirsty, come to the waters; and you who have
no money, come, buy and eat! Come, buy wine and milk without
money and without cost. Why spend money on what is not bread,
and your labor on what does not satisfy? Listen, listen to me, and
eat what is good, and you will delight in the richest of fare."

ISAIAH 55:1–2

God has offered an invitation to His children: get nourished
for free!

God's invitation is not just for those who find favor in the eyes
of the world; it's for everybody: the poor, the disenfranchised, the
broken, and the needy. God isn't stingy with His good gifts.

Few things in this world are truly free, but the love, grace,
and mercy of our Lord is. Yet somehow we spend most of our lives
searching for and worshiping temporary substances that do nothing to fill the Christ-shaped hole in our hearts. Isaiah encourages
us to set aside worldly things and come to the Lord, just as we are,
to eat and drink that which can satisfy our greatest longings.

What are you allowing to take the place of Christ in your
heart, causing you to miss the free gifts of God? Wealth? Security?
Fame? Grades? Relationships? None of them come close to what
Jesus offers: free, lasting nourishment! Let's root out "what does
not satisfy," and accept His invitation today.

Father, help me realize that only You can give me what I seek.

"YES, LORD"

Yes, LORD, walking in the way of your truth, we wait eagerly for you, for your name and your renown are the desire of our souls.

ISAIAH 26:8

"Yes, Lord" is not the easiest thing for us humans to say. Yet throughout Scripture, we see that God works for His glory and our good. He asks everything from us, but He also *gives* us everything. So in humility, we say "Yes, Lord"—yes, to a life spent on living for His glory.

Isaiah said, "Walking in the way of your truth, we wait . . ." But our wait isn't passive or stationary—it's a walk! As a child anticipates opening presents on Christmas morning, we too wait for Him with anticipation, enjoying all the preparations that come with the season. Instead of spending our time gaining material possessions, we offer worship and service to others. Instead of making a list, we discover His agenda and make it ours. We clothe ourselves festively with His truth, making every step one of obedience, of faithful devotion to His purposes.

"Your name and renown are the desire of our souls" isn't just empty praise; it's the confession of our entire lives. So like Isaiah, let's lay our praise before Him, saying, "Take us and make us Yours, so everyone on earth can know how glorious You really are. We say yes, Lord."

> Father, let this verse be a banner waved high over our lives in surrender to You, so everyone might see Your glory and come to know You.

WE HAVE IT ALL

Though the fig tree does not bud and there are no grapes on the vines, though the olive crop fails and the fields produce no food, though there are no sheep in the pen and no cattle in the stalls, yet I will rejoice in the LORD, I will be joyful in God my Savior. The Sovereign LORD is my strength; he makes my feet like the feet of a deer, he enables me to tread on the heights.

HABAKKUK 3:17–19

Our generation so often misses the point of God's grace. We think the purpose behind His faithfulness to us is to add prosperity and comfort to our earthly living. Whether it's money, possessions, or promotions, we tend to thank God when good things come and question Him when they don't. But when we do this, we forget something essential.

God gave us *everything* nearly two thousand years ago: He gave us the blood of His only Son. With Jesus' death on a cross came grace, which gave humanity more than we deserved.

So even if you don't get that promotion, praise God! You have eternal life. If your roommate is annoying you, look past that letdown and remember that the cross washed us clean. No matter the issue hitting you today, massive or miniscule, don't forget this truth: we already possess the greatest gift the world will ever see.

Father, thank You for the cross. Remind us that the meaning of our lives doesn't exist in the things of this world, but in Your kingdom alone.

25

I AM

Moses said to God, "Suppose I go to the Israelites and say to them, 'The God of your fathers has sent me to you,' and they ask me, 'What is his name?' Then what shall I tell them?" God said to Moses, "I AM WHO I AM. This is what you are to say to the Israelites: 'I AM has sent me to you.'"

EXODUS 3:13–14

Have you ever wondered what God calls Himself? God's name, I AM WHO I AM, is powerful. God is the self-existing One. The Lord is the only God who truly *is*, always has been, and always will be. He has all power and authority. He is eternal, unchanging, and faithful.

When Moses was paralyzed by fear and filled with doubts, hearing God's name helped him believe His promise of deliverance. The Lord Jesus identified Himself with this name of God in John 8:58 when He said, "Before Abraham was, I AM." As followers of Christ, we can take comfort in knowing that the Holy Spirit of the great "I AM" lives in us, reminding us of His promises and giving us strength to live as bold witnesses for Him.

In which areas of your life do you need to trust that the Lord has the power to deliver you and the people around you? Pinpoint a few today, and bring them to the Lord—*He is* the source of all strength.

Father, Your very name calms my fears and propels me on my mission. Please increase my faith today.

HE DELIGHTS IN YOU

*Who knows a person's thoughts except their own spirit within
them? In the same way no one knows the thoughts of God except the
Spirit of God. What we have received is not the spirit of the world,
but the Spirit who is from God, so that we may understand what
God has freely given us. . . . for, "Who has known the mind of the
Lord so as to instruct him?" But we have the mind of Christ.*

1 CORINTHIANS 2:11–12, 16

Can you comprehend the mind of God? Our Father doesn't need
to pause to hear one of His children's voices. All in union, the
angels sing to Him, the moon turns upon His charted orbit, and
prayers from every nation kiss His ears, yet He specifically hears
your voice. He sees you. And He is mindful of you (Psalm 8:4). He
never intends for one of His children to perish (2 Peter 3:9). He
is for you, He delights in your presence, and He created your life
with the utmost care and significance.

God is our Father, but He is not like any earthly father. He's
a constant presence in our lives, always giving instruction and
guiding our paths. Ask for God's wisdom—for "the mind of
Christ," so you can show His glory and learn His plans for your
life all the more.

Father, help me see the hidden things that You marvel in
revealing. Help me keep the mind of this world from burying
Your thoughts.

WHOLEHEARTED YES

Samuel replied: Does the Lord delight in burnt offerings and sacrifices as much as in obeying the Lord? To obey is better than sacrifice . . . For rebellion is like the sin of divination, and arrogance like the evil of idolatry. Because you have rejected the word of the Lord, he has rejected you as king."

1 Samuel 15:22–23

God wants our willing and wholehearted *yes*. When God asks something of us, our answer should not be, "Yes, but . . ." God made the ultimate sacrifice by sending His willing and obedient Son. In Jesus, we find the perfect example of obedience. Today's passage shows King Saul giving a "Yes, but . . ." answer—and it didn't end well for him.

Anointed with a message from the Lord, Samuel commanded Saul to destroy the Amalekites; not even animals were to be spared. But when Saul and his armies set out on their mission, they kept the animals, intending to sacrifice them as an offering to the Lord. Saul's sacrifice, lacking in obedience, was of no value to God. Because of his rebellion, God rejected him as king. His "Yes, but . . ." answer backfired.

Even in the difficult moments, let's completely surrender to the Lord. When God sent Jesus to die, Jesus did not say, "Yes, I will make disciples, *but* I will not die on the cross." He said, "Yes, Father." This was not an easy yes, but because of His answer, we too are able to say yes to God.

Father, thank You for Your yes. Make every step I take a step of obedience.

28

HEAR THE KNOCK

"Here I am! I stand at the door and knock. If anyone hears my voice and opens the door, I will come in and eat with that person, and they with me."

REVELATION 3:20

Have you ever experienced a time when you felt like no one understood you or even wanted to listen to you? Do you ever feel completely alone?

During times of despair, it is easy to feel alone, especially working at a new job or being on a college campus for the first time. We can convince ourselves that because of what we have done in the past, there is no way that someone new would love us or even care to know us. Other times, amid the distractions of life, we are not still enough even to hear Him. The believers Jesus spoke to in Revelation experienced all of the above.

But in the middle of our isolation, Jesus knocks at the door of our hearts and is waiting to enter into fellowship with us. He relentlessly pursues us and calls for us to be with Him. He promises to come in and dine with us once we open the door of our hearts. This is the promise of an intimate relationship!

What can we do to be still so we can hear God's voice today? Let us pause to hear His voice, and answer the knock at the door of our hearts.

Jesus, thank You for continuing to pursue me, even when I feel unworthy. Help me seek You today.

COMMANDED TO LOVE

"Hear, O Israel: The Lord our God, the Lord is one. Love the Lord your God with all your heart and with all your soul and with all your strength. These commandments that I give you today are to be on your hearts."

DEUTERONOMY 6:4–6

When God etched the Ten Commandments into two stone tablets, He left no doubt about the obedience He desired from His people. With each command, the gravity of God's perfect standard was confirmed—and so was humanity's sinfulness. As we read through the overwhelming list of dos and don'ts in Deuteronomy, we are forced to face our inability to perfectly keep the law.

Thankfully, God doesn't set an impossible task when He asks us to obey Him. He prefaces the command to love Him with all our heart, soul, and strength with the infallible truth that He is the one and only God. He is holy, sovereign, and eternal, and He deserves our worship and obedience. And if that's not enough, He has reconciled us to Himself through His Son, allowing us to have a personal relationship with Him.

When we grasp the truth of God's unmerited love and kindness, we will inevitably respond with a heart of gratitude and obedience. And although we'll continually fail to love Him with our entire heart, soul, and strength, our efforts should never cease.

> Lord, give me a true understanding of Your commandments and Your gospel, and a heart that responds in thankfulness.

NOTHING TO HIDE

The word of God is alive and active. Sharper than any double-edged sword, it penetrates even to dividing soul and spirit, joints and marrow; it judges the thoughts and attitudes of the heart. Nothing in all creation is hidden from God's sight. Everything is uncovered and laid bare before the eyes of him to whom we must give account.

HEBREWS 4:12–13

Nothing gets by God. He's in every corner of creation, pursuing His people. But He sees through the masks we often put on to impress others, and His Word pierces through the darkness to convict us, to heal and make us whole.

David asked, "Where can I go from your Spirit? Where can I flee from your presence?" (Psalm 139:7). From the beginning of time, humanity has tried to cover its shame from the eyes of God. Adam and Eve immediately recognized their nakedness after they sinned and hid from God in Eden. King David tried to hide his infidelity, sending a man to his death to cover his crimes. Sin separates and shames even those closest to God's heart.

In the Old Testament, God's people had to go through imperfect leaders like Moses or the high priest in order to receive forgiveness for their transgressions. But through His sacrifice, Jesus made a way so that we no longer need to hide from God. We can now enter into rest, knowing that we are welcomed into the presence of God through Jesus' death on the cross.

> God, thank You that because of Jesus, I no longer hide or live in fear, but can approach You as my Father.

ALL IN ALL

He is before all things, and in him all things hold together. And he is the head of the body, the church; he is the beginning and the firstborn from among the dead, so that in everything he might have the supremacy.

COLOSSIANS 1:17–18

We live in a world where value is often quantified in retweets, likes, and favorites. Social media paints a different picture than reality—nobody's life is ever *that* perfect—so we often use it to cover up our flaws and insecurities. While social media did not exist when Paul wrote his letter to the Colossians, the human desire to be valued did.

Paul wrote to the Colossians not only about the supremacy of God, but also the impact His supremacy has on our identities. His power over sin and darkness gives us freedom to stop covering up our blemishes. We don't have to hold all things together, because the Creator of the universe does that for us. We were created by God and for God, but if our primary concern is to look perfect to an imperfect world, we forfeit the opportunity to live our purpose and engage the world with genuine love.

Today, let's love the world around us, not by hiding our failures, but by pointing to the grace in the midst of them. Our scars tell our story, and our story is "I was dead, but Jesus gave me life."

Father, who do You say that I am? Give me the strength and perseverance to walk confidently in that today.

TRUST AND CONTENTMENT

Trust in the LORD and do good; dwell in the land and enjoy safe pasture.
Take delight in the LORD, and he will give you the desires of your heart.

PSALM 37:3–4

Trust. It is a word we are familiar with and hear so often that we may have become numb to it. It's repeated throughout Scripture and talked about often in Christian communities. But what does it really mean to "trust in the Lord" day in and day out?

Trust is wholehearted reliance and dependence—the belief that God will always come through for us. When we fully trust God, we don't have to worry about the future. Trust frees us from fear and allows us to surrender our desire for control and our need to take matters into our own hands. It gives us the freedom to faithfully serve wherever He places us.

Our trust in God grows when we choose to find satisfaction only in Him. When we delight in Him, we see more of who He is, and our hearts are filled with wonder. As we come to know Him and His promises, our natural response is to trust Him! It's a beautiful cycle.

Let's choose to find all joy and contentment in Jesus, rather than the things of this world. When we do, the desires of our hearts become the same as His, and He is glorified!

> Jesus, align my heart to Yours. Teach me what it means to live out of radical trust in You, that I may live fully where You have placed me.

WALKING IN THE DARK

For God, who said, "Let light shine out of darkness," has shone in our hearts
to give the light of the knowledge of the glory of God in the face of Jesus Christ.
2 CORINTHIANS 4:6 ESV

Every day, the sun slowly escorts us out of darkness with its warm light, allowing us to rise and live our lives. Just like the sun, God shines His light into our hearts, taking us from the death of sin into life in Jesus.

When Jesus shines His light and shows us the truth—who we are in our sin, in relation to Him—it can be blinding at first. We may feel overwhelmed by our limitations and smallness. We may not be able to see a way out of our sin, but we can walk by faith through the darkness, just like Paul literally did in Acts 9. After all, we are forgiven, and Jesus is in control now.

God promises that we won't be blind forever. He tells us He will give us the knowledge of His glory, which means one day we will see it—on earth or in heaven. It doesn't matter if we can't see the way forward right now; Jesus has given us truth that sets us free to trust Him and carry on (John 8:32).

Today, walk in faith and keep walking with Christ, even if you cannot clearly see the path before you. Jesus promises He will lift the darkness with His light. So when you are uncertain about the future, press on and choose to trust Him.

> Father, I trust that You are good. Thank You for shining Your light of truth on me. Show me how to actively walk in faith today.

THE PATH OF PURITY

How can a young person stay on the path of purity? By living
according to your word. I seek you with all my heart; do
not let me stray from your commands. I have hidden your
word in my heart that I might not sin against you.

PSALM 119:9–11

Staying on the path of purity might be one of the most significant battles we face. There is a war raging for our hearts and minds, and too often the world's ways are winning. How can we possibly walk in purity when media, peer pressure, and our own selfish desires pull us in another direction?

Today's verse gives us the answer: *by living according to God's Word.* That's easier said than done, isn't it? To live according to God's Word, we have to go "all in" to learn what He says and what He wants. More than simply following the rules, we're called to seek God with all that we are and to bury His Word in the deepest places of our hearts.

Whether you need encouragement today to stay on the path of purity, or to get back on it, know that you can win the battle by choosing to live the life God has called you to live, one decision at a time. Let His Word be your guide.

> Father, teach me how to live according to Your Word and not my understanding. Give me strength and wisdom to walk the path of purity each day.

ABOUNDING IN LOVE

*"The LORD, the LORD, the compassionate and gracious God, slow
to anger, abounding in love and faithfulness, maintaining love to
thousands, and forgiving wickedness, rebellion and sin. Yet he does
not leave the guilty unpunished; he punishes the children and their
children for the sin of the parents to the third and fourth generation."*

EXODUS 34:6–7

Today's verse may seem harsh. How can the Lord be compassionate
and abounding in love when we read that He punishes the children for their parents' sin? The fact is, this scripture teaches us
something very important about the nature of sin: it never affects
just you. Sin always goes beyond yourself and hurts the people you
love: your family, your friends, and even your future children. The
consequences of sin can extend beyond your lifetime.

Consider Adam and Eve and their choice to eat from the Tree
of the Knowledge of Good and Evil. Not only were *they* banished
from the garden of Eden, but their choices also separated their
children—including us—from the Lord. But this is where God's
compassion and abounding love comes in. He reached out to lift us
up from that generational curse, and He forgives our sins through
the blood of Jesus. He loves us so much that He gave us a way out of
our hopelessness and gave life to the generations. He took our guilt
and let us walk—not away, but to *the* Way, Jesus Christ.

Father, thank You that You are abounding in love and slow
to anger. Please forgive me and help me turn to You for the
sake of generations to come.

OUR RESTORER

*The LORD is my shepherd, I lack nothing. He makes me lie down
in green pastures, he leads me beside quiet waters, he refreshes my
soul. He guides me along the right paths for his name's sake.*

PSALM 23:1–3

Sometimes we can feel that every facet of our lives demands our attention at the same time. School, work, friends, family, and social media all vie for our time, while doubts about our purpose, shame from our past, and questions about our future often steal our energy. We can feel frazzled, like we are sailing in a storm with no promise of calmer waters.

In the midst of it all, God sees us. He knows what we need to find true peace and respite. We can't find that peace in a nap—it's not just something we can do to relax ourselves. Jesus doesn't passively stand by while we try to restore our own souls. He *makes* us lie down in green pastures. He *leads* us beside still waters.

Jesus is the Restorer. When we trust Him with our lives and surrender our ambitions to His plan, we can receive and enjoy His rest. Let's approach the cross in worship and awe, because Jesus will give us restoration—and we will not be left wanting!

Father, I trust You. Lead me into Your peace and rest, and restore my soul.

RETURN TO THE LORD

Come, let us return to the LORD; for he has torn us, that he may heal
us; he has struck us down, and he will bind us up. . . . Let us press
on to know the LORD; his going out is sure as the dawn; he will come
to us as the showers, as the spring rains that water the earth.

HOSEA 6:1–3 ESV

Nobody likes being punished. In the shadows of shame and guilt, we go to great lengths to avoid being caught by hiding our wrong-doings. But when we try to conceal our sins, we prevent ourselves from discovering God's ultimate purpose for redeeming our sins: restoration to relationship.

Again and again, Israel turned their backs on God. They sought refuge in alliances with powerful nations and trusted idols to provide for their needs. God loved Israel, but He knew there were consequences for Israel's actions. Though the nation would suffer for breaking their covenant relationship with God, He remained faithful, mercifully drawing them back to Himself.

We do not serve a God who delights in punishment; we serve a God who desires to see us return to His presence. When idolatry and faithlessness take root in your life, don't retreat into the darkness. Repent of your sins and turn back to God, and move forward in His faithfulness. The consequences of your sin may affect you for a time, but as sure as the sun will rise, God's grace remains available to those who draw near to Him.

Father, in times of punishment, bring my heart to repentance so I might once more know Your mercy and grace.

FAITHFUL STEPS

Faith is confidence in what we hope for and assurance about what we do not see. . . . By faith Enoch was taken from this life . . . Before he was taken, he was commended as one who pleased God. And without faith it is impossible to please God, because anyone who comes to him must believe that he exists and that he rewards those who earnestly seek him.

HEBREWS 11:1, 5–6

In the midst of the uncertainties of life, faith is pleasing to God. It is a declaration of our love for Christ and of our trust in God. Scripture tells us that Enoch walked faithfully with God and that pleased Him. Hope and certainty in the unseen defined Enoch's whole life, and his steps reflected that faith.

In order to walk with someone, to move harmoniously in the same direction with the same goals and passions, you must know that person intimately. That's how our faith walk begins—in relationship with God. As we grow in knowing Him, through His Word, prayer, and praise, we grow to trust His goodness more and more. We develop *faith*.

Enoch knew God, so he was able to walk with assurance and confidence in the eternal life that awaited him. Our call is to do the same. When we focus on taking our day-to-day steps with faithful obedience, our hearts align with the mission of Christ. Do as Enoch did: let hope, obedience, and hunger for God guide your every step.

Father, make my pursuit of You the overwhelming desire of my heart.

WHAT IS YOUR GAIN?

Whatever were gains to me I now consider loss for the sake of Christ. What is more, I consider everything a loss because of the surpassing worth of knowing Christ Jesus my Lord, for whose sake I have lost all things. I consider them garbage, that I may gain Christ and be found in him, not having a righteousness of my own that comes from the law, but that which is through faith in Christ—the righteousness that comes from God on the basis of faith. I want to know Christ—yes, to know the power of his resurrection and participation in his sufferings, becoming like him in his death.

Philippians 3:7–10

As we ponder the direction of our lives, our generation is faced with a particular question: *What is your gain?* Some might say money, respect, or, in the apostle Paul's case, a self-righteousness that comes through strict adherence to a set of religious rules. But God tells us through Paul that knowing Christ is our sole spiritual gain; everything else might as well be "garbage" and "a loss."

No doubt, worldly things are magnetic; that's why so many of us run after them. But that pull is an expression of our sinful nature, of our desire to make something other than God our ultimate goal. The truth is, running after those things isn't actually fulfilling; but when we get to know Christ, who is of "surpassing worth," our lives become much more valuable because then we are living with purpose.

Lord, give me the faith to see Christ as my sole gain and the courage to conform my life to reflect it.

OPEN THE GIFT

"Now this is eternal life: that they know you, the only true God, and Jesus Christ, whom you have sent."

JOHN 17:3

Imagine Jesus showing up at your door and presenting you with a very precious gift. You graciously accept it and marvel at how beautifully it has been wrapped, but you never actually open the gift. How strange would that be?

Jesus has given us the precious gift of eternal life. He has saved us from eternal condemnation, and that is beautiful and worthy of rejoicing in. But even more than that, He wants us to unwrap the gift to see what eternal life unveils: intimate fellowship with the one true God.

That's why the Father sent Jesus in the first place: to give us the gift of eternal life. Through Jesus' death and resurrection, He gave us what was impossible without Him: the opportunity to truly and deeply know God forever.

Jesus did not come so we could casually, *sort-of* know about God from a distance. He came so we could personally and intimately know God, to see with our eyes what life is like when we live with Him. If we anchor our lives in the pursuit of knowing God more deeply, we will find true life in the process.

> Jesus, help me desire to know You above all else, for to know You is to be truly alive!

GRACE FOR TEMPTATION

We do not have a high priest who is unable to empathize with our weaknesses,
but we have one who has been tempted in every way, just as we are—yet he
did not sin. Let us then approach God's throne of grace with confidence, so
that we may receive mercy and find grace to help us in our time of need.

HEBREWS 4:15–16

At some point, we all face temptation. This encounter can make us feel as if we are trapped against a wall, alone, in a place where rescue seems far away. Whether we're in a dorm room or in an office building, temptation can turn into a paralyzing fear that leaves us feeling weak, vulnerable, and defeated.

But we have hope. Jesus walked through every bit of worldly temptation. He knows where we are, what we are going through, and that this isn't the end. And in our brokenness He draws near and asks us to simply *follow Him*, holding fast to the path He's called us to.

Though we all face temptations of every kind, in Christ, we are blameless before the Father. Mercy meets us right where we are and calls us up out of our mess. How amazing that He lets us walk forward in freedom!

> Father, enable me to say yes to You today and no to the temptation that is battling for my heart. You are stronger, and You have provided a way out. I choose Your way, believing I am Yours.

GOD REVEALED

"I praise you, Father, Lord of heaven and earth, because you have hidden these things from the wise and learned, and revealed them to little children. Yes, Father, for this is what you were pleased to do."

LUKE 10:21

Before Jesus came, to know God was to adhere to a strict set of laws. But with Jesus' arrival, relationship was available as He revealed God to us! God desires to be known, and the Son shows us the way.

In Luke 10, Jesus sent out seventy-two disciples to preach the gospel and heal the sick. When they returned, they rejoiced because even the demons submitted to them. What power! But Jesus did not come to give authority or power over demons. He came to offer us a lasting personal relationship—like that between a child and a parent. So He rejoiced along with the disciples, but for a different reason: that God chooses to reveal Himself to "little children."

Let's walk as little children today, not relying on being "wise and learned," but relying on Christ, who reveals God to us.

Power, salvation, and closeness to God are unreachable by our efforts. But now Jesus has come near, and we are called to follow Him with childlike simplicity and faith. Though we didn't earn or deserve it, heavenly citizenship is now available to the children of God.

> Father, thank You for the way You reveal Yourself to Your children. Continue to walk alongside me as I fix my eyes on Your grace and glory.

43

FOR OUR OWN GOOD

Israel, what does the LORD your God ask of you but to fear the LORD your God, to walk in obedience to him, to love him, to serve the LORD your God with all your heart and with all your soul, and to observe the LORD's commands and decrees that I am giving you today for your own good?

DEUTERONOMY 10:12–13

When Moses spoke the words in today's verse, the Israelites had just made their way across the wilderness to the edge of the Jordan River. They had fled from Pharaoh in Egypt, crossed the Red Sea on dry land, and fed on manna from heaven. They had constantly wavered between obedience to the Lord's commands and rebellion in favor of their own ways. Now, after forty years of wandering, they stood—barely a stone's throw from the long-awaited promised land. Their new home within sight, the Israelites stood in solemn silence as Moses recounted the law, reminding them to obey the Lord "for [their] own good."

Obedience. Often, we either neglect this duty or focus too much on it, looking for praise for our performance. But true obedience means trusting that the Lord calls us to obey because He has "our own good" in mind.

Today, turn to the Lord in obedience, knowing that we obey not to earn grace, but to fully live the life of grace we have in Jesus.

> Lord, teach me obedience, because my own good is found in keeping Your ways.

FULLY COMMITTED

When you relied on the LORD, he delivered [your enemies] into
your hand. For the eyes of the LORD range throughout the earth
to strengthen those whose hearts are fully committed to him. You
have done a foolish thing, and from now on you will be at war.

2 CHRONICLES 16:8–9

At one time, King Asa trusted that God would provide for the needs of Judah. But toward the end of Asa's reign, something happened in the king's heart—he forgot that God had always been faithful, and he decided to take matters into his own hands. Asa stopped believing God would provide, and he stopped seeking Him. So Asa's once-devoted heart hardened, and he turned to politics, money, and force to get his way. The result? God decreed, "From now on you will be at war."

God knows we are prone to wander and forget His goodness. He is not looking for perfection; He is looking for hearts that trust Him. He wants us to stop trying to control our circumstances and outcomes. Instead, when we choose to trust God and wait patiently for His provision, He promises to be our strength. He gives us peace and softens our hearts in the midst of life's hard seasons. It's a moment-by-moment conscious decision: *I will trust You right now.*

God's eyes are searching for those who are committed to Him. When His eyes fall on us, may He see a heart of trust.

Lord, remind me of Your past faithfulness so I can trust You to be faithful in my present circumstances.

HE IS BETTER

[Jesus] came to a village where a woman named Martha opened her home to him. She had a sister called Mary, who sat at the Lord's feet listening to what he said. But Martha was distracted by all the preparations that had to be made. She came to him and asked, "Lord, don't you care that my sister has left me to do the work by myself? Tell her to help me!"

"Martha, Martha," the Lord answered, "you are worried and upset about many things, but few things are needed—or indeed only one. Mary has chosen what is better, and it will not be taken away from her."

LUKE 10:38–42

How often do we identify with Martha in this story? It is surprisingly easy to view life as a list of tasks to be accomplished, rather than as a personal relationship with the King of kings. When we reduce this relationship to working for God's approval, we exchange intimacy with Him for a misguided faith in our own abilities.

In today's scripture we are reminded that an intimate relationship with God is better than anything we could ever do for Him. Bearing fruit is an important part of our walk with God, but it should not come at the cost of our relationship with Him. Knowing and enjoying Him is the fuel for our actions in His name—not the other way around.

Jesus wanted Martha to understand which came first. Take time today to sit and listen to Jesus, and let His voice move you to glorify His name.

> God, help me know and enjoy You more. May I hear Your voice clearly today.

KNOW HIM BETTER

I keep asking that the God of our Lord Jesus Christ, the glorious Father, may give you the Spirit of wisdom and revelation, so that you may know him better. I pray that the eyes of your heart may be enlightened in order that you may know the hope to which he has called you, the riches of his glorious inheritance in his holy people, and his incomparably great power for us who believe.

EPHESIANS 1:17–19

The Lord gives us a gift when we come to know Him: we get to "know him better." Why would God save us only to have us keep walking in the darkness, treating Him as an unreachable mystery? Far from it! The apostle Paul described growing enlightenment, wisdom, revelation, hope, and power. God is transporting us to far more satisfying ground.

This ground is *knowing God*, and buried in it is a rich treasure of joy that's as inexhaustible as God is glorious. And here lies great comfort: we don't come to know Him more by our efforts alone. That's why the apostle Paul prayed for Christ's followers to reach these depths—he "keeps asking," because only God can get us there.

Are you distracted by the glitz of this world? Confused about God and how faith plays a role in your life? Is there a war raging for the desires of your heart? Are the cravings of our culture drawing you? Dear fellow believer, take heart in God's promises! Keep asking God to give you His Spirit and the ability to know Him better. He will satisfy.

> Father, give me wisdom so I can know You better and experience all You have for me.

POWERFUL WORDS

In the past God spoke to our ancestors through the prophets at many times and in various ways, but in these last days he has spoken to us by his Son, whom he appointed heir of all things, and through whom also he made the universe. The Son is the radiance of God's glory and the exact representation of his being, sustaining all things by his powerful word. After he has provided purification for sins, he sat down at the right hand of the Majesty in heaven.

HEBREWS 1:1–3

We all know that words are powerful, but God operates at a different level. When God speaks, His words have the power to bring life where there was death. The beginning of Scripture tells us God *spoke* everything into existence by His Word alone. He created everything out of nothing, and through Him, all of creation is sustained. Those are powerful words!

As believers, we experience the direct power of God's words in our lives. They have freed us, redeemed us, and made us co-heirs with Christ. So why do we tend to forget the eternal words that mark us as sons and daughters? Why do we listen to so many other voices—the ones that tell us we are unlovable and forgotten?

When those voices overwhelm you, return to the Bible—God's living Word. Because when all else fails, His Word remains, "sustaining all things." When we remember the power of God's words, we can't help but marvel at His power! Let's be overwhelmed all over again by the power of His Word as we pursue God daily.

> Thank You, Jesus, that Your words have the power of life. You are worthy of all my praise!

THE SOURCE OF LOVE

Dear friends, let us love one another, for love comes from God.
Everyone who loves has been born of God and knows God.

1 JOHN 4: 7

What is the source of all love in the universe? Today's passage teaches us that love is from God. And it's contagious—it moves from Him to us. If we have been born of God and know God, then love belongs at the heart of how we treat each other. But if we don't love one another, then how can we say that we know God? Love is the indispensable qualification for anyone who claims to follow Jesus. But so much can get in the way.

What prevents you from living a life of love? Is it pride, self-centeredness, busyness, or insecurity? Who are the people in your life who are the most difficult to love? Take a minute to confess these things to the Lord. When the truth of the gospel fills our hearts, there is no one we can't love. Let's turn to Jesus, our example and source of strength for loving others. Remember He's the one who said, "As I have loved you, so you must love one another" (John 13:34). If that seems like a tall order . . . well, it is. It would be impossible if we weren't connected to the source of all love. Ask Him for an overflowing supply today!

Father, You are the source of all love. Give me strength today to walk by Your Spirit and to follow in Your footsteps.

REMEMBER

Remember also your Creator in the days of your youth, before the evil days come and the years draw near when you will say, "I have no delight in them."
ECCLESIASTES 12:1 NASB

Youth is a blessing. We can use it to boldly seek God, and that's how we gain wisdom and understanding. We often find understanding by dedicating ourselves to the traditions of the church: praying, attending gatherings, participating in small groups, and going on mission trips, among other things.

However, as today's verse tells us, darker days are coming. The remainder of Ecclesiastes 12 describes a time when wisdom seems meaningless, and God seems silent and distant. When those days arrive, we shouldn't expect God to show Himself in the places where He's been in the past. Instead, let's prepare for times when we don't understand God's mysterious ways, knowing that He has a perfect plan—and we can trust Him.

Whether we see Him or not, God is working in our midst. Perhaps God has concealed Himself so we can learn to trust Him and seek Him all the more. In those days when God seems silent, we can show the wisdom we've gained by remembering He is faithful.

Lord, prepare my heart for the evil days that are sure to come. Help me practice wisdom by being silent and patient, remembering that You are the Creator who has all things under control.

NO DARKNESS AT ALL

God is light; in him there is no darkness at all.

1 JOHN 1:5

Darkness cannot occupy the same space in time as light; they are incompatible. When today's scripture describes God as "light," it means He is so holy that no sin or darkness can stand to be in His presence.

In Leviticus, the Israelites were told that if someone had an infectious skin disease, they had to be removed from the community until the priest declared them clean. This was done partly for health purposes, but also because any form of uncleanness could not be in God's presence. The Israelites were a holy people, their land a holy dwelling place. If God was to be with them, they had to be separated from uncleanness in every way.

God gave the Israelites the Law so they would know how to follow Him and be close to Him. But now that we have Jesus, the Law is fulfilled—and He takes away our uncleanness and brings us into God's presence! Jesus makes us holy; He overcomes the darkness with His light. As we follow Jesus, He purifies us; yet it is our task to avoid the sin and darkness that can't coexist with the light of God.

Leviticus 20:26 and 1 Peter 1:16 tell us we must be holy because God is holy. This is our calling. In your choices today, seek Jesus—to know Him, to become like Him, and to be a holy light for this world.

> Father, I yearn to know You. Help me passionately seek You and Your holiness.

HOLY JOY

We wait in hope for the LORD; he is our help and our shield. In him our hearts rejoice, for we trust in his holy name. May your unfailing love be with us, LORD, even as we put our hope in you.

PSALM 33:20–22

David's joy must have been contagious. Psalm 33 begins with David joyfully singing and praising the Lord, exalting Him for creating the heavens and the earth and all that is in them. In today's verse, at the end of this psalm, David's tone shifts to not only praising God, but also expressing hope and trust in Him.

When was the last time you trusted a stranger with something important? David presented trust, hope, and rejoicing as inextricably linked. We can't bring praise and place trust in God if we don't seek Him, or "wait in hope" for Him. After all, God made us to search for and find Him (Acts 17:27).

Why did He make us this way? As we search, we begin to understand His character and experience His faithfulness in our lives. And when we truly understand how great God is, we will inevitably give Him praise the way David did: with our whole hearts, holding nothing back.

God wants us to seek Him above all things. When we wait on Him and hope in Him, our hearts find a contagious joy that nothing else on this earth can give.

> Father, may my heart that once longed to find joy in earthly things now radically shift, longing to know You more.

RESTING WORSHIP

The LORD replied, "My Presence will go with you, and I will give you rest."
Then Moses said to him, "If your Presence does not go with
me, do not send us up from here."

EXODUS 33:14–15

You may think of worship as a purely religious idea, but the concept is much bigger. People are prone to worship all sorts of things because we were created to worship. And whether it's God or something material, what you worship will define who you are.

That's why Moses was worried about the Israelites. Compared to every other nation of their time, Israel was set apart by the presence of the One, sovereign, true God instead of the idols of their neighbors. Fully committed to God and His purposes, Moses knew that without God's presence and leading, the nation was lost; they would start worshiping idols. Moses was afraid that without God's presence to center them in worship, Israel would fall to the evil around them.

The same goes for us. When we only worship God, it centers us around Him. And worship doesn't just happen in church or alone in prayer. We worship God with every single action and choice we make.

> Lord God, thank You for going with me. I choose to worship and rest in You today.

SINGLE-MINDED

Submit yourselves therefore to God. Resist the devil, and he will flee from you. Draw near to God, and he will draw near to you. Cleanse your hands, you sinners, and purify your hearts, you double-minded.

JAMES 4:7–8 ESV

In college, temptations are everywhere. Achievement, popularity, attraction, productivity: we are always pressured to pursue these things. And they can easily become destructive distractions.

Perhaps this is what James referred to when he talked about our "double-mindedness." It's a struggle we face daily: we have to decide if we'll pursue a life for God's glory or for our own. If we try to fulfill our own desires, we will never get enough. However, if we instead seek God's glory in all that we do, then we will always find what we desire—Him.

Let's be single-minded in our pursuits. The more we draw near to God, the more He becomes the reason for our actions. The closer we are to Him, the further we are from prioritizing ourselves. This is because God has placed His Spirit in us and longs for His glory to be shared. Make Him, and not yourself, the reason for your actions. Make His glory what you live for, not your own.

Lord, Jesus Christ, have mercy on me, a sinner.

PURSUE HIM

Grace and peace be yours in abundance through the knowledge of God and of Jesus our Lord. His divine power has given us everything we need for a godly life through our knowledge of him who called us by his own glory and goodness.

2 PETER 1:2–3

Imagine being in a relationship with someone you talk to once a week at most. Someone you call when you need something specific, but rarely think about on a daily basis. Someone you enjoy, but who doesn't affect your daily life. It's safe to say that relationship is not going anywhere.

We might hate to admit it, but sometimes we approach our relationship with God this way. But God desires our full attention—all the time. He wants us to know Him on an intimate level and for us to intentionally pursue Him. How does that affect our relationship with Him? Peter explained that as we grow in our knowledge of God, we experience a grace and peace that we couldn't have apart from Him. As we walk with Jesus, we are given everything we need to live. As we make knowing and enjoying Him the passionate pursuit of our lives, our character begins to reflect the heart of God.

God doesn't want believers who just know about Him; He wants sons and daughters who long to know Him intimately. Make time to pursue Him today.

God, I'm thankful that You desire intimacy with me. Give me a greater understanding of who You are. I want to know You more.

55

A THIRSTY SOUL

As the deer pants for streams of water, so my soul pants for you,
my God. My soul thirsts for God, for the living God. When can
I go and meet with God? . . . By day the LORD directs his love, at
night his song is with me—a prayer to the God of my life.

PSALM 42:1–2, 8

The deer recognizes its need for water. Water is essential for the deer to run, to breathe, and to live. In the same way, we have a desperate need for God, in whom there is life.

Each of us has the desire to live and a thirst for fulfillment. This desire can be satisfied by no other source than the One who ordained life itself. We can all relate to being thirsty. Without water, the body will faint and eventually perish. Without the salvation the Father provides, the soul will perish.

We often go about our days seeking to satisfy this thirst we have for life. We turn to success, sports, relationships, or even social media to fill the longing we have, but these temporary sources return void. True life can only be found in knowing God. Even when we feel distant from the Lord, He is faithful to us. His presence is constant; His love directs us during the day and His song comforts us at night. He is always waiting to fulfill us, with open arms. If you want to truly live, run to the source of life.

Father, Your care is evident in Your presence and Your provision. Thank You for offering me true life in Your Son.

GOD NEAR US

And the Word became flesh and made his dwelling among us. We have seen his glory, glory of the one and only Son from the Father, full of grace and truth.

JOHN 1:14

Have you ever had a friend who lived far away? As much as you love that friend, it's hard to keep up a truly close relationship because you lack proximity. But when you are near each other, you are able to be fully present, both physically and spiritually.

God created human beings for intimate relationship with Him. In the garden of Eden, He walked with Adam and Eve, the pinnacle of all creation, each day. When sin entered human hearts, we were separated from His holiness by rebellion and darkness of the deepest kind.

But God wanted to restore us to the perfect relationship with Him, so He sent Jesus to bridge the divide: "The Word became flesh and made his dwelling among us." Jesus moved near us so we could know Him personally. He became present with us so we could have life and be free.

Jesus is God's central illustration of His purpose for us. He doesn't want to be long-distance friends. His heart is to be with you intimately, sharing your struggles and giving you His endless resources in all circumstances. Knowing and enjoying God is only possible because His Son has already closed the divide by joining us. Rejoice in this truth today.

> God, help me understand the truth of Your incarnation in a more powerful way.

UNWAVERING SOVEREIGNTY

Why do you complain, Jacob? Why do you say, Israel, "My way is hidden from the LORD; my cause is disregarded by my God"? Do you not know? Have you not heard? The LORD is the everlasting God, the Creator of the ends of the earth. He will not grow tired or weary, and his understanding no one can fathom.

ISAIAH 40:27–28

Difficult situations can leave us with defeated, dejected spirits and make us question if God truly sees or even cares about what happens to us. But in these moments, knowing God and seeking Him prove essential to the daily walk of any believer.

After Israel fell to the Babylonians, the Israelites lost everything and were enslaved by their victors. As God's chosen people, the Israelites believed that their defeat meant that God had forsaken them, and in their pain they complained to God. But God had a greater plan for them. Notice God's response to Israel's complaints; it's not a simple consolation, but a strong reminder of His nature. He is "everlasting," proving His majesty; He is "Creator," demonstrating His authority; He is strong, granting His people comfort; and He is wise, providing for a better future.

We may never fully understand why we struggle through certain situations, but we can still trust that God is sovereign over it all. Find hope in the power and love of our Father, who never fails or leaves us.

> Lord, when I feel forgotten, remind me that You love me passionately. I set my trust in Your sovereign plan for me.

CONSTANT PRAISE

Whenever the living creatures give glory, honor and thanks to him who sits on the throne and who lives for ever and ever, the twenty-four elders fall down before him who sits on the throne and worship him who lives for ever and ever.

REVELATION 4:9–10

What a beautiful thought: as we speak, God is receiving the worship He deserves in heaven, and it *never* ceases. We should ask ourselves how we can offer Him the same thing as we go about our lives. If we're honest, we might react, "That's impossible. How can I constantly praise God and get anything else done?"

As imperfect humans, what does it look like to commune with God daily? First, start with motivation. In order to really worship God, we must know just how deserving He is. When we familiarize ourselves with the character and power of God, our hearts will overflow with a desire to enjoy a personal relationship with Him.

The most powerful way to commune with God is prayer. As we spend more time with God, we will long to talk more with Him, so we will set aside time and distractions to prioritize prayer. Prayer will be our response to both happiness *and* to sadness, to sickness and health. And when prayer becomes our natural inclination to any situation, it becomes second nature—a timeless, beautiful conversation.

Let's always approach God in prayer, even with the smallest details, and let His glory fuel constant praise in our hearts.

> Lord, help me confidently approach Your throne and give You the worship You deserve. You are worthy.

HEALTHY FEAR

Indeed, if you call out for insight and cry aloud for understanding, and if you look for it as for silver and search for it as for hidden treasure, then you will understand the fear of the LORD and find the knowledge of God.

PROVERBS 2:3–5

The *fear* of God doesn't mean being afraid of God. Instead, fearing God is reverence and worship from an understanding of who He is. And developing a healthy fear of Him is for our own good (Psalm 34); it helps us constantly acknowledge God's greatness. God created us for Himself, but we fell—and we became separated from the God who guides us. As a result, we often stumble through life because we don't have our internal compass to guide our way: the fear of God and reverence for who He is and what He wants.

Solomon, the wisest man ever to live, understood the importance of developing the fear of the Lord, and so he showed us how to gain it; he encouraged us to seek it and cry out for understanding. So take time to search Scripture with diligence and desperation for understanding. Seek it as something vital to your survival, because then you can understand what it means to fear the Lord—and let that good fear guide you in your decisions.

> Father, grant me wisdom to know You more and understand what it means to fear You, as I study and seek You in Your Word.

FREEDOM, FOR FREE

Formerly, when you did not know God, you were slaves to those who by nature are not gods. But now that you know God—or rather are known by God—how is it that you are turning back to those weak and miserable forces? Do you wish to be enslaved by them all over again?

Galatians 4:8–9

How can the greatest love possible—God's love—be offered freely?

We don't even have to earn this love; Jesus paid for God's love through His sacrifice for our sins. No religion or set of rules can save us. Only in Christ can we find true freedom from sin and from the bondage of trying to do it all on our own. His love frees us to live the life God has designed for us.

Our hearts were created by and for God, and His love is unmatched: no matter how many times we stumble and fall, our chains stay broken and His grace stands available. Let us surrender to Him today and stop trying to earn something that's already been given to us. He requires nothing but an open heart and open hands to receive His grace.

> Jesus, help me live free today and know that You have already done all the work. Let me know the depth of Your love, which has the power to satisfy my deepest longings.

EVER-PRESENT HELP

God is our refuge and strength, an ever-present help in trouble.
Therefore we will not fear, though the earth give way and the
mountains fall into the heart of the sea, though its waters roar
and foam and the mountains quake with their surging.

PSALM 46:1–3

The earth gives way. Mountains crumble. Wars rage. Terror seems to reign. Yet in the midst of all-consuming destruction, Jesus is still there.

Sometimes we view the troubles of life as if they were a car wreck and God as an ambulance en route to the scene: in the midst of the wreckage, we know God is on the way, but we still feel a sense of helplessness because He's yet to arrive. But that's not the picture that today's verse paints. It says that God is "ever-present" in our time of trouble; the very nature of God is not one of absence or empty promises, but one that says, "I am here." He is I AM, not *I will be*. In these hard moments, we can lean on Him and rest, knowing that when we don't have any strength left, He is strong for us. He is already there.

> Jesus, forgive me for underestimating You as someone who's simply en route, but help me see You as the One who is my refuge and strength in all things and at all times. Thank You for your persistent and ever-present love.

OUR PORTION

Whom have I in heaven but you? And earth has nothing I desire besides
you. My flesh and my heart may fail, but God is the strength of my heart
and my portion forever. Those who are far from you will perish; you destroy
all who are unfaithful to you. But as for me, it is good to be near God. I
have made the Sovereign LORD my refuge; I will tell of all your deeds.

PSALM 73:25–28

Every day we are surrounded by a myriad of material things competing for our affection and attention. Some of these objects of desire are good, but some are merely distractions, keeping us from what's really important. Often it's only when every blessing is stripped away that we find ourselves forced to evaluate the foundation we stand on.

Like the psalmist, our spirit may shake when we see the unfaithful succeed as we struggle. Amid our shifting circumstances, our logic forces us to question God's goodness and faithfulness. But when we see the true end of the wicked, our hope in justice is renewed, even during times of sorrow.

The hardships we experience aren't meant to shatter believers. Instead, we can trust God to use our hardships for good; He steers our hearts through them and toward Him. Because knowing God is both the journey and the destination, we can rest in peace today as we press on.

> Father, when my spirit is wavering, set my gaze on You, the unchanging One. Everything I want is found in You—I choose to believe in You today!

KNOWING OUR FATHER

We know that we have come to know him if we keep his commands. Whoever says, "I know him," but does not do what he commands is a liar, and the truth is not in that person.

1 JOHN 2:3–4

God knows us. He is aware of the tiniest detail of our lives; we can have no secrets from Him. Not only does God know *us*, but He also created us to know *Him* and to be in a completely dependent and intimate relationship with Him. But how can we be sure that we know God as our Father?

Today's verse says we can be certain that we know God if we follow His commandments. John went on to say, "The one who keeps God's word is the person in whom we see God's mature love" (1 John 2:5 THE MESSAGE). The most important thing God commands us to do is to love Him above anything else. So, we express our love for God by obeying His commandments.

God doesn't want us to simply know facts about Him: He wants us to know Him personally and love Him. We have a Father who sincerely wants to have a relationship with His children. Do you want to know Him better? In your actions today, seek new ways to follow His commands.

Father, I want to know You deeply. Teach me about Yourself. Please strengthen my obedience and understanding of Your commands.

A GOD WHO PURSUES

"When I shut up the heavens so that there is no rain, or command locusts to devour the land or send a plague among my people, if my people, who are called by my name, will humble themselves and pray and seek my face and turn from their wicked ways, then I will hear from heaven, and I will forgive their sin and will heal their land."

2 CHRONICLES 7:13–14

God is constantly reaching out for His children to come to Him and rest in His peace and forgiveness. But just like the Israelites in Old Testament times, Christians today struggle to remain faithful to God and to follow Him completely. God loves us so much that He disciplines us when we rebel against Him. That's because He wants the best for us—Himself. When we turn back to God, He willingly forgives us, even though we don't deserve His mercy. This cycle repeats itself over and over in our lives, and yet God never stops pursuing us and reconciling us to Himself.

Be thankful that God continually pursues your heart and soul. Even when you wander into a dry, desolate place, know that for every step you take back toward God, He will respond with overwhelming love, forgiveness, and healing.

> Father, thank You for pursuing me. I know that when You discipline me, You are calling me back to You.

TASTE AND SEE

Taste and see that the Lord is good; blessed is the one who takes refuge in him. Fear the Lord, you his holy people, for those who fear him lack nothing.

PSALM 34:8–9

In today's psalm, David invites us to try God out for ourselves—to "taste and see"—to take up His offer of love, grace, mercy, and deliverance and see if it stands in times of trouble. David wasn't simply offering some Christian clichés here; he was speaking from experience. There were many times when David was in massive trouble, on the run for his life. But faithful to His character, God came to David's aid. And David's confidence rested in the fact that he tasted and saw God and found Him to be good.

Do you want to know how to taste and see? Then start with fearing and worshiping God. Take a step of faith, draw close to God through His Word and in prayer and worship, and present your personal requests to Him. As you wait for His answer, reflect on His character, on who He is and what He's done for you, and let your heart rest on the solid truth that "the Lord is good."

Father, through it all You are good and deserving of all praise. Help me pause, remember, and reflect on the sure deliverance I have in You.

LOVING OBEDIENCE

*"Whoever has my commands and keeps them is the one who
loves me. The one who loves me will be loved by my Father,
and I too will love them and show myself to them."*

JOHN 14:21

Jesus' disciples were worried about how they were supposed to live after He was no longer with them. So Jesus assured them that even when He would be physically gone, He would still lead them in their daily journeys through the Holy Spirit.

Today, we are Jesus' disciples. Not only do we get to love Jesus by following His commands, but we also have His Holy Spirit within us through every step of obedience, even when we fall short. By following His lead and having faith that His commands are just, you will experience what living in His grace is truly like. The perfect Father you're obeying is gracious enough to still catch you when you make mistakes, so there is no need to obey Him just to try to earn His favor. Instead, obedience is rooted in love. Today, actively love Him by finding new ways to live in obedience. Trust in His Spirit, and thank Him for His guidance. Though we can't see Him physically with us, He's given us a Guide to lead us on our journeys. And He promises to show Himself to us more and more when we ask and obey.

Father, I give You my decisions and my crossroads. Help me
obey Your commands, and show Yourself to me.

THE FIGHT IS OVER

There is one God and one mediator between God and mankind,
the man Christ Jesus, who gave himself as a ransom for all
people. This has now been witnessed to at the proper time.

1 TIMOTHY 2:5–6

We all have *that* friend, right? The peacemaker. The friend who's always trying to bring calm to a crazy situation or make a fractured relationship whole again. If there is conflict or an argument, that friend is always present to step in and bring peace.

Jesus is that friend for us. God is holy, and we are sinful. Our nature was in conflict with His. So Jesus came to intervene and bring peace between God and mankind. Sin prevented us from having an intimate relationship with a beautiful and loving God until Jesus defeated sin and death on the cross. Through faith in Him we now can be free from the bondage of our sin and intimately know, love, and experience God. He is our "mediator."

Scripture says we are "hidden with Christ," meaning we are no longer defined by our sin, but instead by Jesus' finished work on the cross (Colossians 3:3). When God looks at you, He does not see your shortcomings or your past mistakes. He sees Jesus! Thank God for the gift of Jesus, who made peace and reconciliation possible.

Father, help me walk in the freedom that You purchased for me. Thank You for sending Jesus, our peacemaker.

FIXED ON JESUS

*Therefore, since we are surrounded by such a great cloud of witnesses,
let us throw off everything that hinders and the sin that so easily
entangles. And let us run with perseverance the race marked out for
us, fixing our eyes on Jesus, the pioneer and perfecter of faith.*

HEBREWS 12:1–2

In today's passage, God calls us to some mighty tasks: to throw off every hindrance, to rid our lives of sin, and to run with endurance. No human effort could bring us close to accomplishing these tasks. But God provides for our inability by calling us to fix our eyes on Jesus. He is the "pioneer and perfecter of [our] faith" because He lived the life we could not. Walking in His power, following His example, and ultimately knowing Him enables us to walk according to His Word.

So we commit to spend time with Him, studying His life, and pursuing His wisdom. He is the prize that helps us run in the "race marked out for us," so that we keep our eyes on Him.

Do you find yourself running your race in this mighty manner? If not, could you be fixing your eyes on something other than Jesus? Perhaps it's relationships, pleasures, or your own security. But none of these will ever lead to a triumphant race. We must fix our eyes on nothing less than Jesus—our greatest example, and the pioneer and perfecter of our faith.

> Lord Jesus, deepen my desire to know You more as I look to nothing less than You. Remind me of my dependence on You as Your Spirit enables me to run with perseverance.

REVEALER OF MYSTERIES

But, as it is written, "What no eye has seen, nor ear heard, nor
the heart of man imagined, what God has prepared for those who
love him"—these things God has revealed to us through the Spirit.
For the Spirit searches everything, even the depths of God.

1 Corinthians 2:9–10 esv

There are so many unexplainable things in the universe. Consider the mind-blowing nature of fractals, turbulence, or our complex planetary ecosystems. These earthly mysteries unveil God's infinite creativity. The Creator's ingenuity extends to spiritual mysteries, and with the Holy Spirit's help, we can understand them and know God more deeply through His revelation.

Only by the Spirit can we grasp the life-changing, earth-shattering nature of the cross, the central mystery of God. Since the Holy Spirit intimately knows God's heart and dwells within your heart, He connects you both. He can help you understand the previously unknowable mysteries of God. Therefore, pressing in to the Spirit—seeking His presence, listening for His voice—is a gift by which we can know and enjoy God.

Seek the Holy Spirit through spending quality time with Him and waiting for Him to speak. Study God's Word, and ask the Spirit for understanding. Talk to the Spirit as a dear Friend, who knows you fully and loves you infinitely. He is always present—always with you and ready to reveal God's mysteries.

Holy Spirit, thank You for Your omnipresence. Help me know and enjoy You more deeply.

GOD BRINGS US BACK

"In that day I will make a covenant for them with the beasts of the field, the birds in the sky and the creatures that move along the ground. Bow and sword and battle I will abolish from the land, so that all may lie down in safety. I will betroth you to me forever; I will betroth you in righteousness and justice, in love and compassion. I will betroth you in faithfulness, and you will acknowledge the LORD."

HOSEA 2:18–20

In one of the most powerful metaphors in Scripture, the prophet Hosea was commanded to marry an adulterous woman named Gomer. He was acting out God's relationship with Israel. He physically experienced God's heartbreak in loving Israel, as Gomer broke their marriage covenant time and again. Gomer's acts of betrayal were met with unconditional love, like the love God showed the people of Israel. God continues to show us this same love on a daily basis.

God made a covenant with us to know and be bound to Him forever. We break our end of the covenant when things of this world entice us, but God, in His mercy, calls us back to true love and satisfaction, and He continues to let us back in over and over again. How undeserving we are. How truly precious it is to be bound to our Creator for eternity! Every earthly thing we think we need pales in comparison to the covenant we have entered into with our Father. What more could we ever need?

> Father, thank You for bringing me back to You. Ignite in me a passion to place You above all other things.

THE KNOWN GOD

We know also that the Son of God has come and has given us understanding,
so that we may know him who is true. And we are in him who is true
by being in his Son Jesus Christ. He is the true God and eternal life.

1 JOHN 5:20

There is one aspect of God, at the core of His being, that the human mind cannot fully comprehend: His infinitude. God is unbounded by time, with no beginning and no end. Pause for a moment and think about that.

Dwelling on infinity sends our minds into a spiral because our lives are defined by beginnings and endings. Yet the beautiful thing is that our infinite God, from humanity's first breath until now, has stooped down to the earth-bound and made Himself known to us within forms and boundaries that our finite minds can grasp.

That's the beauty of Jesus! He is the fullness of God, the image of the invisible, come to us in a human form with limits, edges, and flesh that we can understand.

We sometimes seek God because we want a checklist of spiritual to-dos we can manage and cross off when completed. But what if we instead focused our Scripture reading, prayers, and worship on getting to know Jesus? In knowing Jesus we will find our redemption, identity, purpose, and eternal life.

Jesus, thank You for taking on flesh so I could know You. Stir my heart and let me know You even better.

WAITING FOR A NEW ORDER

*Then I saw "a new heaven and a new earth," for the first heaven
and the first earth had passed away . . . And I heard a loud voice
from the throne saying, "Look! God's dwelling place is now among
the people, and he will dwell with them. They will be his people,
and God himself will be with them and be their God."*

REVELATION 21:1, 3

When we talk about heaven, we tend to describe it as an intangible realm of blissful existence. In this far-off place, the chorus of angels echoes endlessly, and time and space disappear into the edge of the cosmos. With every layer of details, this picture of "heaven" slips further from reality. But the Scriptures don't describe heaven in these ethereal terms. For John, the author of Revelation, heaven felt concrete—too wonderful for human language to accurately describe, but still concrete. Its surest aspect is God's eternal presence with His people. Heaven is heaven because God is there.

Conflict, *war*, *genocide*, and *slavery* are all-too-familiar terms in our daily headlines. But a time is coming, not too far from now, when every power in history will surrender before God's throne, and humankind and God will be reconciled. A new order will be established: death will not enter the city gates. God Himself will wipe every tear from our eyes and take us by the hand into His kingdom. Set your hope in the Lord: His coming is sure, and He will reward those who wait on Him.

> Lord, I long to be with You forever. May I walk in a way that
> honors You today.

LOVE FOR THE LOCAL EXPRESSION OF HIS CHURCH

Because Christ established the church for God's glory, I will invest the gifts He has given me in the life and mission of my local church.

What comes to mind when you hear the word *church*? A white chapel with a tall steeple? A worship service? A Sunday school class? It's easy to confuse our past experiences for the church itself. Instead, we must remember the church is not a building, a program, or even a worship service. The church is people—you and me, men and women, young and old, rich and poor, black and white and every color in between—who have been brought back to life through Jesus. It's in these living and breathing people that God's presence lives, and it's through them that He is reconciling creation with Himself. If we don't stop and realize this—that the church is not a *place* of worship, but a *people* who worship—we will cycle in and out of a building every Sunday without ever stepping into the deep, intimate relationships by which God intends to transform us and the world.

The truth is relationships are complicated. It's easier to slip into a seat as the service is getting started and dart to the parking lot as it wraps up than to be vulnerable with another person. Inviting other people to influence and speak into your life can be uncomfortable and messy. But it's exactly there, in the friction of our relationships, where God is glorified in the church. When we have hard conversations and repent for mistakes made, when we cry together after tragedy hits, when we bare our hearts and ask for forgiveness, when we encourage each other in moments of despair, when we buy groceries after someone has lost a job, when we pray for the impossible together, and gather and worship Jesus, we become the physical manifestation of our Father's love, mercy, grace, forgiveness, justice, and holiness. It's in our interactions with one another that His presence becomes real in our lives.

As time marches on, movements will come and go. Buildings will be erected and torn down; books, conferences, and names will be forgotten. But God's people will remain. Even if hell were to swing its gates open and storm the church, she would not be overcome. Christ is jealous for her, and nothing will stand between Him and His bride. But it's up to each of us to live as the church and take our place in this collective journey of following Jesus.

LOVE OF THE LOCAL CHURCH

Let us consider how we may spur one another on toward love and good deeds, not giving up meeting together, as some are in the habit of doing, but encouraging one another—and all the more as you see the Day approaching.

HEBREWS 10:24–25

Togetherness. God created us with an undeniable need for it. He wove the need for the company and encouragement of other believers into us so we could thrive together. God intends for us to be devoted to our churches and to keep us on the straight and narrow, all the while reaching the world with His love.

The church is the earthly representation of Christ's love. The body of Christ is our family—the people who support us in difficult times, rejoice with us in our successes, and consistently lead us toward Jesus. So why do we find it easy to neglect the church, our God-given source of support?

Because we are fallen human begins, we are prone to give up. We get tired, bored, distracted, or angry—and abandon the things that help us grow. But joining other believers at church is too important for us to abandon.

God urges His people to consistently meet together, not as just another rule to follow, but because our church family offers needed love and encouragement. Jesus is our source of faithfulness, and He has provided a community for us to love and be loved in. Let us then follow His example and love each other faithfully.

> Father, please give me the faithfulness I need to continue meeting with and serving my brothers and sisters in Christ.

ON THIS ROCK

"And I tell you that you are Peter, and on this rock I will build my church, and the gates of Hades will not overcome it."
MATTHEW 16:18

If someone asked you, "Who do you say Jesus is?" what would your answer be? For the apostle Peter the answer was clear: "You are the Messiah, the Son of the living God" (Matthew 16:16). Peter's confession is the first from any of the apostles in the gospels. Jesus then told His disciples that the church, the whole body of His believers, would be built upon the apostles with Him as its cornerstone.

In these few lines, Jesus illustrates His lesson by using Peter's name as a clever play on words . In Greek, Peter's name is *Petros*, which means "rock" or "stone" in a building. But Jesus uses another word in Greek—*petra*—which means "bedrock." And this time, He was using the word *petra* to refer to Himself as the structural foundation of the building. So although Peter and the apostles would have key roles in building the early church, Jesus Himself would be the foundation. And when the Son of God is the solid ground of the church, nothing can overcome it.

Christ is still building His church today, and He's inviting us to use the gifts God has given us to be a part of His work. Will you join the apostles and become a rock in your church?

> Lord, give me a passion for investing my love and service into my church.

AN OPEN DOOR

*"These are the words of him who is holy and true, who holds
the key of David. What he opens no one can shut, and what he
shuts no one can open. . . . I know that you have little strength,
yet you have kept my word and have not denied my name."*

REVELATION 3:7–8

Think of a time when God opened a door for you that you couldn't
have opened for yourself. As you remember answered prayers,
restored relationships, ministry opportunities, and conversations
about the gospel, take a minute to thank God for the times He
came through for you, when you couldn't do what you needed
to do in your own strength. When we face trials, suffering, and
doubts, it is essential that we remember the many times God has
provided for us in the past. We can hold on to His promises that
will remain with us and guide us through difficult times.

Today's scripture teaches us that Jesus has the "key of David"—
that is, He has all authority over creation and over God's kingdom.
When Jesus opens a door, no one else can shut it. And through the
cross, He has swung open the doors of heaven for all who call upon
His name. When we were at our weakest, Jesus stretched out His
arms so we could be welcomed in as beloved children.

Let's continue to trust Him, even when we have little strength,
for He is "holy and true," and He will not forget us.

> Father, thank You for the doors You have opened for me.
> Help me remain faithful to Your name, knowing that You have
> already opened the doors of heaven for me!

TRANSFORMING SUBMISSION

Submit to one another out of reverence for Christ.

EPHESIANS 5:21

Submission is not an exercise in manners or proper behavior; submission is allowing Christ to transform our hearts so we can honor Him in our selfless acts of love for the people around us.

Jesus performed the ultimate act of submission. Although He is divine and the omnipotent Creator, He chose to lay down His life for a broken and depraved world. Now He is calls us to follow His lead and do the same: to lay down our own lives and serve others in a world bent on seeking control, power, and fame. To cast aside any desire to elevate ourselves or put people down. To truly love and serve one another.

Submission is against the grain of the control we so deeply desire. Our culture recoils at the mere mention of the word; many people believe to submit is to be weak and passive. But through the power of the Holy Spirit, we submit out of love and strength— not weakness. With Him, we can say no to our selfish ambitions. Today, let's remember that Jesus didn't lord over us—He loved us. And let's freely submit to one another, imitating Christ in our sacrificial love for the church.

> Thank You, Jesus, for embracing submission so that I may live. May Your sacrificial love propel me to put others before myself.

PURPOSEFULLY RUNNING

So flee youthful passions and pursue righteousness, faith, love, and peace,
along with those who call on the Lord from a pure heart. Have nothing to
do with foolish, ignorant controversies; you know that they breed quarrels.

2 TIMOTHY 2:22–23 ESV

This world begs us to take what it has to offer. Advertisements entice us to place our identity in how we look, the Internet leads us to late-night emptiness, and popular culture tells us that the more we have, the more we will enjoy life. Interestingly, the more we gain in these areas, the more broken relationships, shattered self-worth, and identity crises we seem to have.

There is a way out; you can't run *from* something without running *toward* something else. Jesus doesn't want our "put-together" mask; He wants to meet us as we are—He wants the real us. If we turn from the world, fleeing the passions that only rob us of true life, we'll come face-to-face with a Savior who loves us regardless of our past. You have been given the choice: What are you going to run toward? Will you run toward Jesus?

> Father, give me the strength to turn away from my desires and run toward Jesus, in whom righteousness, faith, love, and peace are found.

SURE FOUNDATION

By the grace God has given me, I laid a foundation as a wise builder, and someone else is building on it. But each one should build with care. For no one can lay any foundation other than the one already laid, which is Jesus Christ.

1 CORINTHIANS 3:10–11

In a world saturated by new movements, theologies, and denominations, it's tempting to build our worldview on ear-catching sound bites. While these catchphrases may be current and trendy, they often cause us to miss the fundamental building blocks of the faith.

This isn't a new phenomenon. Nearly two thousand years ago, Paul had to clarify to the church of Corinth that its role was to join the movement of Jesus, not start its own. We are the church, and Scripture calls us to carefully examine the foundation we stand on. When new movements, ideas, and leaders rise, we must remember that *Jesus* is the only unshakable and lasting truth we can build our faith and our lives on.

There are a lot of things we might be unsure of, and even more we might never understand. But one thing we do know is that Jesus is Lord and that in Him is life. Therefore, He is the cornerstone we must always stand on. Build your life on Jesus, the original and true foundation. On Him your faith will stand firm and secure.

> Jesus, You are the solid rock—the sure foundation of our faith. Teach me to look to You, the Cornerstone, as I commit to build up Your church on Your truth.

ACTING OUT OF REMEMBRANCE

Get rid of all bitterness, rage and anger, brawling and slander,
along with every form of malice. Be kind and compassionate to one
another, forgiving each other, just as in Christ God forgave you.
Ephesians 4:31–32

Does it ever feel difficult to be a Christian in your workplace or on your campus? Do you feel pressured by people to act a certain way? Are you sometimes unsure how to act?

The world is constantly looking at us as "Christians," analyzing and noticing how we act and respond to certain situations. We understand that we need to be a light, so we often feel pressure to share with others about Jesus through our own knowledge, which can bring fears and insecurities. Then, we read verses like today's scripture and feel challenged to remember all of the "don'ts" and forget about the other side of the coin: remembering how Jesus forgave us and, out of gratitude, how we should be "kind and compassionate to one another."

When we remember how God forgave us through Christ, we can shrug off negativity and turn to our brothers and sisters in the same kindness and forgiveness. This position of thankfulness and remembrance lends our gaze to Jesus, who is the One working through us to reach those who don't know Him yet. Remember His forgiveness today, and let it be the basis for the way you treat those around you.

> Father, help me remember all You have done for me, so You can use me to impact others.

GENTLE RESTORATION

Brothers and sisters, if someone is caught in a sin, you
who live by the Spirit should restore that person gently.
But watch yourselves, or you also may be tempted.

GALATIANS 6:1

Restoring a person in gentleness is like tending to a broken leg caught in a trap. First the limb must be freed from the trap, then the bone reset and placed in a cast to heal. We should care for a sin-wounded person the same way. God wants us to help each other, even those who have been caught in sin's trap.

But be mindful while freeing your friend, because the same trap that caught your friend can also ensnare you. Restore your friend by wrapping love and words of grace and truth around them like a cast—but don't let pride get in your way, thinking you are superior to your friend or that you don't have to battle against sin, because that's a slippery slope that may send you falling into the trap. As you reset the bone, let kindness and patience be your instruments, since the reset may be painful and healing may not be immediate.

So roll up your sleeves, breathe deep, and bend low. Stop for a friend and care for his or her sin-wound. God's restoration, healing, and freedom are available through you. Will you be a restorer?

Jesus, may You heal and restore as I stop in Your name to do Your work.

THE HEAD OF THE CHURCH

The Son is the image of the invisible God, the firstborn over all creation. . . .
He is before all things, and in him all things hold together. And he is the
head of the body, the church; he is the beginning and the firstborn from
among the dead, so that in everything he might have the supremacy.

COLOSSIANS 1:15, 17–18

We often try to sort life into the things *Jesus* controls and things *we* control. But in today's verse, Paul asserted that Jesus is ruler over *all* creation, and He holds every particle of existence together. And just as Jesus is ruler over the created world, He is also ruler over the church.

How does this change our outlook for the church? That Jesus rules over the church? When we look to Him as our active, listening, speaking leader, obedience becomes a form of worship, and prayer a genuine plea for His guidance. We trust in His leadership, for we know that even though He is perfect, He is still kind and generous, giving us mercy and grace when we fail. Though His power is beyond match or comprehension, we can still approach Him, and He loves us.

We get the opportunity to share in this truth with our community in faith. Let us seek Him as one, for we have confidence that in His love, He will lead us to Himself.

> Jesus, no other name keeps this world in order. Since You have the power to hold even the cosmos together, give me the faith to believe You'll hold Your church together.

STAY IN YOUR LANE

*Brothers and sisters, choose seven men from among you who are known
to be full of the Spirit and wisdom. We will turn this responsibility over to
them, and will give our attention to prayer and the ministry of the word.*

ACTS 6:3–4

We love to get involved in and jump into the things that we see
Jesus doing in our churches, campus ministries, Bible studies, and
student organizations. There are so many opportunities to influence and to be influenced, to lead and be led. But realistically, we
can't be a part of everything!

When we read how the twelve disciples led the church, we
see a beautiful picture of the diverse gifts in the body of Christ.
They model how we are to build the church. The brothers weren't
trying to do everything; they were "staying in their lanes," so to
speak, and entrusted a selected group of others with duties suited
to their talents.

Jesus has given you amazing, unique gifts. You may be tal-
ented in public speaking; you could have a great compassion for
people whom society tends to neglect; you might have the gift of
hospitality. No matter the gift Jesus has given you, excel in it! By
tending and growing your own talent, you allow others to operate in their gifts while you do the same, building up the body as
intended—each member doing its part.

> Jesus, show me how I should invest the gifts and passions
> You've given me in Your church.

CLOTHED IN HUMILITY

You who are younger, submit yourselves to your elders. All of you,
clothe yourselves with humility toward one another, because,
"God opposes the proud but shows favor to the humble."

1 PETER 5:5

If we're being honest, humility is especially difficult for our generation. As we transition from our teenage years to young adulthood, we seek independence. And as we try to establish our own lives, we get more confident—but in our confidence in our new lives, we sometimes believe that we know better than those who have built their lives before ours.

In today's verse, Peter gives us a reality check, instructing us to submit to our elders' leadership by living humbly with one another. Still, as Peter pointed out earlier in 1 Peter 5, this doesn't mean the elders are the totalitarian rulers of the church and have no obligation toward the younger men and women they are responsible for. Peter said the elders should lead as humble servants.

To live as a Christ-follower means we need to conform ourselves to His example—and Jesus was the perfect example of humility. Though He was still fully God, Jesus considered others more important than Himself and took on the role of a servant. Since our Lord humbled Himself that much, we have no reason *not* to humble ourselves and live a sacrificial life worthy of Christ.

> Lord, just as You came in humility to serve, let me do the same in my church.

TRUE GENEROSITY

*Now about the collection for the Lord's people: Do what I told the
Galatian churches to do. On the first day of every week, each one of you
should set aside a sum of money in keeping with your income, saving
it up, so that when I come no collections will have to be made.*

1 CORINTHIANS 16:1–2

Generosity. It's a term that may not cross our minds too often—
except maybe when we see the offering plate. But Paul reminds us
that we ought to consciously practice giving to our brothers and
sisters in need.

If we skim over today's passage, it might sound like an administrative detail. But if we look closer, we see that God calls us to
be generous with our possessions and, ultimately, everything we
have belongs to Him. The Lord blesses us so that we can be a blessing to others. When we are generous with what we have received,
the Lord can use that portion to supply others' needs.

Paul asked for money, but the Lord may ask more of you.
He may ask that you invest your time and talents in serving the
church or maybe even that you open your home to others. How
can you open your hands and bless your brothers and sisters in
need with what you have?

Father, please help me be generous with the blessings You
have given to me. I pray that as I go through life, I remember
that everything is Yours, and I am the steward.

A NEW MISSION

*Although I am less than the least of all the Lord's people, this grace was
given me: to preach to the Gentiles the boundless riches of Christ, and to
make plain to everyone the administration of this mystery . . . His intent
was that now, through the church, the manifold wisdom of God should be
made known to the rulers and authorities in the heavenly realms, according
to his eternal purpose that he accomplished in Christ Jesus our Lord.*

EPHESIANS 3:8–11

After Paul's conversion, he not only experienced new life in Jesus;
he also received a new mission. He was no longer to use his gifts
to persecute the church, but rather to build it—to champion the
church's mission by preaching salvation to the Gentiles. In God's
perfect wisdom, through Jesus, He opened the door for all people
in all nations to know Him. What had been a mystery was now
known, and Paul used his life to speak this truth to as many
people as he could.

As a follower of Jesus, you have also received new life and a
new mission. You are a part of the church and are to carry out its
mission: to share the news about God's salvation with the world.
We believers proclaim what Jesus accomplished: freedom for all!
So how will you use your life, talents, and gifts to champion God's
mission for the church?

> Lord, thank You for making a way for all to know You. Show
> me how to invest my life in the active plan for the world's
> salvation.

CHURCH FAMILY

Do not rebuke an older man harshly, but exhort him as if he were your father. Treat younger men as brothers, older women as mothers, and younger women as sisters, with absolute purity.

1 TIMOTHY 5:1–2

What does it mean to be a member of a family? As Christians, we have been adopted into Christ's family—the church. No matter where we've come from, because of Jesus, we now belong in His family for life.

Today's verse tells us we should love our family with "absolute purity." How do we do that? Psalm 119:9 says being pure is living according to God's Word. So we must show love to each other in the way we see it carried out in the Scriptures: to treat others with respect, faithfulness, dignity, honor, and sacrifice. And just as our Father has loved us with patience and forgiveness, so must we also love our family members in the faith.

Remember what life was like before you knew Jesus? Remember wanting to feel like you belonged? Wanting to be loved and known? These desires can only be fulfilled by Jesus, the One who made us. In response to His love for us, we get to stretch out our arms and invite those who are still searching into the family of Jesus. As members of His family, we are woven together with the purpose of caring for each other, so let's not wait any longer to start loving the church fully and deeply.

> Jesus, thank You for calling me to Your family. Grow in me a deeper love for my family members.

DISCERNING THE BEST WAY

This is my prayer: that your love may abound more and more in
knowledge and depth of insight, so that you may be able to discern
what is best and may be pure and blameless for the day of Christ.

PHILIPPIANS 1:9–10

When asked what the most important Jewish law was, Jesus explained that it is love for God first, then love for your neighbor that fulfills all the laws of the prophets (Matthew 22:36–40).

Through His ministry, Jesus exemplified a lifestyle of love. As followers of Christ, we're called to infuse that love into every aspect of our lives. But this is not always easy. We're often faced with difficult situations with no clear prescription on how to love a friend or neighbor well. How can we best meet others' needs when we don't know what to say, or when we don't feel loving?

Paul understood this difficulty and prayed for our love to "abound" in knowledge and insight, so we can discern the best way forward. We don't have to come up with the answers on our own; God gives us that knowledge and insight. Loving others can be challenging, but through prayer and Christ's Spirit, we are empowered to navigate life with love and grace.

Jesus said the world will know His followers by the way they love each other (John 13:35). So let us excel in love for one another, as a testimony to the love and glory of Christ.

God, help me love You above all else. May my love for my brothers and sisters serve as a testimony about You and bring You glory.

SELFLESS LEADERSHIP

Deacons are to be worthy of respect, sincere, not indulging in much
wine, and not pursuing dishonest gain. They must keep hold of the deep
truths of the faith with a clear conscience. They must first be tested;
and then if there is nothing against them, let them serve as deacons.

1 TIMOTHY 3:8–10

Christian leadership is a selfless pursuit. Contrary to the paradigm given by the world, the Christian leader seeks to advance not his or her own name, but Christ's. That leader is motivated not just by personally devised convictions, but by God's eternal principles. Paul gave special attention to the character of these leaders in order to preserve the inner strength of the church and its ability to witness to the world.

Paul called leaders to be sincere, to exercise self-control, and to lead upright lives. Leaders in the church are entrusted with the responsibility of teaching and keeping the deep truths of the faith. They must be found to be trustworthy, because this is no small task. A leader's strength must be rooted in Christ, and not fame or personal abilities. Above all, a biblical leader is motivated by a deep desire to advance God's kingdom by making Jesus' name known.

How can you become a strong leader? How can you foster authentic community, something the world is desperately looking for? Instead of focusing on our own reputations, let's focus on advancing Christ's mission.

Lord, make my own motivations plain to me, so I can serve
Your people with a sincere heart.

ROOT YOURSELF IN GOD

The time will come when people will not put up with sound doctrine.
They will turn their ears away from the truth and turn aside to myths.
But you, keep your head in all situations, endure hardship, do the
work of an evangelist, discharge all the duties of your ministry.

2 TIMOTHY 4:3–5

In today's world, there are many different places we can run to for help and teaching. God's truth often makes us uncomfortable and challenges our pride, so we're tempted to run to worldly "teaching" that boosts our egos, appeases our self-centeredness, and numbs our appetite for truth. With so many self-help promises vying for our attention, it's all the more pressing that we find and serve in a church that's not about pleasing ourselves.

God gives us the gift of His church, led by Jesus, so we don't fall for the "myths" set out by worldly teachers. Church is where we meet with God, align our lives with His truth, and invest in His kingdom. It's a local expression of the global body and bigger mission of Christ. In a generation that is always chasing the next high or ego-boosting achievement, we must be the people who root down and completely invest in God's life-affirming work.

Consider how you can serve the church. Rather than suiting our own desires, let's focus on keeping open hearts, asking God where He wants us to serve, and fully investing where He directs.

> Lord, purify my motives. I do not want to satisfy my own desires; I want to completely invest in Your body wherever You have me.

NO SHAME

Do not be ashamed of the testimony about our Lord or of me his prisoner.
Rather, join with me in suffering for the gospel, by the power of God.
2 TIMOTHY 1:8

Have you ever been "shamed" for your faith? Maybe you've sat through a lecture on the "ignorance of Christianity." Perhaps you have a coworker who passionately believes that God is just a crutch for weak people. Regardless of your situation, these interactions can often be awkward or intimidating.

Paul was very familiar with the world's rejection of Christ's message. In fact, he wrote today's scripture while he was in prison! Despite his circumstances, Paul told his protégé, Timothy, to be unashamed of the gospel—the very thing that put Paul in prison. This is not simply a command, but a hope-filled firework intended to bring God's beautiful light into darkness. We are to be unashamed because God has given us His Spirit. And it's not a Spirit of fear, but of power, love, and self-control (2 Timothy 1:7).

The world we live in is filled with hostility because a person determined to gain power is the complete opposite of the service-filled life God desires. But if the Spirit of God dwells within you, you can walk confidently, knowing that you bring life wherever you go.

Father, thank You for the life You have given me. Make me an unashamed instrument for You.

UNARMED, YET UNSHAKEN

Peter was kept in prison, but the church was earnestly praying to God for him.

ACTS 12:5

When God established the church, He gave us the gift of prayer. As a form of worship, prayer gives us direct access to Him. Worship was designed to bring glory to God, and prayer connects us to God by reminding us that we are dependent on Him for everything.

Even in the beginning of the church, persecution and affliction were constant. Peter, a faithful follower of Jesus, was sent to prison to be executed for his witness of the gospel. There was nothing he could do to free himself from the chains King Herod set to bind him. His circumstances seemed insurmountable. Having no other resource than to run to God in their great need and helplessness, the church "earnestly prayed." God heard their prayers and, through a miracle, freed Peter from prison!

God began building His church through its persecution, and prayer was their weapon. The church grew and became strengthened because the early believers remained persistent in prayer, trusting in God's promises, and utterly dependent on Him for help. Let's strive to act with the same urgency as the early church. Let's invest ourselves in praying for one another, asking God to use us to make Jesus' name known throughout the earth.

Lord, let our prayers for Your church become dependent on Your power and expectant that You will do immeasurably more than we could imagine.

ANSWER THE CALL

Now to him who is able to do immeasurably more than all we ask or imagine, according to his power that is at work within us, to him be glory in the church and in Christ Jesus throughout all generations, for ever and ever! Amen.

EPHESIANS 3:20–21

More often than not, when we study today's verses the focus rests on the promise of "immeasurably more." This is not wrong; God has already done more than we could ask for or imagine in our lives through Jesus, and He continues to do so even today. But Paul's message doesn't stop there. He reminds us that the purpose of the church is to worship and glorify God.

Paul called us to participate in this great task: to make God known among the world and to celebrate Him forever. Paul invited us to glorify God through the church because the church is the primary agent for proclaiming God's fame to the world.

How are you contributing to the glory of God through your church? Paul called all generations to serve in this way, which definitely includes us. Today, rejoice in the One who has already accomplished the impossible for us. Devote your gifts and talents, whatever they may be, to His glory, and respond to His grace by lifting up His name with your local church.

> God, help me answer Your call with my life today, and show me ways to contribute where I am.

PURPOSEFULLY GIFTED

By the grace given me I say to every one of you: Do not think of yourself more highly than you ought, but rather think of yourself with sober judgment, in accordance with the faith God has distributed to each of you.

ROMANS 12:3

Paul, the author of Romans, spoke these words out of deep gratitude for the gifts God gave him. God gave us particular gifts for a purpose. And when we use our gifts to serve others, God is glorified.

God has invited us to be a part of the story He is writing by allowing us to use the gifts He has given us. We believers find our meaning not within ourselves alone, but as a part of His body—we collectively belong to Christ and, therefore, to each other. When we realize this, we can stop wishing we had a different role, or different talent, or different personality so that others will think highly of us. Instead, we can begin to work together, using our own unique gifts that complement other believers' gifts. When we have more diverse talent at our disposal, it's only natural that we will attract even more people to join God's kingdom.

Let's turn from the thoughts of self-importance, and instead remember Christ's example, which challenges us to give up our own ambitions so we can serve others and glorify God.

Lord, help me rest in the strengths You have given me and use them wisely, so others can join the beautiful story You are writing.

BUILT TOGETHER

You are no longer foreigners and strangers, but fellow citizens with God's people and also members of his household . . . with Christ Jesus himself as the chief cornerstone. In him the whole building is joined together and rises to become a holy temple in the Lord. And in him you too are being built together to become a dwelling in which God lives by his Spirit.

EPHESIANS 2:19–22

When we say, "Jesus is the foundation of the church," what does it mean? We know that when Jesus rose from the dead, He made a way for humanity to reach God. Once strangers and outsiders, the Gentiles became one with the Jews and were invited to become members of God's family; they became recipients of all the benefits of a citizen of heaven. So Jesus, bringing the whole world together, is the cornerstone of this new, unshakeable foundation. When we're "built together" in Him, we all have a secure and purposeful place.

Upon His foundation, a holy temple is being built, composed of the children of God—no matter their gender, race, or social status. This unity, the church, is God's design. His children are stronger together and are a necessary support for each other.

As our lives are intertwined, His building rises in strength, creating a dwelling place for the Spirit of God. In love and service, devote yourself to Christ and to His church—your brothers and sisters—so that your lives may be built together into something greater.

> Jesus, help me love Your church so we become a family where the Spirit rests.

MINISTERS OF MERCY

"Which of these three do you think was a neighbor to the man who fell into the hands of robbers?" The expert in the law replied, "The one who had mercy on him." Jesus told him, "Go and do likewise."

LUKE 10:36–37

In the parable of the good Samaritan, Jesus described the importance of showing love and mercy to all people, even when it isn't convenient. He told a story about a man who had been robbed and left for dead on a road. A priest and a Levite, two prominent and upright figures in Jewish society, saw the stranger, and each continued on his way, not bothering to help the man. A Samaritan, however, stopped to care for the afflicted traveler, tending his wounds and even paying for his medical treatment.

Samaritans were a people group that the Jews considered unclean. But this Samaritan showed practical love by caring and providing for a man he didn't know. The Samaritan did not pause to consider if this man had the same spiritual, racial, or social identity. Rather, he was moved to help out of love and compassion.

Christ demonstrated perfect love for all mankind when He sacrificed His life for the sins of both righteous and unrighteous people. Just as Christ died for those in every life situation, let's seek to serve people of all backgrounds, looking on them with compassion and a desire for them to know Jesus.

Father, challenge me to serve people as Christ did, pursuing them with mercy, grace, and love.

A BIGGER FAMILY

He replied to him, "Who is my mother, and who are my brothers?" Pointing to his disciples, he said, "Here are my mother and my brothers! For whoever does the will of my Father in heaven is my brother and sister and mother."

Matthew 12:48–50

Jesus' disciples chose Him over anyone else in their lives, including their families. And Jesus showed His love for His disciples when He gave them equality with His own mother.

Jesus wants hearts that are dedicated to Him. Taking a leap of faith can be scary, but the rewards greatly outweigh the risks. God promises to hold us in His hands; all we have to do is let go and give Him first priority in our lives.

When Mary and Martha opened up their home to Jesus, only Mary decided to welcome the interruption and listen to what Jesus was trying to tell her (Luke 10). Martha was so fixated on her duties that she missed out on the important gift God had offered her; she didn't make Jesus her first priority. Jesus asks that we put Him first, trusting that the life He offers us is more than anything we could plan for ourselves. When the disciples left their families to follow Jesus, He promised a larger, eternal family, bound together in His love, that we can all be a part of. Isn't that greater than we could imagine?

> Father, thank you for taking me into Your family. Teach me how to keep You first in all things.

LOVING OTHERS

*If I speak in the tongues of men or of angels, but do not have love, I
am only a resounding gong or a clanging cymbal. If I have the gift
of prophecy and can fathom all mysteries and all knowledge, and if
I have a faith that can move mountains, but do not have love, I am
nothing. If I give all I possess to the poor and give over my body to
hardship that I may boast, but do not have love, I gain nothing.*

1 CORINTHIANS 13:1–3

In some of the most poetic verses in the Bible, Paul taught us
about love. And it's love that gives value to our actions, because
love gives us the servant's heart that God wants us to have. Love
is not about personal fulfillment, a goal, or heightened emotion.
It is not egotistical. In these verses, Paul intentionally included
things that exist for the benefit of others: the gifts of prophecy
and knowledge are used to teach others; faith demands trusting
in something other than ourselves; and surrendering possessions
means nothing unless there is a recipient.

In all ways, love is as much about giving as receiving. Loving
others means opening our lives to others, even when it's not
convenient for ourselves. It means listening long and intently
to others while they share themselves with you; it means forgiving others because holding grudges is selfish. Let's intentionally
think about the love we give to others, and be thankful for the
love we receive in return.

God, help me participate in love by promoting others in my
life, being concerned with them more than myself.

101

DEVOTED TO FELLOWSHIP

Those who accepted his message were baptized, and about three thousand
were added to their number that day. They devoted themselves to the
apostles' teaching and to fellowship, to the breaking of bread and to prayer.

ACTS 2:41–42

There's no way around it. Relationships can be challenging. Because we're imperfect humans dealing with other imperfect humans, we need God's Spirit to fill us with a supernatural stream of patience, forgiveness, and wisdom. But the good news is that when we accept Jesus as Lord, not only is our relationship with God redeemed, but also our relationships with one another. And the best place to experience redeemed relationships intentionally is within the church.

God established the church for His glory and for the good of those who love Him. As members of the church, we celebrate God's grace in Jesus, never forgetting that the price of our redemption was Jesus' body broken on the cross. We are called to build each other up in the image of Christ. Together, we joyfully share the good news with others, welcoming new believers into our family.

The church is an incredible gift, created by God to be the embodiment of Christ on earth. And as that embodiment of Christ, we're literally hands and feet of God, faithfully serving others for His glory. Until our time on earth is over, let us draw on God's strength to support each other in our eternal purpose.

Father, allow us, as the church, to be a unified body, on mission together in Your name to advance Your kingdom.

JUST DISCIPLINE

*With whom was [God] angry for forty years? Was it not with
those who sinned, whose bodies perished in the wilderness?*
HEBREWS 3:17

When studying Scripture, context is key, and it's important to understand the background of the truth we are trying to grasp. The story of the Israelites reveals a lot about the character of God. Since believers today tend to behave much as the Israelites did, we can learn a lot from the way God interacted with them.

God extends undeserved grace and love toward us, but His love is not always the warm and fuzzy kind we like to feel. As a loving and just Father, sometimes God must discipline us away from sin that ultimately leads to death.

Even after God delivered the Israelites from Egypt and continually provided for their needs, the Israelites forgot God's faithfulness and turned from Him with sinful, unbelieving hearts. Because the Israelites placed their trust in their own hands instead of God's, they were forced to wander in the wilderness for forty years and never entered the promised land (Numbers 32).

Like the Israelites, we often become fearful, lose trust, and seek sin as a way to control our circumstances; when we do that, we miss out on the plans God has in store for us. Instead, trust and obey God, and you will live a life beyond anything you could imagine!

Jesus, open my eyes to Your faithfulness so I am not deceived by the ways of the world.

REGARD FOR OUR LEADERS

Now we ask you, brothers and sisters, to acknowledge those who work hard among you, who care for you in the Lord and who admonish you. Hold them in the highest regard in love because of their work. Live in peace with each other.

1 THESSALONIANS 5:12–13

It can be easy to overlook everything our leaders do for us. In our universities, families, workplaces, and especially our churches, God has placed men and women to care for our physical and spiritual well-being. But often, when leaders work the hardest, they are criticized the most. Sometimes, instead of receiving honor, they encounter scorn.

Paul spoke to the Thessalonians about a similar relationship dynamic with their leadership. While the people may have wanted to ignore authority and reject leadership, Paul pleaded with them to praise their leaders for all the hard work they had done. Though their work seemed burdensome at times, their leaders admonished the Thessalonians because the leaders cared for them. Their goal as leaders was not to be popular among the people, but to ensure the church was following Jesus faithfully.

This message is extremely timely today. How often has our society praised rebelling against our leadership? It takes humility and maturity to honor leaders who sacrifice so much for us. Let's live in peace and hold these hard workers in high regard, for God has placed them in our lives for our own good.

Jesus, help us encourage and honor those who lead us.

THE POWERFUL WORD

*I solemnly charge you in the presence of God and of Christ Jesus,
who is to judge the living and the dead, and by His appearing and
His kingdom: preach the word; be ready in season and out of season;
reprove, rebuke, exhort, with great patience and instruction.*

2 TIMOTHY 4:1–2 NASB

Timothy was a rising leader in the church who was so close to Paul that the apostle called him his spiritual son. This scripture was likely one of the last things Paul wrote to him. "Last words" are typically some of the most important gifts and instructions passing leaders leave behind. In this letter, Paul emphasized the importance of God's Word. Why would he do this?

Earlier, Paul wrote, "All Scripture is God-breathed and is useful for teaching, rebuking, correcting, and training in righteousness" (2 Timothy 3:16). The Scriptures are a gift. They are the most useful means we have for training for a pure life. God's Word is powerful (Hebrews 4:12), purposeful (Isaiah 55:11), and it will endure forever (Isaiah 40:8). Paul wanted to impress this on Timothy's heart.

Gifted speakers often repeat phrases or concepts they want their audience to remember. Paul frequently talked about Scripture and the importance of teaching and training others from it. Pay attention to Paul's encouragement. Since we have this gift from heaven, let's use it!

Father, thank You for Your Word. Continue to remind us of the power and purpose of the Scriptures.

DIFFERENT GIFTS, ONE GOAL

We have different gifts, according to the grace given to each of us. If your gift is prophesying, then prophesy in accordance with your faith; if it is serving, then serve; if it is teaching, then teach; if it is to encourage, then give encouragement; if it is giving, then give generously; if it is to lead, do it diligently; if it is to show mercy, do it cheerfully.

ROMANS 12:6–8

Paul didn't skirt around the idea that the body of Christ is diverse. Yet in the church's diversity, each member has a specific role to unify and build up the body. Our roles are designated by our spiritual gifts—the talents God gives us through His Spirit. Just as grace was freely given, so our spiritual gifts are given to us simply because we are children of God.

Our spiritual gifts are just that: gifts. And God challenges us to exercise them accordingly, as instruments of service. Whether you have the gift of prophecy, meaning you aptly speak truth at the right time, or you have a heart to serve, use your gift as worship. Some gifts may seem flashier than others, but we don't exercise them for our own recognition. Instead, let's present ourselves as living sacrifices to God. He is the One who gave us the greatest gift: His Son, Jesus.

> Father, show me how to worship You by giving my gifts back to You.

CLEANSING CONFESSION

Therefore confess your sins to each other and pray for each other so that you may be healed. The prayer of a righteous person is powerful and effective.

JAMES 5:16

Sharing our struggles and sins with another human being is difficult. This kind of vulnerability destroys our pride—and it shows us how much we need Jesus and the church. Yet Scripture tells us there is power in confession and prayer.

Jesus speaks about making the church spotless and blameless for His glory and our good. As members of this body, we get to take part in this process. When we confess our struggles and pray with each other, God is always present and always brings us encouragement. He is glorified as we humble ourselves and admit we need Him. When we are honest, we typically find other people in the church have similar experiences, and they can share how they dealt with particular struggles. This is the power of Christ-centered community!

When we confess our sins to each other and humbly ask for prayer, we outwardly express our need to live for Jesus with the help of brothers and sisters. God never meant for us to walk alone. As we confess to each other and pray with each other, God restores us so that we can live a life that glorifies Him.

> Lord, help us pray for one another and shoulder others' burdens, so Your name may be glorified through Your church!

REMIND ONE ANOTHER

*We always thank God, the Father of our Lord Jesus Christ, when
we pray for you, because we have heard of your faith in Christ
Jesus and of the love that you have for all God's people.*

COLOSSIANS 1:3–4

How easy it is for us to forget things. Though we might do our best, our attention spans and memories are often limited. That applies to remembering what God has done in our lives too. At one moment we are overwhelmed in amazement of Jesus' sacrifice on the cross, and the next we forget the gospel and cling to the empty promises this world has to offer. But God knows we're forgetful! That's why He provides us with community where we can continuously remind each other to live out the heartbeat of the gospel.

Paul wrote this letter because the church at Colossae had accepted false teaching. Although Paul had never visited the church in person, he cared about them and saw they were going down a path that could only lead to a loss of faith. So Paul sent this letter to reinforce the gospel in their hearts and to encourage their faith and love.

When those of us who are members of the church are engaged in each other's lives, we see our faith strengthened. This is what community is about. How can you remind someone today of the truth of the gospel?

Father, teach us how to encourage and remind each other of the gospel so Jesus' character can echo through the halls of our church and out into the world.

WE KNOW, SO OTHERS CAN KNOW

God placed all things under his feet and appointed him to be
head over everything for the church, which is his body.

EPHESIANS 1:22–23

Think for a second about how beautiful the natural world is. Think about stars, oceans, animals, and people. Now think about this: you can know the Creator of everything, and get to enjoy everything He made. Creation reflects Him and shouts aloud His magnificence!

Scripture says we are God's most marvelous creation, and together as the church, we are His body on earth. Today's verse calls us to understand that Jesus, who created everything and has authority over all things, is leading His body, the church, today and for all time. As His church, we are the chosen instrument through which He speaks, moves, and acts on the earth. He leads and fills us to make His glory known. We respond by emptying ourselves to reflect this glory to others!

The church is a beautiful part of God's creation meant to shine His glory to those who desperately need a glimpse of heaven. Remember what it was like before you knew Jesus? Remember the moment your heart jumped as you glimpsed a glory beyond this world?

Take a moment to thank Jesus for inviting you to partake in His glory, and ask Him to reflect it through you today.

Jesus, use me as a vessel to help other people see how beautiful You are!

HOLINESS OVER HAPPINESS

With minds that are alert and fully sober, set your hope on the grace to be
brought to you when Jesus Christ is revealed at his coming. As obedient
children, do not conform to the evil desires you had when you lived in
ignorance. But just as he who called you is holy, so be holy in all you do.

1 PETER 1:13–15

Have you ever heard the phrase "do more of what makes you happy"? Though it would be easy to live our lives based on this philosophy, God calls us to a different standard. He calls us to a life that can feel like the complete opposite of doing what makes us happy: a life of holiness—of walking away from what might feel good or look enticing and, instead, walking toward the things that make us more like Christ.

In today's verse, Peter drew a clear line between children of obedience and those who "conform to evil desires." He was aware of the worldly temptations that wage war for our attention, but he emphasized our ability to choose holiness in spite of them. Fortunately, we're never alone in our attempt at perfection. We can rely on Jesus, the perfecter of our faith and our source of righteousness. Although it is our responsibility to choose obedience and to make God-honoring decisions, we can rest in the finished work of the cross—the only way we will ever be made holy.

Daily, we choose between holiness and the desires of our flesh; yet when we truly grasp the hope of the gospel, the choice is simple.

Lord, let the awareness of Your gospel create in me a desire for holiness.

ENCOURAGING WORDS

Do not let any unwholesome talk come out of your mouths,
but only what is helpful for building others up according
to their needs, that it may benefit those who listen.

EPHESIANS 4:29

Every single day, Jesus fills your life with grace. When you mess up, when you ignore God, when you've run out of strength, He gives you grace upon grace (2 Corinthians 12:9–11). We are called to follow His example and use our words to extend grace to those around us, including the church.

As brothers and sisters in Christ, we are united by Jesus' miraculous work, but often we divide ourselves by words that tear others down. We criticize and gossip instead of speaking words of life like Jesus did. Sometimes we are insensitive to others and try to say good words at the wrong time, like trying to push cheerfulness on someone who is grieving. Conversation is messy business, but it's crucial to relationships. So let us seek to speak with our fellow Christians with care.

Consider your words. Were there any moments this last week where you gossiped, slandered, cursed, rejected, or mocked? Think about what kind of harmful talk you tend to indulge in, identify it, and ask God to help you break this cycle of hurtful words. He is faithful to draw us closer to Himself, and He will replace unkindness in our hearts with encouragement.

Lord, fill me with encouraging, grace-filled words for my fellow believers today.

STEWARDING OUR GIFTS

Each of you should use whatever gift you have received to serve others,
as faithful stewards of God's grace in its various forms. If anyone
speaks, they should do so as one who speaks the very words of God.
If anyone serves, they should do so with the strength God provides,
so that in all things God may be praised through Jesus Christ.

1 PETER 4:10–11

Learning to use our spiritual gifts is a lifetime journey. Once we think we have a handle on them, we find ourselves discovering something new. There are, of course, many spiritual gifts, but in today's passage, Peter focused on two categories as examples: speaking gifts and serving gifts. Those of us with speaking gifts are to speak of God's truth with reverence, not using our gift as a megaphone for our own ideas, but as an instrument to carry the gospel. Those of us with gifts of serving are to serve wholeheartedly, drawing strength from the Lord, not ourselves, so that God is praised through the strength Jesus provides us. In all things, we are to use our gifts to serve the church and to praise Jesus.

Your gifts, whether serving or speaking, or something completely different, are yours to steward and leverage wisely. These gifts are not meant to earn us acceptance or praise in the eyes of our peers, but for God's glory and for your fellow believers. Today, reflect on what kind of gifts you have. Where does your strength come from? How are you using your gifts?

God, continue to show me more about the gifts You've entrusted to me and how You would have me use them.

SERVANT LEADERSHIP

I appeal as a fellow elder . . . be shepherds of God's flock that is under
your care, watching over them—not because you must, but because
you are willing, as God wants you to be; not pursuing dishonest gain,
but eager to serve; not lording it over those entrusted to you, but
being examples to the flock. And when the Chief Shepherd appears,
you will receive the crown of glory that will never fade away.

1 PETER 5:1–4

We live in world that is all about self. We take selfies. We talk
about what we want and where we are going without giving any
thought to those around us. Yet in this self-centered world, God
gives us something that should never be about us: leadership.

Christ-centered leadership is beautiful; it is an opportunity for
us to serve others. It is a gift that God entrusts to us to use to build
the church. But the minute we take His purposes out of leadership
and put ourselves at the center, the beauty is gone. No longer are
we able to find joy in serving others. Instead, we seek recognition
for ourselves. Instead of viewing leadership as a service-oriented
privilege, we see it as a burden. When we put ourselves in the
center, actions become self-seeking rather than life-giving.

If you are in a position of leadership or would like to be, ask
the Lord for a heart of humility and grace to lead His people well.
If you are not in a position of authority, pray that God would give
your leaders wisdom and humility.

> Lord, thank You for the opportunity to serve You. Never let
> my pride get in the way of showing others Your truth.

WALK IN LOVE

*Follow God's example, therefore, as dearly loved children and
walk in the way of love, just as Christ loved us and gave himself
up for us as a fragrant offering and sacrifice to God.*

EPHESIANS 5:1–2

When love goes beyond just a feeling and becomes an action, we begin "walking in the way of love." Paul told the Ephesians that if they could grasp what a life of love is, they would not only be overwhelmed by the amount of love God had for them, but they would also know the love He wanted them to show to each other.

God's extravagant love for the church is so abundant that it cannot be measured. He loves us even when we are hard to love. And He keeps coming back for us, delivering us, and ministering to us in our weakness. That's why we base our love for each other on His example of love.

Whether it's outside or inside the church walls, we always have the opportunity to respond like Christ and love others the way He loves us: in action, not just in thought. As we walk in the way of love, may our decisions always reflect His actions. Let's seek opportunities to share the greatest love of all, telling others of Jesus' sacrifice on the cross for our sins. It's the greatest love anyone could give or receive.

> Dear Father, help me respond to the world with whole-hearted love, even when it's so much easier not to. Show me how to walk in the way of love.

WISDOM FOR THE YOUNG

Don't let anyone look down on you because you are young, but set an example
for the believers in speech, in conduct, in love, in faith and in purity.

1 TIMOTHY 4:12

If you are reading this devotional, you are probably considered by most to be young. And because of that, you might run into some conflict with people who scoff at the way you live your life. In our society, the young are typically considered impulsive people who make plenty of mistakes and have no idea how they are supposed to conduct themselves or treat others. Even older believers in our community may struggle to see our worth in guiding other believers closer to God. It doesn't have to be this way!

Just as Paul encouraged Timothy, we must set an example for other believers with the way we live, regardless of any opposition we may face because of our age. Our faith can change and inspire people. So don't be afraid to follow your convictions, and show others how to live like Christ. It is Jesus, not your age, who defines your worth in God's kingdom.

> Father, thank You for seeing value in me, despite how little experience I have in this world. Give me Your wisdom and knowledge so I can set an example even though I am young.

REJOICE IN SUFFERING

Now I rejoice in what I am suffering for you, and I fill up in
my flesh what is still lacking in regard to Christ's afflictions,
for the sake of his body, which is the church.

COLOSSIANS 1:24

How could Paul rejoice in suffering? Because he was doing it for something much greater than himself—the church. Paul's heart was focused on the gospel—the good news—which says that God has reconciled us to Him and made us "without blemish and free from accusation" (Colossians 1:22). This was so revolutionary that it overwhelmed his pain to the point that he rejoiced!

Paul's instinct of self-preservation had faded away and was replaced by a "kingdom perspective." He was prepared to lay his life down with expectancy that others would see who Christ is and what He has done for humanity.

We too can get rid of our instinct for self-preservation. That comes by knowing that any amount of suffering is completely worth the trade. Because Paul had this perspective, he could rejoice in the suffering that comes with death to self and life to Christ.

All believers will face suffering at some time in their lives. But when we're in the midst of pain, let's rejoice and take the opportunity to proclaim Christ, knowing that His body of believers will thrive and grow from our selflessness.

Father, help me grow in love for my brothers and sisters, to the point that I can rejoice in hard times and good.

116

TUNED TO GOD

Rejoice always, pray continually, give thanks in all circumstances;
for this is God's will for you in Christ Jesus.
1 Thessalonians 5:16–18

When a conductor leads an orchestra, he or she unifies an assortment of disparate parts to perform one act of harmonious beauty. Yet, if just one instrument is out of tune, the piece's full loveliness cannot be expressed.

God also uses His children as participants in His orchestra. Each of us has a unique role to play as a member of the church, but when we do not abide in Christ through faith, we become just as dissonant as an out-of-key instrument to the masterpiece God is creating in His body of believers.

How do we stay in tune? By doing the will of God through rejoicing, praying, and living a life of thanksgiving. These intimately connected commands are God's clear-cut, practical ways to walk in integrity according to His will.

When our hearts are sanctified, we are free to fulfill the role God has for us in His church. Serve your community through tuning your heart to God and becoming a perfectly tuned instrument in His orchestra.

God, give me the discipline to walk in faith by rejoicing always, praying without ceasing, and giving thanks no matter what. Attune me to Yourself and the great work of Your church.

SACRIFICIAL SERVICE

God is not unjust; he will not forget your work and the love you have shown him as you have helped his people and continue to help them. We want each of you to show this same diligence to the very end, so that what you hope for may be fully realized. We do not want you to become lazy, but to imitate those who through faith and patience inherit what has been promised.

HEBREWS 6:10–12

Have you ever been in a situation where you were serving in your church, and it felt like you were doing tons of work to amplify God's glory and name without results or acknowledgment? Take heart; Scripture promises that He will remember the selfless love you've shown for Him and His people.

Let that sink in for a second. Even if it seems like your service goes unnoticed, God sees what you've done and gives you the unwavering promise of eternity spent enjoying Him. The God of the universe created you to serve others through His church here on earth. By serving the church, you are serving Him!

Even though times may get tough, deadlines may build up, and you may get tired, stay firm and continue the course, because God is filling you every step of the way. He has created you for Himself and His church, and He will continue to fight for you as you faithfully steward what He gives.

Lord, ignite a new passion in my heart for Your church, the expression of Your grace and glory here on earth.

CONFLICT AND UNITY

We are co-workers in God's service; you are God's field, God's building.

1 CORINTHIANS 3:9

Have you ever been frustrated with someone you thought was on your side? Have you tried to work together with someone toward a greater common goal, only to find conflict slowing you down? It's amazing how different perspectives can make or break a great team of intelligent, God-fearing people.

As believers, we all have the same purpose of working to expand God's kingdom. But since the beginning, disunity has been one of the church's greatest struggles—at times even becoming the greatest hindrance to our ability to share the gospel. Discord comes when we fail to love each other, yet we have been commanded to even love our enemies (Matthew 5:44)! Unity, then, takes great effort and patience: the same kind of back-breaking labor and teamwork it takes to sow a field or construct a building. But the reward is worth the struggle.

When you run into conflict with another believer and find yourself constantly contradicting his ideas or questioning her motives, *stop*. Remember you are a servant of the Lord and are only a steward of everything He's given to you, including your time and energy. Do not waste them bickering!

> Lord, in frustrating situations, grant me wisdom to see myself and others through Your eyes, and grant me the submission to obey faithfully and preserve unity.

ENCOURAGE ONE ANOTHER

Encourage one another daily, as long as it is called "Today," so that none of you may be hardened by sin's deceitfulness. We have come to share in Christ, if indeed we hold our original conviction firmly to the very end.

Hebrews 3:13–14

None of us can operate in a vacuum. If we become isolated, if we stop exposing ourselves to the truth, if we focus on worldly concerns in our lives, our hearts will grow hard. We will forget and turn away. We continually need to be reminded that God provides for us, gives us strength and peace, and is always with us.

And to help us remember His faithfulness, God gave us our church communities. The Bible cautions us that when life becomes challenging and tests our faith, it becomes much easier for us to doubt God and forget all He has done for us. Staying on the straight and narrow is tough, and it goes against our natural tendencies. So we acknowledge this, and as a church, we look out for one another.

When we see a brother or sister struggling, let's offer encouragement. When we see someone becoming isolated, let's reach out. And if we become discouraged ourselves, we can ask someone for help, knowing we don't have to go through it alone.

As long as we have *today*, let's remind each other of all God has done for us. Let's encourage each other to keep the faith, because we know that in our weakness His strength is made perfect in us.

Father, help me keep my eyes open to the needs of my fellow believers and show me where I can give encouragement.

THE GREATEST IS LOVE

Now these three remain: faith, hope and love. But the greatest of these is love.
1 CORINTHIANS 13:13

How can we understand the love of God—not in superficially, but in a deep-within-our-souls comprehension? How can we begin to learn how infinitely expansive His affection is for us? God expresses His love for us endlessly, in new ways every day. Part of the adventure of faith is learning to recognize these expressions—and reflecting this love in the way we treat others.

Today's verse tells us that faith, hope, and love are all intimately connected within God's plan for us. These virtues are developed within our hearts and fulfilled in our actions. Yet Paul said the most important virtue of the three is love. Earlier in the same chapter, Paul expounded on the crucial role love plays as the motivator that gives meaning to everything we do, including serving the body of Christ (13:1–12).

With this in mind, think of your local church. How can we find and reflect expressions of God's love in the church? Serving the church out of a sense of duty instead of love is missing the point. Love, bolstered by faith and hope, should be the thing that propels us to serve the church. Do you feel like you don't have enough love to make this a reality? Don't worry—God has an endless supply. Remember that God is faithful to give to those who ask (Matthew 7:7–8).

> God, infuse in me a passionate love for You and Your purposes, and help me serve Your church motivated by that love.

121

LEADERSHIP REQUIREMENTS

*Here is a trustworthy saying: Whoever aspires to be an overseer desires
a noble task. Now the overseer is to be above reproach, faithful to his
wife, temperate, self-controlled, respectable, hospitable, able to teach,
not given to drunkenness, not violent but gentle, not quarrelsome,
not a lover of money. He must manage his own family well.*

1 TIMOTHY 3:1–4

If this list of attributes sounds demanding, it should. Leadership is
serious business—and a testament to how Christ loves and builds
His church. The qualities in today's verse point to a type of leadership marked by consistent service and powered by grace. The risk
is too great and the cost too severe for those overseeing the flock
to be weighed down by worldliness. How many churches have
been seared by scandal, shaking the faith and witness of those
in the church? It is critical that those in church leadership take
responsibility for their actions and words—their impact goes far
beyond just one person.

To represent Christ and His church in a leadership position
is to be fiercely committed to one's growth in holiness for the
sake of others. Of course, that's not to say that everyone in the
church shouldn't exhibit these qualities, leader or not; but those in
leadership certainly must. Meditating on the requirements of the
overseer, let us come to Jesus, the Chief Overseer, and ask for His
grace and power upon our leaders.

Lord God, strengthen the overseers in Your church, so we all
can grow to know You more.

NO EXCLUSIONS

He said to them, "You are well aware that it is against our law
for a Jew to associate with or visit a Gentile. But God has shown
me that I should not call anyone impure or unclean."

ACTS 10:28

Have you ever found it difficult to welcome someone into your church? Maybe their culture differed from yours, or maybe your personalities clashed. No matter the reason, God calls us to accept everyone who seeks Him, because *everyone* has been offered His gift of grace.

In Acts 10, Peter received a vision and obeyed the Holy Spirit's call, going to share the gospel with the Gentile centurion Cornelius. Peter's missional act was a key shift in the church, which moved from evangelizing only Jews to preaching the gospel to the entire globe. Peter's choice to welcome Gentiles into Christianity was highly controversial in the Jewish community, but it was definitely God's will according to the vision He sent Peter.

God's will is not bound by human laws; He does not exclude those who seek Him. As members of His church, may we welcome those of diverse backgrounds with open arms, for the body of Christ is made up of many members (1 Corinthians 12:12). Ask God to help you overcome your prejudices and welcome those who seek Jesus in your community.

> God, give me the grace to love each of Your children and accept them wholeheartedly.

MARRIAGE, CHRIST, AND THE CHURCH

Husbands, love your wives, just as Christ loved the church
and gave himself up for her to make her holy.
EPHESIANS 5:25–26

For many of us, marriage is something for the future. But it's not too early to understand God's vision for marriage, letting it change not only your motives *in* marriage, but also *for* marriage—and any romantic relationship. After all, God's vision for marriage is closely related to His vision for the church.

You may have heard the church described as the "bride of Christ." In today's scripture, Paul looks deeper into this metaphor and shows how marriage parallels the relationship between Jesus and His bride. When we consider that God authored marriage and made it an example of the depth of Jesus' love, it's easy to see how loving our spouse correlates to loving the church and being Christlike.

So when we think about sacrifice in marriage, every act of submission to one another in love turns into a reflection of Jesus giving Himself up for the church. Every kindness to our loved one, every forgiven wrong, is a display of Jesus' endless grace toward us. Our faithfulness in hardships mirrors Jesus' faithfulness to His bride.

How can we make this image the basis of all our relationships? Married or not, by being Christlike in our love, we display the glory of Christ.

Lord, thank You for Your example and for showing me how to love. Help me become Christlike in my love for Your bride, and for my spouse.

THE GIFT OF COMMANDMENTS

By this we know that we love the children of God, when we love God and obey his commandments. For this is the love of God, that we keep his commandments. And his commandments are not burdensome.

1 JOHN 5:2–3 ESV

Regardless of the family we were born into, our adoption into God's family made us brand new. We were given a new life through faith in Jesus, a new family, and a new direction. In our heavenly Father's family, we are known intimately and still loved relentlessly.

But how do we respond to our Father's perfect love? John told us that to truly love God means to keep His commandments. Do we keep His commandments in order to earn His love? No—we could never measure up. We keep His commandments because they are good for us. God does not give us commandments to burden us, but so we can glorify Him before the world and enjoy healthy relationships within our family of faith.

We must make many decisions as we journey through life, and trying to fit all of God's commandments into our everyday choices can be intimidating! But remember—God helps us. We just start with the two greatest and simplest commands: first loving Him and then our neighbor (Matthew 22:34–40). We can leave everything else up to Jesus, who loves us unconditionally and has given us His Spirit when we need help.

> Father, thank You for adopting me into Your family and for giving me the gift of Your commandments.

125

CALLED TO FREEDOM

You, my brothers and sisters, were called to be free. But do not use your freedom to indulge the flesh; rather, serve one another humbly in love. For the entire law is fulfilled in keeping this one command: "Love your neighbor as yourself."

GALATIANS 5:13–14

Have you ever tried to follow Jesus, but then came under a lot of judgment from people who thought you weren't doing enough?

The Galatians were still learning about their new belief in Jesus. They were trying to live the right way, but false teachers were criticizing them for the way they lived and telling them they weren't working hard enough.

Paul's response can encourage you with clear direction: following Jesus means you love and humbly serve others. Just keeping that one command fulfilled the "entire law"—there was nothing else for the Galatians to worry about. So often we feel pressure to judge our lives by a checklist of our rights and wrongs, but we must remember that Jesus has set us free already! He paid the entire price, and no matter how many "good" items we check off our list, we can't pay for something that was already bought.

So walk in freedom today, using every opportunity to serve and love your brothers and sisters in Christ. Letting go of needless worry will free your heart to love, worship, and attune yourself to your neighbors.

Jesus, please increase my faith to believe the promise that I am truly free. May my love and service to others reflect that!

UNIQUELY GIFTED

God has placed in the church first of all apostles, second prophets, third
teachers, then miracles, then gifts of healing, of helping, of guidance,
and of different kinds of tongues. Are all apostles? Are all prophets?
Are all teachers? Do all work miracles? . . . Now eagerly desire the
greater gifts. And yet I will show you the most excellent way."

1 CORINTHIANS 12:28–31

Did you know that God has a unique role for you to play in His amazing story? Do you know what it is? Whether or not you've figured it out, know that God created you to have a special place in His church. We aren't just spectators who are supposed to enjoy a good sermon and sing some songs, absorbing the benefits of being saved and playing no part in Christ's body. Rather, our job is to meet the needs of our community with the gifts and talents we have received from God. It's easy to get caught up in trying to decipher how we can be most useful, but that's not the point. Using our gifts—whatever they may be—contributes to the strengthening of the church; that's the purpose of every gift.

So if you've felt a desire to become more involved with the church, don't hesitate; dive in! Your role is far from insignificant. Don't get stuck questioning whether you have anything important to give, and don't be discouraged by how small your role may seem. No one gets left out. Take the opportunity to play your part in Christ's glorious story.

> Lord, show me how I can play a role in Your church with the
> gifts You have given me.

BETTER TOGETHER

I remember you in my prayers at all times; and I pray that now at last by
God's will the way may be opened for me to come to you. I long to see you
so that I may impart to you some spiritual gift to make you strong—that
is, that you and I may be mutually encouraged by each other's faith.

ROMANS 1:9–12

Think of a time when you worked with someone toward a common goal. How did it feel when others came alongside you for a common purpose? Was it encouraging?

Paul understood that there was something powerful about people working together. While he was on a missionary journey, he wrote a letter to the church in Rome, which we know today as the book of Romans. Paul had never been to the early church in Rome, yet he was deeply encouraged by their faith in Jesus, and he constantly prayed for them, asking the Lord for an opportunity to go visit them. Paul knew that fellowship with other believers was essential for his and their faith.

Communion between believers is an indispensable part of our faith. We need to help each other live the life Jesus has called us to; we cannot do it on our own. So seek fellowship with other believers, and surround yourself with other Christians who are working toward a gospel-centered life. You can both be encouraged by your ministry and fellowship.

> Lord, lead me toward rich community with other Christians.
> Use me to encourage them to serve You, and use them to
> encourage me through their faith.

FAMILY FIRST

Anyone who does not provide for their relatives, and especially for their own household, has denied the faith and is worse than an unbeliever.

1 TIMOTHY 5:8

Our faith starts with those closest to us. In today's verse, Paul even said that we must first practice our faith by caring for the people God has placed in our family. When we start by caring for our family, we can then focus on the other people who may be in need. Family relationships, no matter how difficult, can be beautiful examples and training ground for selflessly loving and caring for others.

Paul wasn't the only one who placed high priority on providing for others. James, the brother of Jesus, emphatically instructed believers to let the Word of God transform the way we treat those who cross our paths. James 1:27 says, "Religion that God our Father accepts as pure and faultless is this: to look after orphans and widows in their distress and to keep oneself from being polluted by the world."

The gospel tells us to place the needs of others we encounter above our own. This is one of the greatest ways the world can see Christ in us. We don't even have to look far: look at the people closest to you and love them, for they may very well need the love of Christ the most.

> Father, thank You for my family. Allow me to put my faith into practice by serving and caring for them the way You care for the ones You call Your own.

LIFT UP THE CHURCH

I commend to you our sister Phoebe, a deacon of the church in Cenchreae. I ask you to receive her in the Lord in a way worthy of his people and to give her any help she may need from you, for she has been the benefactor of many people, including me.

ROMANS 16:1–2

It can be hard to figure how to plug in to our local church. But in today's verse, Paul notes three clear ways we can interact with one another. First, much like Paul, we are to be *ambassadors* for one another, championing and recognizing others' service and dedication to the church. Then, like Phoebe, we are to be *servants* of the church by providing selflessly for the needs of our brothers and sisters. Finally, in the same way the local Romans were asked to do, we are to *receive others* and give them a seat at our table.

So if you're wondering about your place in your local church, a great place to start is to look for ways to recognize someone's work, provide for a need, or make a new person feel welcome. There may already be opportunities to serve wrapped around these goals, or perhaps there's room to start a brand-new endeavor. In ways big and small, let's take these principles and foster a genuine and active love for the local church. By loving each other, we become better equipped to show His love to the world.

> Jesus, thank You for giving me a chance to incorporate my story into Your grand plan. Show me how to encourage, aid, and welcome all those who come through my church's doors.

LOVE WITHOUT JUDGMENT

Love does not delight in evil but rejoices with the truth. It always protects,
always trusts, always hopes, always perseveres. Love never fails.

1 CORINTHIANS 13:6–8

How is it that the church, the place that teaches us about true love, is so often not allowed to be in need of love?

We know no church is perfect. Every church is composed of imperfect people who constantly make mistakes and need grace, yet we judge the "bride of Christ" harshly. We compare her shortcomings with those of the church down the street as we try to determine which church has the best services, worship teams, and facilities. But what we often forget is that the church is not an event or a building, but people—people who, through God's love, have been brought to life in Jesus.

What if, instead of pointing and judging, we plant ourselves at our local church and start investing our love there? Paul tells us that love never fails. When programs, pastors, and worship bands fail, love won't. Trials may come and storms may arise, from outside and within the walls of the church. Yet if we root ourselves in loving devotion to the church, Jesus' name will be glorified in us.

Let us not forget the beautiful love story between Christ and the church. Since Jesus calls the church His bride, let us then see her as He sees her: radiant and holy before Him.

Jesus, let me see Your church the way You see her. Help me love her the way You love her.

131

SHARE FREELY

All the believers were one in heart and mind. No one claimed that any of their possessions was their own, but they shared everything they had.

ACTS 4:32

If you've ever been around a group of toddlers, you've probably heard one of them shouting, "Mine!" while hanging on to a toy. One of our first lessons in life is to share—and it's a hard one. We have to keep learning it over and over again throughout our lives. As we grow older, it's not just toys we have to share; it's our time, our resources, our money, and our energy. But as Christians we have the benefit of knowing that none of it was "mine!" in the first place.

As we strive to become more Christlike, we begin to forget our own selfish desires and learn to love each other fully, like Christ loves. Just like the new believers in Acts, we know that everything we have is from God and for God. That means what we own is not meant to be a blessing just for us, but for others as well.

We learn to love others by sharing our gifts, talents, and lives freely with one another. No longer do we claim our gifts or possessions as our own, but we steward these gifts appropriately for God's sake. God has entrusted you with certain gifts and possessions for His kingdom. How will you use them to make a difference and bless His church?

> Father, thank You for Your many blessings. Teach me how to share them freely with the body of believers.

BURDEN BEARERS

Carry each other's burdens, and in this way you will fulfill the law of Christ.

GALATIANS 6:2

It's often hard to know how to share in someone's sadness, listen during times of stress, and help manage hurts and struggles. Yet bearing one another's burdens is the truest expression of a Christlike love. In our calling to fulfill the law of Christ, we must love others with purpose and endurance.

Imagine the love that compelled Christ to go to the cross—the overwhelming hatred for sin, but the overpowering love that prevailed. By literally carrying the weight of our sins, He became the ultimate example of bearing one another's burdens. That same sacrificial love, humbly laying down oneself for another's good, is what we are called to give one another.

Jesus told His disciples that they were to love each other with the same endurance, purpose, and intentionality that He loved them (John 13:34). In practice, carrying the burdens of others looks like an active and selfless investment in people who cross your path. Pray for those you encounter, speak truth in love, give with compassion, serve one another humbly, lend and expect nothing in return. Call back those who have turned away; minister to the ones who are struggling and hurting. Giving the love of Christ is the way of living the love of Christ.

Father, help me view love the way You do. Prepare my heart to carry the burdens of others unconditionally and with endurance.

GIVING GLADLY

"Bring the whole tithe into the storehouse, that there may be food in my house. Test me in this," says the LORD Almighty, "and see if I will not throw open the floodgates of heaven and pour out so much blessing that there will not be room enough to store it."

MALACHI 3:10

Money, and how we handle it, can be a touchy subject. Yet God doesn't leave us in the dark when it comes to our finances. We are to give generously to God's work, in faith, and trust that He will provide.

The Old Testament law set a standard of giving one-tenth of income to the Lord. Earlier in Malachi, before today's verse, we see that a curse was coming on the nation of Israel because the Israelites had not honored God in their tithes and offerings. Instead of bringing a thankful offering from their best, they were offering Him their leftovers. God challenged His people to test Him, essentially saying, "Be faithful in giving what I have asked of you, and watch Me bless you beyond what you can even handle."

As Christ followers, our entire lives belong to God. How can we fully give ourselves to God if we are withholding in our finances? In order to fully pursue His will and receive the fullness of His blessings, we must faithfully give of what we have. Do not hold back from God what is His. Give freely to His house, the church, and watch as He blesses His people in return.

Father, thank You for freely giving Your love to us. Unclench my fist, so that I may honor You in my finances.

CARE FOR YOUR TEMPLE

Do you not know that your bodies are temples of the Holy Spirit, who
is in you, whom you have received from God? You are not your own;
you were bought at a price. Therefore honor God with your bodies.

1 CORINTHIANS 6:19–20

Let's say your neighbor asks you to watch her dog for the night. Is that dog then yours to give away, starve, mistreat, or do with what you like? Of course not! Your neighbor trusted you to take care of *her* dog—you should treat it the way she would.

Just like the dog, we are not our own; we belong to God. When Christ died on the cross for our sins, He purchased our lives through His blood. And we're supposed to honor Him with the temple He has given us.

And honoring God with your body means more than eating healthy and exercising. It means being mindful of the actions you take, the places you go, and the way you interact with others. And don't forget: what you do with your body has a direct effect on your heart and soul. Often, the first step to taking care of your spiritual self is to take care of your body. Its habits and health can nourish or starve your heart.

Does your body carry you into sin, or into God's presence? Are you using it to serve others, or to serve your own desires? Christ has saved us from sin so we wouldn't have to live a life without hope. Treat your body as a sacred space He inhabits!

Lord, help me honor Your name with my body and not give leverage to the sin You have purchased me from.

TRUSTED SERVANTS

This, then, is how you ought to regard us: as servants of Christ and
as those entrusted with the mysteries God has revealed. Now it is
required that those who have been given a trust must prove faithful.

1 CORINTHIANS 4:1–2

When Paul wrote his first letter to the Corinthians, he emphasized his position in the church: that he was not to be considered
higher than a servant. In Paul's eyes, there was no greater position than to humbly serve the Most High. He devoted his entire
life to carrying out the tasks God assigned, since he had been
"given a trust."

Our position, like Paul's, should be humble servitude. But we
don't serve human masters; the Master we serve entrusts us with
great treasure—Himself, revealed in Jesus! Paul called us not to
serve lackadaisically, but with diligence and awe that we've been
entrusted with the great work of making Him known. Think
about this: God trusts you to tell others about Jesus!

Today, be thankful that He gave you the greatest gift in the
universe, and serve Him with a humble heart. He put you where
you are for a reason; you are uniquely suited to make Him known
in your city and in your social circles.

> Thank You, Jesus, that You have entrusted me with Your
> work. Show me how to serve faithfully today.

THE SELFLESS GOSPEL

Let us not grow weary of doing good, for at the proper time we will reap a harvest if we do not give up. Therefore, as we have opportunity, let us do good to all people, especially those who belong to the family of believers.

GALATIANS 6:9–10

The believers in Galatia had lost sight of the gospel. A group of false teachers had convinced the once faithful Galatians that faith alone simply wasn't enough. These apostolic imposters imposed a return to the law, arguing that ceremonies and traditions were required for true salvation. So the apostle Paul rebuked those claims, reminding the Galatians that they were no longer slaves to the works-based religion they had escaped from; they had found freedom in the message of Jesus. But Paul went further, encouraging the Galatians that this setback was not the end of their story.

Piling on rules and an unreachable standard of perfection can tire us out, making us want to just give up. It makes us feel we'll never be as good enough. And that's true. We can't make ourselves perfect, but we don't have to; Jesus takes that burden from us. And Paul invited believers to live as Christ lived: persistent in love and wholly dedicated to the needs of others. We press on, as our imperfect selves, and "do good."

Father, bless me with patience and perseverance, and help me press on for the good of others.

REMEMBER YOUR LEADERS

Remember your leaders, who spoke the word of God to you. Consider the outcome of their way of life and imitate their faith.

<small>HEBREWS 13:7</small>

Who would you consider worthy of modeling and imitating? We decide for ourselves each day which people we will allow to influence us, and thereby give them a unique power in our lives. Their influence can mold who we become in the future.

The last chapter of Hebrews provides encouragement and reminders for followers of Jesus, specifically about leadership. Hebrews defines a leader as someone with faith in God, who *speaks* the Word of God and lives out its "outcome." True leaders sharpen us, causing us to reflect on our own walk with Christ. Can you think of anyone who spoke the Word to you in a way that struck you to the core? What can you learn from "remembering" them and considering "the outcome of their way of life"?

Yet, before we seek leadership from others, we must consider if we are wholeheartedly looking to follow Jesus before others. If we seek Him first, we become more like Him and His priorities become our priorities. Then, our obedience to Jesus informs how we look to—and choose—other leaders.

Let's boldly seek and pray for leaders who challenge and call us up to the fullest potential of living life with Jesus.

> Jesus, bless Your church with discernment and leaders who fear You. We want to see what it means to walk with You to the fullest!

THE GREAT PROJECT

"Moses was faithful as a servant in all God's house," bearing witness
to what would be spoken by God in the future. But Christ is faithful
as the Son over God's house. And we are his house, if indeed we
hold firmly to our confidence and the hope in which we glory.

HEBREWS 3:5–6

When each person in a group fully trusts the leader, that group functions best. In the same way, the body of Christ functions most effectively when each member has unwavering confidence in Jesus, the head and leader of the church.

You may not realize it, but you are part of a building project that's been going on for generations. The death and resurrection of Jesus allows us, His people, to be built into the eternal church, His house. Moses was a foreman: he and the rest of the Old Testament prophets served God by building up His people. Today, we bring glory to God by serving together and building the church, which belongs to Jesus—the leader of the entire project.

What unshakeable confidence comes from abiding in Jesus, trusting His purposes, and resting in His love! This confidence unifies our Christian community—we are being built into one house under Him. As we keep our eyes focused on Jesus, He provides us with a united plan to fulfill His purposes. Rest in your faith in our leader, Jesus—He is trustworthy and guiding His project to a glorious end.

> Lord, thank You for the vision You have for Your people. Show me how to hold fast and be a solid part of Your great house.

THE CALL TO COMMUNITY

If one part suffers, every part suffers with it; if one part
is honored, every part rejoices with it. Now you are the
body of Christ, and each one of you is a part of it.
1 CORINTHIANS 12:26–27

The city of Corinth was so diverse in population and economic opportunity that it attracted people from all over of the world. Led by the Spirit, the apostle Paul traveled to Corinth and eventually established a church there. But not long after Paul left, he began to receive discouraging reports. The believers in Corinth were divided. Differences in wealth and social position caused some in the church to treat other members as inferior or, worse, unnecessary.

Recognizing the dangers of this hostile behavior, Paul reminded the Corinthians of their unity in Christ. They had been brought together by the Holy Spirit, so they no longer lived to promote themselves—they were to proclaim Jesus. Joy and suffering were no longer reserved for the individual, but affected every person in the body.

There is no room for superiority in the church. When we exchange humility and sacrifice for self-interest, we reject the blessings of community. Respond to this gift by growing in relationship with other believers, freely sharing everything. Serve them as if they were a part of you, because we are united as one in the body of Christ.

Father, You have blessed me with community. Show us how to be unified in everything—both in suffering and in joy.

WHAT'S MINE IS YOURS

All the believers were together and had everything in common. They
sold property and possessions to give to anyone who had need.

ACTS 2:44–45

Whenever we hear about the early church's communal living, it almost shocks us. This fellowship concept sounds extremely radical for the individualistic society we live in. Our culture tells us, "What's yours is yours, and what's mine is mine," but these verses are a glimpse of the heartbeat of the early church. They lived with extravagant generosity.

The bond that characterized the early believers was so fundamentally unique that Luke, the author of Acts, defined it by a simple word that means "sharing" or "having in common." That's the kind of fellowship the early church practiced; selfless, abundant generosity was the standard. They protected, helped, and loved each other; in practice, they gave themselves wholly to one another.

We have a generous God who gave Himself to us in His only Son, Jesus. That's the framework for generosity He established. When we understand that God, who owed us nothing, gave everything for us, our mentality changes from living for ourselves to living for others. Embrace the culture of the early church, which challenges us to say, "What's mine is yours."

> Lord, all I have is Yours. Give me a generous heart that reflects an understanding of the gospel, and wisdom so I can be a good steward of everything You have given me.

LIVING WITNESSES

Encourage the young men to be self-controlled. In everything set them an example by doing what is good. In your teaching show integrity, seriousness and soundness of speech that cannot be condemned, so that those who oppose you may be ashamed because they have nothing bad to say about us.

TITUS 2:6–8

How do you react when someone accuses you or persecutes you with words? It's tempting to lash out. We want to blame the things and people around us for the turmoil they cause us and to accuse them in turn. Today's passage challenges us to silence critics with our self-control, integrity, and good works. Our mission is not to prove the "others" wrong, but to live the life God called us to live. This life, as Paul implied, is one that all can see is good—one that repels attempts at slander.

Paul's message underscores the importance of living virtuously and sincerely. Though cultures will change in what they believe is good, the path Jesus laid describes a life that all can see is good, no matter the context or time period. Therefore, commit yourself to following Jesus, and silence the world's critics by abounding in the good works He sets before you.

> Dear God, let Your Spirit build self-control in me. Show me the good works You have planned for me, and help me walk in obedience to Your call.

LIVING STONES

As you come to him, the living Stone—rejected by humans but chosen by God and precious to him—you also, like living stones, are being built into a spiritual house to be a holy priesthood, offering spiritual sacrifices acceptable to God through Jesus Christ.

1 PETER 2:4–5

When Peter's letter reached its recipients, they were in exile. Their national and religious identity lay, literally, in a pile of rubble. Rome had systematically persecuted the believing population, scattering them to outer provinces. Not one stone of their former lives was left on top of another. Many were killed, but some survived in exile. Among them was a group of Jewish converts who were still learning how to live out their new faith in Jesus.

It was during this dark time that Peter reminded them of their living hope in Christ. Though the temple had been torn to pieces, God was still building His church. His followers are the living, breathing stones that house His presence on earth. Wherever His people go, He can be worshiped.

Like these exiles, we sojourn in a foreign land. As we learn what it means to be a Christian in this century, we must not forget that our faith is not built upon what is physical, but on what is spiritual. Let's then see beyond the material things that we so often call "church," and remember that God's house is made up of people, the living stones of His true church.

Jesus, You are the cornerstone of our faith. Please build us into Your true church, so we can offer sacrifices that honor You.

BETTER THAN WINE

Do not get drunk on wine, which leads to debauchery. Instead, be filled with the Spirit, speaking to one another with psalms, hymns, and songs from the Spirit. Sing and make music from your heart to the Lord, always giving thanks to God the Father for everything, in the name of our Lord Jesus Christ.

EPHESIANS 5:18–20

Boozeday Tuesday. Wine Wednesday. Thirsty Thursday . . . We could go on and on about the strong relationship alcohol has with college life. We, as followers of Jesus Christ, can see in this passage that the Lord commands us plainly to "not get drunk" because it leads to "debauchery," meaning excessive indulgence in our own pleasures. We all know how alcohol affects the body; it changes us and can make us someone we are not. It can lead us to make terrible decisions that are followed by damaging actions.

Jesus *does* call us to be filled—not by wine, but by the influences of His Holy Spirit! When the Spirit controls us, we are no longer indulging in our desires, but the Lord's. The Spirit can lead us to encourage our brothers and sisters in ways we couldn't think of by ourselves. He can fill us with boldness to share God's truth in difficult situations.

So let's allow God's Spirit to take over our thoughts and actions, for when we do, our life-focus changes from pleasing ourselves to praising and glorifying God with everything we are!

Lord, help me be filled with Your Holy Spirit. I want to drink deeply from Your Word today so I may overflow with Your truth to those around me.

FREED FROM SHAME

The third time he said to him, "Simon son of John, do you love me?" Peter was hurt because Jesus asked him the third time, "Do you love me?" He said, "Lord, you know all things; you know that I love you." Jesus said, "Feed my sheep."

JOHN 21:17

Through Peter's life, we get a glimpse of Christ's unending grace. In Jesus' darkest hour, Peter, one of Jesus' closest friends, denied knowing Jesus *three times* for fear of his own life. But that was not the end of Peter's story.

After Jesus rose from the dead, He appeared to Peter, asking him *three times*, "Simon son of John, do you love me?" Jesus wasn't asking this to remind Peter of his denial. Jesus was redirecting Peter's shame of the past toward an invitation to "feed [His] sheep"—His people. Jesus knew that Peter's mistake didn't disqualify him from discipleship: Peter still had a role to play in building the early church. And he's influenced countless Christians since then.

Perhaps you've messed up and feel unfit to follow Jesus. But Jesus is the One who gets the final say in our lives—not our mistakes. Despite our tendency to act out of our desires and turn from God, Jesus still forgives, even though we don't deserve it. Setting aside condemnation, He does not point back toward our wrong, but forward to the potential of future glory in Him.

He's not done with you. Listen to His call and join His work.

Jesus, You are merciful. Help me to look up from my mistakes and become a caretaker of Your flock.

FRUIT TO SHARE

The fruit of the Spirit is love, joy, peace, forbearance, kindness, goodness, faithfulness, gentleness and self-control. Against such things there is no law. Those who belong to Christ Jesus have crucified the flesh with its passions and desires.

GALATIANS 5:22–24

A healthy fruit tree uses water, light, and nutrients from the earth to produce fruit. Likewise, when we are rooted in and watered by the Spirit, we produce fruit too. It comes when we walk in God's ways and when we are refreshed by His strength and wisdom. But the fruit of the Spirit is not just for our own benefit, or even about us! Today's verse tells us that the fruit of the Spirit is all about how we treat each other.

When we rely on the Spirit to guide us, we begin to change, transforming into people who live and think like Christ. We bear fruit that's meant to be shared. So strive to live harmoniously among those around you by walking with the Spirit, listening to Him in prayer and study, and allowing God to develop His fruit in you. Then you will dwell in love, joy, and peace; be patient and kind, full of goodness, faithfulness, and gentleness to those around you; and practice self-control as you walk through life. If this fruit grows in you, the world around you will see the character of our perfect God.

> Father, You have created me uniquely to impact my realm of influence. Allow fruit to grow in me so I can share it with those around me.

CHRIST IN THE BEGINNING

*In the beginning was the Word, and the Word was with God, and
the Word was God. He was with God in the beginning. Through him
all things were made; without him nothing was made that has been
made. In him was life, and that life was the light of all mankind.*

JOHN 1:1–4

Yes, we only hear the name Jesus in the New Testament—but He
didn't just come along halfway through the story. Jesus was present
at the beginning. He was not an afterthought; He was necessary.
Everything was made through Him and nothing passed by Him
untouched. His work started long before we were born, and before
sin broke the perfect world He created. Jesus is the Creator of all
things, and His life is our light. As His followers, what does this
mean for us?

Jesus is "light" in the darkness. Even after humankind
accepted sinful life over the eternal, He came to His created world
and offered access to His life again. He broke through the darkness to show the world just how incredible God is.

Every day, we have the opportunity to be a part of His plan,
to let His light be stunningly evident in every situation, to show
others how to find life. How will you shine your light to the people
in your life?

Jesus, show me Your amazing power in incredible ways
today. Thank You for letting me be part of Your story.

SUBMIT TO SELFLESSNESS

And you, my son Solomon, acknowledge the God of your father, and serve him
with wholehearted devotion and with a willing mind, for the LORD searches
every heart and understands every desire and every thought. If you seek him,
he will be found by you; but if you forsake him, he will reject you forever.

1 CHRONICLES 28:9

David is remembered for some horrible sins. Giving into lust, David committed adultery, and then had the woman's husband killed in battle to conceal it. Even after confessing his transgressions and receiving forgiveness, David watched the devastating consequences of his sin infect every aspect of his life. Hoping to spare Solomon the destructive effects of unrighteousness, David implored him to earnestly pursue God and obey His every command. If Solomon rebelled, the downward spiral of brokenness would drag him and the nation of Israel further from the presence of God.

This plea came with a heavy weight and an even greater promise. If Solomon chose unrighteousness, he would be rejected from the Lord's presence forever. But, if he chose to seek the Lord with his whole heart, the Lord promised He would be found. We live in the same promise!

When we answer Christ's call to follow, we relinquish control over our lives and go where He leads. As you follow Christ, live surrendered to His will and purpose, ready to makes the sacrifices He will call you to. In your seeking, you will get Him!

> Father, forgive me of my disobedience. Draw me near to You
> so that I do not stray from Your path.

UNFAILING SUPPORT

When Timothy comes, see to it that he has nothing to fear while
he is with you, for he is carrying on the work of the Lord, just
as I am. No one, then, should treat him with contempt.

1 CORINTHIANS 16:10–11

Remember field day back in elementary school? It usually happened at the end of the year, and everyone was working for the top prize. There were jumping contests, tug-of-wars, and most importantly, the relay races. Just a few chapters before today's verses, Paul tells us that we are racing for an imperishable crown (1 Corinthians 9), and the race continues today. We are on Christ's team—the church—racing alongside each other for His glory!

When we see brothers and sisters going through different seasons of the race, we are called to serve them, encourage them, and to stand up next to them. Timothy came to the church in Corinth as a young man, perhaps not as respected as Paul himself. But Paul said that shouldn't matter because Timothy was doing the Lord's work, just like he was. No matter the season we find ourselves in, we should be able to walk confidently because we have the church and our heavenly Father beside us.

Let's work toward unity as we follow our captain, Jesus, and run toward His glory.

> Lord, allow us to see our brothers and sisters in Christ the way You do. Help us stand unified as Your church, encouraging each other as we run the race set before us.

WORSHIP WHERE YOU ARE

"Yet a time is coming and has now come when the true worshipers
will worship the Father in the Spirit and in truth, for they are
the kind of worshipers the Father seeks. God is spirit, and his
worshipers must worship in the Spirit and in truth."

JOHN 4:23–24

Jesus' encounter with the Samaritan woman at the well had all
the ingredients for controversy: He was a man, she was a woman;
He was a Jew, she was a Samaritan; He was a rabbi, she was an
adulteress; He worshiped in Jerusalem, she worshiped in Samaria.
John couldn't have painted a clearer picture of clashing national
identities, cultural norms, and religious practices. Yet in the midst
of this potentially volatile scene, Jesus teaches us that none of these
attributes make a true worshiper of God. He tells us true worship
is defined by "Spirit and in truth." It's not about the physical quali-
fiers, which we so often think are necessary to approach God, but
about the spiritual, intangible disposition of our hearts.

The Samaritan woman thought worship was about finding
the right *place* to worship. Jesus teaches us, though, that it's about
the right *kind* of worship. God can be worshiped at any time and
in any place if we seek His truth through His Spirit. How can we
worship Him this way today?

> Jesus, You've taught us that true worship is defined by the
> power of Your spirit and Your truth. Awaken our hearts to this
> truth so we can worship You today.

UNITY AMONG BELIEVERS THAT AMPLIFIES HIS NAME

*Because God's fame is amplified when believers love each other,
I will strive for unity among all Christians on my campus.*

The strongest statement Christians can collectively make about the love and truth of Jesus is through our unity. So crucial is unity to Jesus Himself that it was the focus of His prayer just prior to entering the Garden of Gethsemane (John 17:20–26), the night before He was tried, beaten, and crucified. This should be evidence enough that unity is at the heart of God.

True unity is rooted in humility. It can only happen when we place ourselves in a posture of "others first." In a world that continues to be more and more *me* driven and focused on the conviction *I have to get mine,* a humble heart that sees *we* as greater than *me* is incredibly powerful. This is the opposite of the flow of the world. This is the kingdom of God.

Jesus said that the world would know we are His by our love (John 13:35). Interestingly, He did not say "by our doctrine" or "by our denomination," but *by our love.* The heart of unity can see the bigger picture and say to our fellow Christians, "Although we may not agree with one another on every little thing, I love you and will walk alongside you, because we are each sons and daughters of God."

There is great power in unity. Conversely, there is debilitating weakness in division. Just as Scripture teaches us, we are all part of one body and Jesus is the head. God wired each of us uniquely with different gifts, and when our gifts are brought together under the banner of one great name, Jesus, the world is changed.

For me, it's the same with music. Play just a single note by itself, and it is not really all that exciting. Actually, it gets annoying pretty quickly! But when different notes begin to play together in harmony and in tune, chords begin to form, and beautiful songs arise. Notice I said "in tune."

May we begin to see the church as a symphony, and God as the great Maestro. Let's play the notes He's given us to play. Let's play in tune together. And may the world hear the music—the music of His grace and mercy for all.

—CHRIS TOMLIN

THE PERFECT MODEL

Now about your love for one another we do not need to write to you,
for you yourselves have been taught by God to love each other.

1 THESSALONIANS 4:9

How does God teach us to love? His very nature is wrapped up in holy, consuming love—revealed in His Son, Jesus Christ. In all His actions and words, Jesus, the perfect image of the Father, became the only tangible display of true love that the world has ever known. Completely God and completely man, Jesus taught humanity how to love perfectly—with their hands, feet, mouths, and hearts.

Love is kneeling in the dirt with the prostitute and extending grace instead of judgment. Love is praying for your enemies and giving them food and drink. Love is leaving the ninety-nine sheep to pursue the one that is lost. And love is sacrifice—laying down your life for a brother or sister. Jesus Christ showed us the essence of love: a sinless man bearing the sins of the world so that humanity could be free, forgiven, and righteous.

Jesus is your perfect teacher and model. God asks you to be like Him: holy and full of love for one another. Bask in His love and learn about it, and it will drive you to imitate Him.

> Jesus, thank You for teaching us how to love each other. Help me grow in understanding and experiencing Your love so that my life increasingly reflects Yours.

BUILDING UNITY

What then shall we say, brothers and sisters? When you come together, each of you has a hymn, or a word of instruction, a revelation, a tongue or an interpretation. Everything must be done so that the church may be built up.

1 CORINTHIANS 14:26

Paul's letter to the Corinthians arrived at a time this young church was breaking apart. Aside from rampant sexual immorality, the church was being torn apart by factious leaders who were using their spiritual gifts for their own glory. Division was gnawing away at the fabric of the church. Not surprisingly, the church was ineffective in ministering to the broader city and advancing the gospel. But Paul's call for the church was clear: "Everything must be done so that the church may be built up."

Like the Corinthians, we also become ineffective when we use our gifts to amplify our own names instead of the name of Jesus. As God's vehicle for His mission, we should strive for unity and love in Christ. God has given each of us gifts to help build His church. Let's use our gifts to minister to our brothers and sisters. When we gather as believers, our gifts come together in harmony for the purposes of building each other up and advancing God's kingdom.

Thank You, Father, for the gifts You have given me. Help me elevate Your name above all else in my heart so I can use my gifts to unify and build up Your church.

CELEBRATE EACH OTHER

Is not the cup of thanksgiving for which we give thanks a participation
in the blood of Christ? And is not the bread that we break a
participation in the body of Christ? Because there is one loaf, we,
who are many, are one body, for we all share the one loaf.

1 CORINTHIANS 10:16–17

Have you ever thought about the complexities of the human body and how many working parts contribute to serve one function? Just think of a machine as complex as the eye or as unfathomable as the human brain.

The church is the same way; it's made up of many gifts, ethnicities, cultures, stories, and talents, all serving the same God in a beautiful, complex way. However different we all may look from each other, we have all recognized that living for Jesus is more important than anything else we could spend our lives doing.

This generation of young believers has an opportunity to impact the trajectory of the global church community. If we center ourselves on this fact—that we have been rescued from our sinfulness and have been called to walk into light—the world will see a powerful, unified church. God has created each of us in unique ways, but He's also called us to serve Him together. Unity doesn't happen by chance; it requires us to be intentional with our actions. Take time today to encourage a fellow brother or sister to stay unified in the faith.

> Jesus, help us celebrate each other's gifts so, together, we can carry out Your amazing purposes.

MADE FOR MORE

As iron sharpens iron, so one person sharpens another.

PROVERBS 27:17

A community centered around Jesus, the church, is intended to be authentic. And with authenticity comes honesty—the easy kind *and* the hard kind.

The Bible tells us that as believers, we're called to sharpen one another. And you know what happens when you strike an iron flint against another? Sparks fly! It's how you handle the aftermath that determines if you make a pile of molten ash or if you create a more refined product.

There will be days when you'll speak truth to a friend, and there will be days when you're on the receiving end of such truth—but that's how God designed relationships to be. No matter which seat you find yourself in, God calls you to always humble yourself, live authentically and honestly in community, and ultimately help each other journey toward Jesus. And a true friend will be willing to tell you things that you don't want to hear.

Don't do life alone, dwelling in fake community. Even when it hurts, true community will lead you to life.

> Father, help the people I surround myself with speak the truth into my life, and please give me wisdom to speak truth into their lives as well.

YOUR PEOPLE

Just as a body, though one, has many parts, but all its many parts
form one body, so it is with Christ. For we were all baptized by
one Spirit so as to form one body—whether Jews or Gentiles,
slave or free—and we were all given the one Spirit to drink.

1 CORINTHIANS 12:12–13

It is hard to fit in sometimes. Groups are everywhere—the athletes, sororities, fraternities, the studious, the student government, the religious, the gamers . . . the lists go on and on. Although these groups can sometimes turn into cliques, we can also admit that once we fit into a group, we feel secure. We feel known. Once you find "your people," it is easy to become yourself without shame or fear of rejection.

Paul told us in this passage that once we are in Christ, we become part of a large body of believers. We are in Jesus' group. This body is made up of many different groups and types of people, but we all have the same goal: to bring God glory with our lives. Though we have differences, we are called to love, serve, and accept those in the body so we can work together to win everyone to Christ.

God made you just as you are and placed you just where you are for His purpose. So invest yourself in serving His church, for He has given you something special to contribute by bringing you together with His family!

God, help me use my unique abilities to bring You glory. Let me serve other believers around me to further Your kingdom.

DIVIDED WE FALL

May the God of endurance and encouragement grant you to live in such harmony with one another, in accord with Christ Jesus, that together you may with one voice glorify the God and Father of our Lord Jesus Christ. Therefore welcome one another as Christ has welcomed you, for the glory of God.

ROMANS 15:5–7 ESV

Commanded by Christ to preach the gospel, the apostle Paul spent much of his life visiting churches throughout the Mediterranean. During his ministry, Paul collected offerings for believers in need, corrected false teachings, and encouraged the churches to persevere in the faith. But for all the issues he addressed, Paul placed special importance on Christ's followers being united in mind and purpose for the sake of the gospel. The churches that slowed down the spread of the gospel were plagued by divisions and disagreements. But the churches that saw the most dramatic changes in believers and nonbelievers alike operated as one body, never losing sight of the goal to make Christ known.

The church exists to empower and encourage believers to proclaim the gospel. When anything diverts our focus from this calling, the church inevitably struggles to impact the culture.

While we may struggle with petty disagreements, the church is called to love people and share Christ. In your community, how can you make service and love a priority, reminding each other that you are part of the greater mission of God?

Father, show me new ways our unity can bring life to our surroundings and spread Your gospel.

SPEAK WELL, NOT ILL

Brothers and sisters, do not slander one another. Anyone who speaks
against a brother or sister or judges them speaks against the law and
judges it. When you judge the law, you are not keeping it, but sitting in
judgment on it. There is only one Lawgiver and Judge, the one who is able
to save and destroy. But you—who are you to judge your neighbor?

JAMES 4:11–12

Living in Christian community allows us to interact with people who have different perspectives and interests. Because we are interacting with so many people on a daily basis, we can easily become frustrated by someone who deals with situations differently than we would. If we don't handle our frustrations well, we can bring great harm and division to the church.

James exhorts Christian believers not to *slander*—not to use harmful speech against one another. Slander not only goes against God's law, but it forgets His authority. James is quick to remind us that judgment belongs only to Him.

As we learn to engage with people who are different from us, we will naturally get frustrated; and sometimes it's easier to tear down someone than it is to build them up. But in the midst of our frustration, God gives us an opportunity to show steadfast love and patient problem-solving. Today, when you interact with your church family, will you choose love and acceptance over judgment and slander?

Father, I pray for those who frustrate me within the church.
Help me love them as You do.

NOT FOR US TO JUDGE

"Do not judge, or you too will be judged. For in the same way you judge others, you will be judged, and with the measure you use, it will be measured to you."

MATTHEW 7:1–2

It is easy to see the debauchery all around and focus with laser-like precision on condemning and fixing it. But when we get wrapped up in the sins of others, we ignore our own shortcomings. Sin is not merely brokenness, issues, or problems—sin is a mind-set that separates us from God! So if we want to stay connected to God, it's imperative that we turn our eyes inward first and deal with our own hearts before we start judging others' mistakes.

We humans were not created to judge; we were created to love people so that they will want to know Christ. And He's the only One who can judge hearts and save souls, anyway! Christ commands us to love one another as He loves us—unconditionally and without reserve. So let's focus on our job—extending love to others—and let Jesus be the one who judges and forgives our hearts.

> Lord, You have already forgiven me and set me free. Help me bring others into this freedom by showing them how much You love them, instead of condemning them as if I am You! You are the perfect judge. Thank You for Your forgiveness; help me extend the same to others.

AS JESUS LOVES

"A new command I give you: Love one another. As I have loved you, so you must love one another. By this everyone will know that you are my disciples, if you love one another."

JOHN 13:34–35

Toward the end of Jesus' time on earth, He spoke with His disciples about a new standard of love. Prior to this conversation, it was understood that we should love each other as we love ourselves, but here Jesus takes that a step further. He explains that His followers are to love as *He* loves.

We hear this so much in our Christian life, but what does it really mean for us? Jesus' love far surpasses societal norms. His is a love that is unconditional, outside of circumstance. It's a love that is rooted in the acceptance we receive from Jesus, not from our friends, family, or the world. The strength to love in this manner is only birthed from the grace we've been given. And because it's so far outside the norm, we will need to pursue it and constantly refocus on it throughout our lives.

Why does Jesus tell us that loving one another is a "command," not a suggestion? Because this holy love is how the world recognizes what Jesus is like and that we are His followers. Our love for our brethren shows God's grace more clearly than anything else. So refocus your heart and mind on this supernatural love, and let the world come to know Jesus through your love.

Jesus, help me grasp the weight of Your love for all people today, that I may love as You first loved me.

CIRCLE OF LOVE

Let no debt remain outstanding, except the continuing debt to love one another, for whoever loves others has fulfilled the law. The commandments, "You shall not commit adultery," "You shall not murder,"... and whatever other command there may be, are summed up in this one command: "Love your neighbor as yourself." Love does no harm to a neighbor. Therefore love is the fulfillment of the law.

ROMANS 13:8–10

Love knows no boundaries; it's a beautiful full circle between God and believers. God sent His only Son down to earth to bear our sins because He loves us. What He asks in return is that we love Him and that we love those near us. Love is at the beginning and end of our story of redemption because it's the channel by which we see God's faithfulness, mercy, and forgiveness.

However, this ideal love is not always easy. Every day, we run into circumstances that seem contrary to love. When we see loved ones divorce or get a serious illness, or when we are in pain ourselves, it is difficult to extend love to those around us. But we must remember that our joy and love come from Jesus Christ. He loves us even when we're at our lowest, and He reaches down and picks us up. In the same way, we extend to others the love that Jesus shows to us—completing the circle of love that He began.

Christ showed us that we ought to love each other in action. How will you love someone today?

> Lord, thank You for showing me love and how to love. Show me new ways to give this love to others.

A MULTITUDE MADE ONE

Behold, a great multitude that no one could number, from every
nation, from all tribes and peoples and languages, standing before
the throne and before the Lamb, clothed in white robes, with palm
branches in their hands, and crying out with a loud voice, "Salvation
belongs to our God who sits on the throne, and to the Lamb!"

REVELATION 7:9–10 ESV

The earth contains 195 countries. 6500 languages. 7 billion people. The diversity is mind-blowing, and yet God knows and loves each person intimately and fiercely. He moves in the heart of each God-lover with tailor-made precision and works all things perfectly for the glory of His name.

When you meet another follower of Jesus, you can have an instant connection because of your mutual best Friend. But siblings fight, and God's children are no different. Diversity is beautiful, yet causes inevitable conflict in a sinful world. How do we respond?

Seek Jesus, the Prince of Peace, the Lamb of God. Remember that one day, all will stand together, clothed in purity and waving branches of praise, singing to Jesus. God loves unity and will provide wisdom to help you find harmony.

Today, invest in your community and love them intentionally. Don't be afraid of conflict, but acknowledge that God uses everything to grow us into the people we are meant to be.

> Jesus, give me a heart that loves unity. Let me glorify Your name through passionately loving You and others today.

FELLOW WORKERS

Dear friend, you are faithful in what you are doing for the brothers and sisters, even though they are strangers to you. They have told the church about your love. . . . We ought therefore to show hospitality to such people so that we may work together for the truth.

3 JOHN VV. 5–6, 8

The early church spread the gospel through intense mission work, both near and far away. Jesus' instructions were to spread the gospel to the ends of the earth. But no matter where we go, we are supposed to be united in the spread of the gospel.

In today's passage John commended his friend, Gaius, for exemplifying unity in his mission work. Gaius had welcomed some brothers and sisters in Christ who were traveling to carry the name of Jesus. Because they were united in this cause, Gaius joined with them in advancing the gospel by providing supplies for their physical needs.

Likewise, we can also contribute to this type of unity and commitment in the spread of the gospel. Don't skip opportunities to support people in the mission field, because you can help grow God's family. No position or responsibility in His church is any more important than another! Though you may not be going to the ends of the earth today, you can still "show hospitality." What part does God have for you in this season, and how can you support those around you whose roles are different?

Lord, help Your children to work together to share Your good news everywhere.

BEYOND OUR DIFFERENCES

"My prayer is not for them alone. I pray also for those who will believe in me through their message, that all of them may be one, Father, just as you are in me and I am in you."

JOHN 17:20–21

How do you relate with Christians outside of your church? Do you pay no attention to them, or is there a little resentment brewing in your heart?

We have more important things to do than to get hung up on our differences. We are called to love fellow believers, and we do this by actively caring for them and praying for them—like we would for our own fellow church members. You don't have to become best friends with every other Christian you meet; rather, approach all Christians with open hearts, paying attention to who God puts in your path, and think about how He might want you to minister to them.

Stay tuned-in to the believers around you. God uses us to help each other—and He could be guiding you to contribute in ways that may not be obvious to you. When believers love each other, the church also grows in its witness. Our love goes beyond just each other; it serves as evidence of the gospel to those observing from the outside. Let's reflect Jesus' love by approaching each other with openness, for God is love, and His people ought to love one another.

Lord, teach me to love other believers with Christ's love and to seek a unity that glorifies You in the world.

THE ACTION POINT

We know that we have passed out of death into life, because we love the brethren. He who does not love abides in death.

1 JOHN 3:14 NASB

In today's verse, John had just explained to his readers that God's children could be known by their righteous deeds. He cited the example of Cain: we could tell Cain didn't belong to God because Cain hated his brother, and this hate led to evil action. Children of God are marked by a love that inspires not only feeling, but also right action. Our active love toward our brothers and sisters practically demonstrates our identity.

The sad reality is that Christians' actions often tell a story that's the opposite of what we want to tell. Disunity in the church causes Christians to lose their credibility before nonbelievers. This is not a new critique; both Jesus and Paul repeatedly warned the early church of the effects of disunity. And although unity is not directly mentioned here, John speaks about the foundation of unity, which is love for one another. If we have truly passed from death into life in Jesus, we cannot just claim to love each other, but must actually love in action and deed. The world is watching us, judging our message by our actions. Commit to taking decisive action today—the kind that shows our love for each other with sincerity and transparency, so the world may see that God's love truly abides in us.

Jesus, please show me specific, love-inspired actions You want me to take today, as I work with Your people to demonstrate Your love.

A NEW NAME

"I will remain in the world no longer, but they are still in the world, and
I am coming to you. Holy Father, protect them by the power of your
name, the name you gave me, so that they may be one as we are one."

JOHN 17:11

When Jesus prayed today's prayer, He was preparing to leave the disciples and return to His Father. But He wasn't about to leave His people empty-handed. Among the many gifts He left, He included a family name.

Have you ever thought it would be fun to join a famous family and be able to open doors at the drop of your name? Here on earth, for better or worse, fame and influence can be passed down from generation to generation, along with wealth and power. But how many more perks come with God's name? He adopted you when you accepted His Son. Your new family name doesn't give you a mere earthly inheritance or fleeting popularity, but true adoption and family. Protecting us with the "power of [God's] name," Jesus cleanses us. The broken find healing, and the lonely find a huge group of siblings who live under the very same name.

This kind of adoption makes us one—one family, with one purpose: glorifying God. Jesus prays that we will be one "just as we are one." Imagine the closeness of the Trinity. How can you build and celebrate the same kind of closeness with those who share your family name?

Jesus, thank You for adopting me into this amazing family. Show us how to become one as You and the Father are one.

167

SUPPLIER OF OUR NEEDS

Our desire is not that others might be relieved while you are hard pressed, but that there might be equality. At the present time your plenty will supply what they need, so that in turn their plenty will supply what you need.

2 CORINTHIANS 8:13–14

Do we really believe that God is good and will provide for us?

That little seed of doubt has been part of human nature since Adam and Eve's original sin, and this same doubt has been rooted in our nature ever since. There are two ways we could deal with this doubt: we could let it motivate us to try to be our own saviors and proprietors of our welfare—but that would keep us from living sacrificially and generously. Or, we could hang our doubt on the truth of the gospel and be set free from it, for all of our needs and desires can be met by Christ and the abundance of His work.

Spiritually, we were all equally desperate and in need of a Savior. And through Christ's goodness, we who believe have now become rich. The gospel does not exempt us from hardships in this world, but it does free us so that, in either abundance or deficit, we can trust in God for our sustenance. He always faithfully provides what we need most. Just as the Israelites had the *daily* task of trusting God for provision through the gathering of manna, we too should practice trusting in God's goodness daily. When we share our time and resources with one another, we let Him work through us in providing for His children.

Father, thank You for Your abundant provision and grace. Help me trust in Your goodness every day.

WISDOM AND PEACE

But the wisdom that comes from heaven is first of all pure; then peace-loving, considerate, submissive, full of mercy and good fruit, impartial and sincere. Peacemakers who sow in peace reap a harvest of righteousness.

JAMES 3:17–18

Wisdom isn't just found in the mind; it's a living gift from God that shapes our actions, which drives us to produce "good fruit." So why do we need to approach each other with wisdom? The world's view of Jesus is largely shaped by the words and actions of His church. When our words and actions are filled with selfishness, we forsake the needs of others. And as we begin to splinter off from other believers, the world sees a squabbling church, which turns people off instead of enticing them to join in a different kind of life. But if we allow God's wisdom to shape our hearts and produce good fruit, the world sees peace, humility, mercy, and sincerity—attributes that make Jesus' love shine and appeal to a world that is hurting and in need of that kind of love.

As today's verse says, God's wisdom produces peace. If we desire a "harvest of righteousness," we must be willing to do the hard labor of "sowing" peace around us—both within our church and outside of it. Try to be a peacemaker, and see how God's wisdom yields a harvest much bigger than you could imagine.

Thank You, Father, for so generously giving me Your wisdom. Show me how I can promote the love of peace where You have placed me today.

PROMOTING UNITY

What, after all, is Apollos? And what is Paul? Only servants,
through whom you came to believe—as the Lord has assigned to
each his task. I planted the seed, Apollos watered it, but God has
been making it grow. So neither the one who plants nor the one
who waters is anything, but only God, who makes things grow.

1 CORINTHIANS 3:5–7

We identify ourselves by our names. And our instinct tends to be to "make a name for ourselves." Much of what we do and say is based on a desire to better our visible identity—who we associate with, what we wear, who we claim to know. At the heart of this is self-promotion: seeking self-glory over God's glory.

Our struggles today aren't much different from the ones the Corinthians encountered. They too identified themselves by worldly names. They argued and judged each other on whether they followed Paul or Apollos, two famous preachers. And where any other name is elevated above God's, discord and disharmony soon follow. As Christians, we have one purpose: to elevate the name of Jesus above *every* name. When the church is unified in this purpose, self-promotion fades away. We are servants, given different tasks, but God alone makes things grow.

Today, when tempted to elevate our names, or any name other than Jesus', let's shift our eyes to God's glory, uniting our hearts around the One Name that sustains us.

Lord, let all other names in my life fade away, and in my unity with others, let the name of Jesus rise.

GROWING VERTICALLY

Instead, speaking the truth in love, we will grow to become in every respect the mature body of him who is the head, that is, Christ. From him the whole body, joined and held together by every supporting ligament, grows and builds itself up in love, as each part does its work.

EPHESIANS 4:15–16

How do we measure growth? In this world, we often measure a community's growth numerically and horizontally: that is, by how many separate individuals there are and how far they've spread. But in Ephesians 4, we see that a spiritual community also grows vertically in our relationship with God—individual and corporate growth are correlated. As one grows, the other grows.

Paul, the author of Ephesians, wrote that personal spiritual growth has a direct impact on the numerical growth of the church. Rather than counting horizontally, they count vertically; the church will grow in the number of believers and built *up* in Christ.

No matter our situation, growth is possible. Christ gives us all the tools we need. He gives gifts and grace that build us together and in Him. Abiding together in Christ, we experience personal growth; our hearts shift to His, our lives speak His truth, and our feet are rooted in Christ. All things—both good and bad—will build us up.

From Him, we then grow as the church. Seek Him today, and in your seeking you will grow.

> Christ, I want You to be the root and source of everything I do. Help all of us in the church grow together toward You.

A HEART TRANSFORMED

Put on then, as God's chosen ones, holy and beloved, compassionate
hearts, kindness, humility, meekness, and patience, bearing with one
another and, if one has a complaint against another, forgiving each other;
as the Lord has forgiven you, so you also must forgive. And above all
these put on love, which binds everything together in perfect harmony.

COLOSSIANS 3:12–14 ESV

Behavior modification says, "I can change because of what I do," while a heart transformation says, "I am changed because of what Jesus has done." Putting on something new usually requires us to remove something first, but this exchange between our old, sinful life and our new Christian life can't happen through our own desire to change. We can only change when we understand *whose* we are and *who* we are: God's chosen ones, adopted and redeemed to new life in Jesus Christ.

With this knowledge we can move forward with compassion for the people around us, with confidence because God has adopted us, and with peace because we know God is in control. We walk in love, not in order to obtain salvation, but because He has already clothed us in it. We are free to love when it is hard, free to deny ourselves when the world tells us to take what we want, and free to forgive when we have been hurt and wronged. Through our own behavior modification, we are unable to truly change; but when the Lord transforms our hearts, the victory is already won. We are free.

> Father, transform my heart, that I may put on Your new way of life.

WORTHY CONDUCT

Whatever happens, conduct yourselves in a manner worthy of the gospel of Christ. Then, whether I come and see you or only hear about you in my absence, I will know that you stand firm in the one Spirit, striving together as one for the faith of the gospel.

PHILIPPIANS 1:27

Paul calls us to conduct ourselves "in a manner worthy of the gospel." But what does that mean? And what does that look like in our lives?

Earlier in Philippians 1, Paul answered this question. He told us in Philippians 1:21, "For me, to live is Christ and to die is gain." A life worthy of the gospel is one that has decided that glorifying Jesus is its chief purpose. Even when times are rough, the desire to know Christ and advance God's kingdom overwhelms any difficulty we might face. To better understand what "worthiness" looks like, imagine an old produce scale—but instead of measuring weight, this scale measures worth. If you were to put your life on one side and the gospel on the other, would the weight you place on your life be out of balance with the weight you place on the gospel?

Notice how Paul closed today's verse: "I will know that you stand firm in the one Spirit, striving together as one." If we want to seek unity in the Spirit and our work for the gospel, we must first live in a manner that matches the gospel.

> Lord, show me how to walk in a manner worthy of Your perfect and precious gospel, and how we as believers can strive together.

ROOTED IN LOVE

*I pray that you, being rooted and established in love, may have power,
together with all the Lord's holy people, to grasp how wide and long and
high and deep is the love of Christ, and to know this love that surpasses
knowledge—that you may be filled to the measure of all the fullness of God.*

Ephesians 3:17–19

For a seed to grow, it must be planted in the right soil; its roots
need to dig deep to secure itself to the ground. If its roots aren't
secure, the seed will be easily plucked up when animals or stormy
weather comes, and the plant will die. The same principle applies
in your walk with Jesus: in order for you to blossom, your life must
be rooted and established in the soil of Christ's love.

But how do you root yourself in love? By spending time with
Jesus and imitating Him. He was a humble seed who allowed
Himself to be buried, so you must also sacrifice yourself for
others. Love in action as He did—give generously, serve freely. As
you plant your feet firmly in loving others, you will encounter His
love—and it will leave you basking in wonder and living in the
unexplainable fullness of God.

You were never destined to remain a seed, a life of unborn
potential. God made you to be a tree with wide branches that provide shade and rest to many in need. Ground yourself in love that
you may be "filled to the measure of all the fullness of God."

> Jesus, let me love like You do, and bring me to depths of love
> that I've yet to reach.

THE MIND-SET OF CHRIST

In your relationships with one another, have the same mindset as Christ
Jesus: Who, being in very nature God, did not consider equality with God
something to be used to his own advantage; rather, he made himself nothing
by taking the very nature of a servant, being made in human likeness.

PHILIPPIANS 2:5–7

If you were "in your very nature God," what would you do with your life? Would you aim to please yourself, remaining comfortably above everyone else? Or would you step down from your throne, and lay down your power to serve others?

Jesus chose the second option. His love for us drove Him from a position of power to one of weakness, and He daily chose to consider others' needs before His own. He willingly took a less glorious role to love a bunch of sinners—sinners He knew would eventually reject Him. In this world there is a constant temptation to live for ourselves instead of pouring out our lives for others, yet God calls us to take on a life like Jesus'—to love and serve in humility and to consider others' needs before our own.

How can you show the attitude of Christ toward the people in your life? When we see how much Jesus gave for us, we can't do anything less than love, serve, and consider others in the same way. Let the Holy Spirit transform your relationships by taking the time to daily develop this mind-set of Christ.

> Lord, open my eyes to the people You want me to serve.
> Grant me the humility to consider their needs above my own.
> Teach me to love others as Jesus loves me.

TEAMWORK MAKES THE DREAM WORK

How good and pleasant it is when God's people live together in unity!

PSALM 133:1

Have you ever been away from your family and friends for an extended period of time? Do you remember the joy you felt when you reunited with them?

God loves His church and wants that kind of joy for His people when they're together. He designed the church to be more than a team or a unit—He designed us to be a family.

In the days of the early church, the first believers would gather in homes, not to sit around and have a church service, but to eat and spend time together. Acts 2:46 says that the early church "broke bread in their homes and ate together with glad and sincere hearts." Their genuine love and care for each other extended past Sunday mornings into their daily lives. This deep fellowship not only filled them with great joy, but also gave God pleasure, because when His people live in harmony, His name is glorified!

Church is not a building we go to, but a family we belong to. Let's then love each other genuinely today, inviting each other into our everyday lives beyond the church. That way, we can truly come to enjoy each other in a "good and pleasant" way, knowing that God desires for His people to live together in unity.

Jesus, thank You for designing the church to give us close, personal relationships. Help my church family come together and enjoy the blessing of family You've given us.

BUILDING THE BROKEN

*We who are strong ought to bear with the failings of the
weak and not to please ourselves. Each of us should please
our neighbors for their good, to build them up.*

Romans 15:1–2

Christ came for the weak and the broken, to provide hope in a
hopeless world. His selfless life is the model we should live by. He
saved us when we were broken, so in turn we should build up the
weak until they become strong, thus creating more voices raised
in praise for God's goodness and compassion.

Mark 2:15–17 reminds us that, much like a doctor serves the
sick rather than the healthy, Jesus came not for the righteous but
for the broken. That's good news, because we all qualify as weak
and broken at some point. And being broken, we can recognize
the brokenness in those around us. Whether it is someone clearly,
visibly suffering, or someone quietly exhausted and weakened
by secret pain, we each encounter human weakness daily. That's
when we forfeit our own needs to serve and uplift others. Like the
doctor helping the sick and Jesus saving the broken, we are called
as strong believers to care for the weak, helping them stand firmly
in their faith and ministering to their needs.

Today, find new ways to bear with one another's failings and
build up your brothers and sisters, practicing this biblical truth
that is rooted deeply in love.

Father, use me as a source of comfort and guidance for
those in need.

SELFLESS COMMUNITY

Therefore if you have any encouragement from being united with Christ, if any comfort from his love, if any common sharing in the Spirit, if any tenderness and compassion, then make my joy complete by being like-minded, having the same love, being one in spirit and of one mind. Do nothing out of selfish ambition or vain conceit. Rather, in humility value others above yourselves, not looking to your own interests but each of you to the interests of the others.

PHILIPPIANS 2:1–4

There is one essential message to Paul's words: community really is valuable to Christians! Living in community is foundational to the Christian faith. Having authentic community is not merely cooperating or putting up with each other; it's living selflessly for one another. Jesus showed us how to have community with others: He served them perfectly by giving His life for them.

We live in a divided church in a divided nation. How do we get past those differences? The answer is right here in today's verse. Do nothing selfishly, regard others as better, and look to others' interests. Putting another before yourself is the Christ-follower's joy because it's the living model of Jesus' selflessness. In this completely countercultural move, we acknowledge that He has already given us all we need, and we are free to direct our actions outward to others. So disregard the urge to make petty distinctions, and aim to live accountable and in service to one another. Set your mind on the goal we all share: proclaiming the glory of God to all.

> Father, You are the truth that holds us all together. Help us put aside our differences and focus on what matters.

THE BIGGER PICTURE

*I appeal to you, brothers and sisters, in the name of our Lord Jesus Christ,
that all of you agree with one another in what you say and that there be no
divisions among you, but that you be perfectly united in mind and thought.*

1 CORINTHIANS 1:10

Conflict is inevitable, and the church is not above the harm that division can cause for God's people.

In today's verse Paul noted a division in the church of Corinth, when differing opinions drove them apart. While Paul wasn't saying that conflict will be absent in the church, he was calling the Corinthians to resolve things, come to an agreement, and refocus on Jesus. As Paul wrote to the church, he reminded them of who they were: sanctified in Christ Jesus and called to be holy (v. 2), brothers and sisters (v. 10), and grace-receivers (v. 4).

Remember who has unified you, for He encourages us to love each other. Unity involves the practice of remembering: remembering the bigger picture, purpose, and calling of our lives. We are not incapable of agreeing with one another. He has equipped us spiritually to rise above our feelings and inadequacies to become a unified people.

Think about the church's potential when unified. What might it look like for us to set Christ before us in every situation? What could we accomplish as a church?

> God, help me in times of conflict to look outside of myself and look to You, who You say I am, and what You call me to do.

DISCIPLINE AND UNITY

"If two of you on earth agree about anything they ask for, it
will be done for them by my Father in heaven. For where two
or three gather in my name, there am I with them."

MATTHEW 18:19–20

Taken out of context, today's verse could be interpreted as a magic trick: two people come to God for requests and, like a genie, He grants their wishes because more than one person is asking. But when we take time to understanding the rest of Scripture, there's so much more to it.

In the previous verses, Jesus taught His disciples about church discipline. He talked about confronting a straying church member in order to reconcile them to the body of believers. These verses then take the concept further, explaining how Jesus will be there with His disciples when they bring the burden of truth to a brother or sister.

Jesus offers growth and restoration through the process of discipline among believers. Rather than sweep problems under the rug, He calls us to meet together, pray, and lovingly speak with His guidance. The key is to come together with a desire for unity and reconciliation, using God's truth to anchor our decisions. Discipline can be hard to take and awkward to give, but let's not shy away from it, for God can bring unity to us through it.

Lord, thank You for disciplining the ones You love. Let us humbly accept truth in our own lives from those who care for us, and give us courage to love others in the same way.

BE WASHED

"Now that I, your Lord and teacher, have washed your
feet, you also should wash one another's feet."

JOHN 13:14

Knowing His time on earth was nearing a close, Jesus, the Word made flesh, set a compelling example for His followers.

"Unless I wash you, you have no part with me" (John 13:8), Jesus responded to Peter, who couldn't get over the thought that His Master would wash the dirt off his feet. But what Peter didn't see then is that Jesus must serve us first before we can serve others. This order, which He modeled through His life, reminds us that we have to come and receive His love before we can ever go and give. After all, "even the Son of Man did not come to be served, but to serve" (Mark 10:45).

True service is impossible if we are not intrinsically motivated by love. To love is to serve and to put others above yourself, and to serve is to surrender pride and to place intentional yet genuine kindness on display. Jesus did that for us.

Unity in Christ is not possible without love. So let's pause and allow Him to serve us, knowing that we can only *give* love after we have *received* His love and mercy.

> Jesus, help me walk in love today. Make me an agent for unity among believers. Thank You for the kindness You've shown me and for being the ultimate example of a servant and friend.

GLIMPSES OF GLORY

So then, no more boasting about human leaders! All things are yours,
whether Paul or Apollos or Cephas or the world or life or death or the present
or the future—all are yours, and you are of Christ, and Christ is of God.

1 CORINTHIANS 3:21–23

Glory is a complex concept. We believe we catch a glimpse of it every day as athletes accomplish feats beyond comprehension or scientists discover uncharted territory. We simply want to be remembered. Our nature is to seek glory. However, we are here for one exceedingly important purpose: giving glory back where it belongs—to God. Every glorious thing we celebrate is but a glimmer of His greater glory.

Cephas, or Peter, was a disciple, an apostle, and a martyr for Christ. Paul was an apostle who was shipwrecked, beaten, and martyred for Christ's name. These men had plenty of reasons to be proud of what they'd achieved. Yet, they understood that Christ-followers do not boast in our human accomplishments, but we lay our successes along with our sufferings at the feet of Christ. We are not here to take the praise, but to point each other toward Jesus, so we may see God's greater, all-encompassing glory.

If we are Christ's, then we are God's, and if we are God's, all things are ours. Get rid of boasting and self-importance, and instead seek God's glory. That's where the real glory is.

> Lord, thank You for displaying Your greatness on the earth.
> Let me not get caught up in the vessels You show it through,
> but celebrate Your glory together with You.

PLAYING FAVORITES

My brothers and sisters, believers in our glorious Lord
Jesus Christ must not show favoritism.

JAMES 2:1

Nothing destroys the unity of any group like "playing favorites." Families have been fractured, churches have been split, and relationships weakened all from the perception that someone is choosing one person over another for special, unfair consideration.

There are many examples of the negative effects of favoritism in Scripture. Isaac and Rebekah made their own sons, Jacob and Esau, into mortal enemies because they chose favorites between their children. Jacob followed the model his parents established and treated his children in the same way, which caused seeds of jealousy to spring up in their family. Unity has never come from showing favoritism.

As believers in Jesus, we are a family. And familial love is steadfast, regardless of what a member may or may not have to offer at a certain time. In today's verse, James is warning against treating rich and poor neighbors differently. Let's then stop playing favorites, and let us love each other the way Jesus loves us. The world will see what it's like when families love not because of perceived value or personal preference, but from the overflow of God's endless love and passion for His mission.

> Father, if there is any place where I've been withholding love, open my eyes. Fill me with a surplus of Your love—and thank You that there is more than enough to go around.

SURPASSING LOVE

Finally, brothers and sisters, rejoice! Strive for full restoration,
encourage one another, be of one mind, live in peace.
And the God of love and peace will be with you.
2 CORINTHIANS 13:11

In his final words to the Corinthians, Paul urged the church to seek unity. In a world defined by varying degrees of hate, selfishness, and greed, Jesus tells us that our love for Him and for one another is our defining characteristic. Instead of listening to a world that tells us to look out only for ourselves, we are called to rejoice with those who are rejoicing, and mourn with those who are mourning (Romans 12:15). When our differences attempt to tear us apart, the foundation of our faith stands firm.

The world often rejoices in division, but the church seeks restoration. The world promotes selfishness, but the church encourages selflessness. The world celebrates the spectacle of disagreement, but the church rallies around one mission.

Demonstrate a love that surpasses the world's understanding, and you will spread God's fame. Be the safe and secure place where your brothers and sisters feel restored and renewed to seek Christ. Whether on campus, at work, or within your home, strive to display God's love by being a source of comfort and encouragement for others.

Father, thank You for giving beautiful alternatives to the world's answers. Help me demonstrate Your all-surpassing love more and more each day.

CONFOUNDING LOVE

*No one has ever seen God; but if we love one another, God
lives in us and his love is made complete in us.*

1 JOHN 4:12

God lives in us, and His presence is especially evident when we love each other, even when it inconveniences us or we'd rather do something else. Thankfully, God showed us how to love, and His Spirit gives us the power and strength to show love to others, especially when it's hard.

God's selfless love has always confused our broken world, a world that holds selfishness and greed as the standard. When we have God's love in our hearts, its presence immediately sets us apart from others because we embody the selflessness God showed to us. God's love inspires us to forgive others, so grudges disappear. It inspires us to give to those who have none, so poverty shrinks. Regardless of whether people believe in God, God's love moves us to hold the hands of believers and nonbelievers alike, so dissentions disintegrate, and we become one body.

When we allow God to show His love through us, we are *in* the world but not *of* it. Rely on God today to fill you with His love, and ask for opportunities to show it in ways that make the world wonder.

Lord, help me love when it's hardest. Help me depend on You in all things and to show others Your love. Use me to invite others into Your love.

A SACRED TEMPLE

Do you not know that you are God's temple and that God's Spirit
dwells in you? If anyone destroys God's temple, God will destroy
him. For God's temple is holy, and you are that temple.

1 CORINTHIANS 3:16–17 ESV

You have value in the eyes of God. Just as the ancient temple was sacred to God, so are you. He has chosen to dwell within each of us, His children, and by His Spirit we are made holy. These truths are important not only because they can help us find our own worth in God, but also because they show us the worth in others.

It can be tough to always see each other as God does. Our vision is limited, and disagreement and bitterness between Christians can quickly pull our attention away from Him. In these times, stop, breathe, and remember: that person is God's temple, and God's Spirit dwells there. Why would you pull that temple down? Practicing patience and understanding helps us enjoy each other and makes us more effective in sharing the message of Jesus.

So for today, strive to see others through His eyes. This will unite us as believers, and ultimately help us shine the light of Jesus to everyone we meet. Remember how God chose to love you and dwell in you, and aim to show this love to others in how you live.

> God, help me see the world through Your eyes today. Teach me to treat others with the same grace and humility You have given to me.

ETERNAL FAMILY

*Now that you have purified yourselves by obeying the truth so that
you have sincere love for each other, love one another deeply, from
the heart. For you have been born again, not of perishable seed, but
of imperishable, through the living and enduring word of God.*

1 PETER 1:22–23

God loves us so much He chose to redeem us. Not with something earthly or perishable, but with the blood of His precious and
blameless Son. His sacrifice cleanses and purifies us permanently
for eternity. We join in His resurrection and are born again to new
life here on earth and forever with Him.

What does this new, imperishable life look like? First, Jesus
gave us access to God, so we can walk with Him daily. He will
ask us to follow Him and trust where His Spirit leads. Because
God is love, obeying His truth and living in relationship with Him
directly results in a genuine love for others.

Your new life is also intrinsically linked with others. As you
build on the friendships you've made with other believers, allow
your love for God to be demonstrated to those who don't know
Him; this has an eternal consequence too. This love—free of
hypocrisy, greed, and selfishness—unifies us with believers and
draws others into this family.

> God, thank You for Your everlasting love toward me. Give me
> the ability to love others with authenticity and sincerity so
> that Your eternal family can grow.

WAIT

When the day of Pentecost came, they were all together in one place.
ACTS 2:1

Have you ever been assigned a group project? Did you notice how destructive it was if each group member tried to act independently? Or, on the other hand, did you experience the power of unity if the group joined together to fulfill the assignment?

This was the case with the early believers as they waited for the Holy Spirit to come. At this time, they were some of the few people on planet Earth to intimately know Jesus. And just before He ascended to heaven, Jesus had told them to go and spread His gospel across the earth. Jesus then told them to wait, that He would send a Helper to aid them in carrying out His mission on earth. So they waited together for Him to send the help He had promised to carry out their commission. They all shared the same mind and same heartbeat: Jesus' name and renown.

The church today is called to the same mind: to spread His glory on earth. As we gather together in like mind and mission, we can truly sense the power of God working through a diverse, but united body across the earth. So remember the purpose and the name we center around. Gather together with His church to make His name known.

> Jesus, the only thing we want is to tell the world about You. Help us wait on Your Spirit together, and move through us to reach people from here to the ends of the earth.

UNITY IN PRAYER

They all joined together constantly in prayer, along with the women and Mary the mother of Jesus, and with his brothers.

ACTS 1:14

What is one thing that every denomination has in common? Despite stylistic differences, we reach out to God through prayer.

If we are going to see Jesus at work through our generation, then we need to be united around a clear purpose. That's what we see in this scripture: believers gathered together to pray. There was no spiritual elitism going around in Jesus' family because the cross had leveled the playing field. They were united and speaking the same language: prayer.

Just as language must be the common denominator for a group of people to able to achieve anything they propose to do, so must prayer be at the center of the church's work. Prayer can never be peripheral—it's what unites us. When we don't see the whole picture, prayer binds us to the One who's painting on the canvas of history, linking us together as a family to our heavenly Father! So before we pursue any endeavor or set ourselves on any purpose, let's come together before our Father in prayer. He hears us and knows what we need before we even ask.

Jesus, unify Your followers with prayer, bringing us together as we seek Your will and provision.

LAY DOWN

"My command is this: Love each other as I have loved you. Greater love has no one than this: to lay down one's life for one's friends."

JOHN 15:12–13

Have you ever met someone who has genuinely served and loved in a surprising and supernatural way? Were you shocked by their grace and selflessness? Did it cause you to wonder what was different about that person?

Chances are, that person loved with the sacrificial love of Jesus, the love He calls us to display. Jesus said there is no greater love "than to lay down one's life for one's friends." In this particular moment, He foreshadowed the fact that He would lay down His life for us, showing us the highest and most perfect love.

We may not have an opportunity to physically die for someone else, but we have ample opportunities to put our wants and ambitions aside to serve the Lord and others. This is often mind-blowing in a culture that tells us to look out only for ourselves.

Loving like Jesus could look like staying an extra hour at work to cover a shift, helping a student in a class who is struggling, having that hard conversation that will lead to reconciliation, or giving someone a ride. These sacrificial acts of love can cause people to ask questions and can ultimately lead them to Jesus!

Can you think of any opportunities to lay yourself down to serve someone else today?

Jesus, thank You for the beauty of sacrificial love. Direct my path so I can show this kind of love to someone in need.

UNITED WE STAND

If we claim to have fellowship with him and yet walk in the
darkness, we lie and do not live out the truth. But if we walk in
the light, as he is in the light, we have fellowship with one another,
and the blood of Jesus, his Son, purifies us from all sin.

1 JOHN 1:6–7

Living a life in community with other people isn't *just* a good idea; rather, John tells us it is a natural part of walking with God. God Himself *is* a community, and He invites us to share in the fellowship He enjoys with the Son and the Spirit.

Sharing our lives with others helps us walk "in the light" and keeps us from stepping into darkness. In isolation, we can lose sight of reality and wander off into confusion and ineffectiveness. But community raises the lantern and leads us along the way of truth. We bear each other's burdens, wage war on sin through collective prayer, and keep each other accountable to higher standards of godliness. These actions give us strength, and they are only possible in community with other believers.

So for today, draw near to God through fellowship. Allow the community around you to strengthen your relationship with God. Dive into meaningful relationships with other believers, and worship together with them today. And as we hold each other in the light, Jesus continues to purify us from the things that bind us.

God, help me to live fully in community today. Let me walk with others in Your bright light.

ABOVE ALL

Above all, love each other deeply, because love covers over a multitude of sins. Offer hospitality to one another without grumbling.

1 PETER 4:8–9

Most of us have a lot on our plates. We juggle responsibilities for school, work, relationships, and more. This constant bouncing around can prevent any one priority from rising to the top.

Scripture says that we are to love one another "above all" else. This is because love, when rooted in forgiveness and reconciliation, "covers over a multitude of sins." Many people today have deemed the church to be ineffective, individualistic, and lacking in love. To counteract this, love must be our top priority. Though disagreements may arise, if we embrace deep love, unity is quick to follow. After all, unity is simply love in motion. When we show other people this love, like when we're hospitable without complaining, then the church comes together and true unity is accomplished.

How can love rise to the top in your daily life? What would it need to take precedence over? What "multitude of sins" would it cover? Imagine the unity we could see if authentic, selfless love were to permeate our churches and lives—the world would come to know Jesus *much* faster!

> Lord, teach me to love deeply with a humble heart and to prioritize Your love over all else.

REJOICE TOGETHER

I will extol the LORD at all times; his praise will always be on my lips. I will glory in the LORD; let the afflicted hear and rejoice. Glorify the LORD with me; let us exalt his name together.

PSALM 34:1–3

There's something addictive about sing-alongs. One moment you're in the car with friends, and the next you're belting out your favorite song at the top of your lungs together. You can't help yourselves; you feed off the collective energy. But when you're alone, the energy and passion are not the same.

Being alone in our relationship with Christ has a similar effect. For a while, we start the day with time in the Word; we pray; we walk the walk. Everything seems okay. Then the fire burns out, and the flame goes dim. What was once excitement to praise Jesus turns into the continuous drone of daily life. We go from passionate worship to dry routine. Why?

It's hard to live the life of following Jesus alone, off our own energy. It's not meant to be that way. Exalting God, being the church, means worshiping in community—standing alongside believers in order to keep our heads up. We suffer together. We rejoice together. Stand hand-in-hand with your brothers and sisters in Christ, so that today will be lived in awe and worship of the greatest Lord of all. Renew your passion by rejoicing in Him together.

Father, help us worship You as one. Show us how to bring our voices together so Your name will echo across the earth.

193

HUMBLE WORTHINESS

I urge you to live a life worthy of the calling you have received. Be completely humble and gentle; be patient, bearing with one another in love. Make every effort to keep the unity of the Spirit through the bond of peace.

EPHESIANS 4:1–3

When Paul told the Ephesians to "live a life worthy of the calling you have received," he meant something that might surprise people who look for worthiness the world's way. Our culture tells us to "fake it till we make it," stand out, reinforce our qualifications, and project an air of confidence. It tells us to put up a front to convince people we're deserving of our position. How exhausting.

Instead, Paul offers a better way: humility and community. His words apply to both our individual callings and our corporate calling as the church. Christ-inspired humility, gentleness, patience, and—most of all—love are the hallmarks of worthiness. Glorifying God is the benchmark of success. No amount of posturing or bravado can match His beauty. And no one can accomplish alone what can come through community—the "bond of peace" that shows the world what God's Spirit can do.

In our private and vocational callings, we're all working toward the same goal: spreading God's love. Let's make humility and unity our go-to response as we chase after our calling. Then, together, the Spirit can move through us in far greater ways than we could dream up on our own.

Lord, make me completely humble and devoted to peace in Your family—for the sake of the calling You've given me.

LOVE FOR CHRIST'S BRIDE

Therefore let us stop passing judgment on one another.
Instead, make up your mind not to put any stumbling
block or obstacle in the way of a brother or sister.

ROMANS 14:13

Full of love and wonder, the Groom gazes upon His beautiful bride as she walks down the aisle. A passion burns within Him, a holy zeal to lead, protect, and love her with all His heart.

Heaven is passionate for His bride, the church. What a mistake would it be, then, to judge she whom Christ has approved, to tempt she whom Christ adores?

All too often, the bride of Christ suffers judgment from her members. By placing a stumbling block, an expectation, or a temptation, we create a snag in the aisle for the bride to slip and fall. When we walk in judgment, we bring condemnation and confusion, but Christ has called us to walk in love.

To walk in love is to regard others in the church as Jesus does. While humans naturally dwell on the external, judging on incomplete information, Jesus focuses on the heart. So do not approach the bride of Christ antagonistically by judging one another. Instead, remember everything Jesus did to prepare her for Himself. And discover freedom and growth as you respect her and love God without restraint.

Jesus, let my thoughts become like Yours so I treat Your bride as You do.

WATCH OUT

I urge you, brothers and sisters, to watch out for those who
cause divisions and put obstacles in your way that are contrary
to the teaching you have learned. Keep away from them.

ROMANS 16:17

Do you ever wonder why Paul's letters are so insistent that church members watch out for division? Why does this come up so much? Perhaps because it's a key symptom that something in the church isn't aligning with Christ's teaching. Paul warned that when individuals bring their own agendas to the church, they can lead others away from its intended purpose.

Of course, we are all called to reach out to people who are separated from Christ. But if we constantly, exclusively surround ourselves with influences that don't bring God glory, we can easily begin to absorb lies that lead strong believers astray. That's why we're instructed to "watch out." Yet the more we surround ourselves with God-driven, God-following believers who cling to His teaching, the more we will learn to walk like Jesus—together. If we strive for godliness, seeking unity in the cross of Christ, we will experience genuine community. Let's take advantage of every breath God gives us be wise and vigilant, seeking the goodness of serving the Lord in unity.

Father, all we want is You. Allow us to become Your church, waiting desperately for You to move.

REMEMBER

Remember what the apostles of our Lord Jesus Christ foretold. They said to you, "In the last times there will be scoffers who will follow their own ungodly desires." These are the people who divide you, who follow mere natural instincts and do not have the Spirit. But you, dear friends, by building yourselves up in your most holy faith and praying in the Holy Spirit, keep yourselves in God's love as you wait for the mercy of our Lord Jesus Christ to bring you to eternal life.

JUDE VV. 17–21

We all need reminders. We have so much information cycling in and out of our brains that it is impossible to keep track of it all. When it comes to God's Word, it's absolutely in our best interest to remember it; His Word is the bread that feeds our hearts.

Jude instructed us to remember one of the apostle's most important lessons: we should not be surprised when we encounter people who scoff and sow dissent, because they do not have the Spirit and do not have the gospel as a priority. These people set their minds on the flesh and are slaves to it. However, Christ's followers set their minds on the Spirit and are freed and united by it.

We are liberated to live in God's love, praying and building together and seeking His wisdom. In community, we work to remind each other of the good news of the gospel. In unity of the Spirit, we pray for one another, and by the help of brothers and sisters, we work to keep each other in God's love. How can you remind yourself and others of these basic truths today?

> Father, grant me the faith and patience to persevere with my fellow believers.

197

HEALING PEACE

He himself is our peace, who has made the two groups one and has destroyed the barrier, the dividing wall of hostility, by setting aside in his flesh the law with its commands and regulations. His purpose was to create in himself one new humanity out of the two, thus making peace, and in one body to reconcile both of them to God through the cross, by which he put to death their hostility.

EPHESIANS 2:14–16

Jesus' death was the ultimate act of peace. On the cross, sin was defeated, and death's power was lost. Through Jesus, God brought Himself to humanity, making unity possible among all humankind.

Today's verse refers to two feuding groups: the Jews and the Gentiles. They were continually at odds—one group was God's chosen people, and the other didn't know Him. But when Jesus fulfilled the law on the cross, both Jews and Gentiles were set free to obtain righteousness. Ethnic distinctions were no longer necessary, because Jesus tore down the wall of hostility that sin and broken people had made.

Jesus does not see denomination, ethnicity, language, or gender; He sees one family saved through His blood. Everyone can come to Him—no matter who they are or where they come from. So treasure that unity. In the face of hostility, look to the Prince of Peace, for there is no feud, animosity, or division that cannot be made whole in Christ.

Jesus, thank You for oneness with You. May I too be an agent of peace.

ENCOURAGING REMINDERS

Strengthen the feeble hands, steady the knees that give way; say to those with fearful hearts, "Be strong, do not fear; your God will come, he will come with vengeance; with divine retribution he will come to save you."

ISAIAH 35:3–4

Have you ever wondered why believers gather together as a church? There are many reasons to come together as a body, but one of the main reasons is to strengthen each other and encourage each other.

Life is difficult and painful at times. Maybe someone you know is in the middle of difficult times causing them exhaustion, fear, doubt, or weakness. Or maybe that person is *you*. Though filled with hardship, these moments are beautiful opportunities for the church to encourage one another, to remind one another that the promises of God are unfailing and unwavering and that Jesus is walking with us in love. One of our functions as a family is to constantly remind each other of who God is, what He has promised, and what He has personally done for us.

How can you make encouragement a way of life? Who can you encourage today? Take time to think about who may need a reminder of God's perfect love, and approach them with support and words of truth.

> Jesus, thank You for Your church, and help us lift each other up in Your name.

SHARE THE GRACE

"I have the right to do anything," you say—but not everything is beneficial. "I have the right to do anything"—but not everything is constructive. No one should seek their own good, but the good of others.

1 Corinthians 10:23–24

In today's passage, Paul redirected our definition of God's grace. He said that although we have freedom through Christ from the strict laws of the Old Testament, it doesn't mean that everything we want to do is beneficial for God's kingdom. God's grace is not meant to help us help ourselves; it's meant to help us help others.

In Christ, we have more freedom than anyone could imagine. When we use this freedom only for our benefit, we take away the chance to demonstrate His grace to those who do not know Him. We can read, listen to sermons, educate ourselves, and fill ourselves with as much godly insight as we can hold, but unless we turn that outward, it is not "constructive" to anyone but us. Goodness shouldn't be hoarded or kept to ourselves; it was meant to be shared joyfully. Let's not just seek our own good, but the good of those around us. How can you turn outward today with something that was once for your own good, but can be a blessing to someone else?

Father, I pray that I don't disregard Your grace as a bandage for myself, but rather as a lifeboat bringing me closer to You. Direct my focus toward the good of others because I already have all I need in You.

THE NEW SELF

But now you must also rid yourselves of all such things as these: anger, rage, malice, slander, and filthy language from your lips. Do not lie to each other, since you have taken off your old self with its practices and have put on the new self, which is being renewed in knowledge in the image of its Creator.

COLOSSIANS 3:8–10

Take a second to remember what it was like before you met Christ. How did you feel? What did you think each day? What did you long for?

When we were in bondage to sin, we acted out in many different ways. We didn't know Christ, or the hope that we cling to. Because of our insecurities, some of us portrayed a false version of ourselves, because we wanted to fit in. Some of us turned to substance abuse to fill that longing. Our behavior when we were trying to fill the pre-Jesus void is considered our "old self."

But in Jesus, those longings are completely filled! And because Jesus paid for our sins on the cross, we praise Him and thank Him for setting us free from our old selves. But He doesn't just allow us to bask in His redemption; He asks us to put on the "new self," which is a life of faith, hope, love, and encouragement to all of our brothers and sisters and those who do not know Him yet. It's a daily process, though, and we need Him to help us put on this new self every day. Follow Jesus every morning as He leads you further from the old self and shows you more about the new.

Lord, show me how to put on the new self today so that You may be glorified in me!

SUPERNATURAL KINDNESS

*Finally, all of you, be like-minded, be sympathetic, love one another,
be compassionate and humble. Do not repay evil with evil or insult
with insult. On the contrary, repay evil with blessing, because
to this you were called so that you may inherit a blessing.*

1 PETER 3:8–9

Throughout his first letter, Peter addresses how church members should relate to others. He instructs us in relating to authorities, masters, husbands, wives, and finally, other members of the church.

In relating to other Christians, Peter isn't telling us to do *x*, *y*, and *z*. He's calling us first and foremost to *be* a kind of people. On our own, we can't fulfill all of the characteristics in today's scripture. But because we have experienced a "new birth" by God's mercy (1 Peter 1:3), we have access to this inner transformation.

This new birth comes from God's living Word—"a life conceived by God himself!" (1 Peter 1:23 THE MESSAGE)—giving us complete access to Him. It enables us to share His mind-set, respond with sensitivity, view each other as family, and be humble in our dependence on Him. Because of this inner transformation, there will be a spiritual unity in the church and a transformation of the way we act. So in all your interactions today, be conscious of the inner transformation Christ has worked in you. He enables you to respond in kindness, no matter what comes your way.

God, I want to be all that You have called me to be. Show me how to react with Your supernatural love.

UNIFIED VISION

Do we not all have one Father? Did not one God create us? Why do we profane the covenant of our ancestors by being unfaithful to one another?

MALACHI 2:10

What holds the church together?

In today's verse, Malachi speaks of the people of Judah. After dwelling in the promised land and enjoying God's blessings, the people of Judah had lost their faith. The men abandoned God's command to love each another by deceiving and being unfaithful to each other—marrying the foreign women God had forbidden them to associate with and leaving behind the wives they had committed to. In their selfishness, the people of Judah forgot that God cared not only for offerings and sacrifices, but also about how they treated each other. Now they wept because God rejected their halfhearted offerings.

Division in the church arises when the church's vision is no longer centered on Christ's commands of loving one another. If we are looking to love as Jesus commanded us, we must remember how He loved us and how He calls us to love one another. Sacrificial, patient, faithful, and sincere love is what holds the church together. We set aside distractions that might be attractive in the moment and take instead the pure commitment of God's covenant with us. Let's love one another as God calls us to do, because when the church does this, the world knows we are His disciples (John 13:35).

Lord, let us never forget how You have loved us. Help us remain united around You.

PREPARE YOUR HEART

"Therefore, if you are offering your gift at the altar and there remember that your brother or sister has something against you, leave your gift there in front of the altar. First go and be reconciled to them; then come and offer your gift."

MATTHEW 5:23–24

The act of worship takes reflective preparation. Before we worship God, we express reverence by preparing our hearts to come before Him. That, Jesus says, requires that we reconcile any strife with fellow believers.

The temple offerings Jesus refers to in Matthew equate to the tithes and offerings that we give to our local church. Jesus is clear that we can't give to God until we work out existing conflict with our neighbor. Offerings do not act as atonement for wrongdoings in our lives. The only way to come before God is through Jesus Christ, who gave Himself up so that our relationship with God could be reconciled. In the same way, Jesus asks that we seek reconciliation in our relationships with one another. When we humble ourselves and work through relational strife, we honor God by making our relationships right before we come to worship God.

Preparing for any act of worship, we must reflect on our hearts and examine our motives, relationships, and desires. Are there disagreements between you and a brother or sister in Christ? Go and seek peace, and then come worship with a clean heart.

> Before You, Lord, I want to offer a pure heart. Guide me in making my relationships right so that I can come humbly before You in worship.

WORSHIP TOGETHER

*A very large crowd of people assembled in Jerusalem to
celebrate the Festival of Unleavened Bread in the second month.
They removed the altars in Jerusalem and cleared away the
incense altars and threw them into the Kidron Valley.*

2 Chronicles 30:13–14

When Hezekiah became king over Judah, sin and disagreement had divided Israel into two kingdoms, Israel and Judah; this turned both kingdoms away from their loving Creator. Hezekiah, however, sought to reunite the people in God's name. Led by the Spirit, Hezekiah removed idols from the land and gathered members of the twelve tribes in Jerusalem to celebrate the first unified Passover in more than two hundred years. The people of Israel worshiped and glorified God together as one body, and God heard their prayers and healed the people.

Praising God is what truly unifies His people. He designed us to live as a one body so we could enjoy His favor and show the world a clear picture of His love. Like the people of Israel, we see God's glory when we come together and seek Him in worship. And as we move toward God as one body, we grow closer to seeing His will fulfilled. As believers, let's become one in Jesus, so that through our unity the world might know God makes us one.

Father, lead us to be a more unified body. Allow us to throw aside what hinders us, uniting in praise of You.

THE LADDER

"Whoever wants to become great among you must be your servant, and whoever wants to be first must be your slave—just as the Son of Man did not come to be served, but to serve, and to give his life as a ransom for many."

MATTHEW 20:26–28

If you've ever seen someone use a ladder, you know that there is usually one person climbing up—and another person holding it steady from the bottom. As young adults, we are rallied to climb the ladders of life. From school to internships to the workplace, we live and operate on the rungs of success. But Jesus flips the script in Matthew when He calls us to descend from our high places and, instead, hold the ladder for others.

While the world is climbing and gaining more power, He says, "Not so with you." In Jesus' terms, serving—not climbing—is the true embodiment of leadership. Jesus told His disciples this because He knew that when our desire to lead shifts from a perspective of accumulating power to one of serving others, we are then be able to make a way for those around us to see His grace more clearly.

Jesus didn't call us to the back of the line simply to stand idly. How can you get off the ladder and actively serve others today?

> Jesus, thank You for setting an example of what a servant leader looks like. Remind me that when I am last, I am becoming more like You.

MOTIVES MATTER

You, then, why do you judge your brother or sister? Or why do you treat them with contempt? For we will all stand before God's judgment seat.

ROMANS 14:10–11

When Paul wrote this passage, certain members of the Roman church had started making rules about food, Sabbath days, and fasting. Because of the freedom Jesus brought, these rules shouldn't have been a requirement for the Christian life, but certain church members had started to treat them like they were. They looked down on those who didn't share their practices, and this inflated their pride.

Paul urged the church to abstain from judging each other about such trivial things because *what* we do is less important than *why* we do it. Our motive is crucial. Fasting, restricting certain foods, and practicing the Sabbath are beautiful ways to draw near to Jesus, but these actions don't save us. If we look to activities and rules for our salvation and hold others to standards not laid out in Scripture, we are susceptible to pride and disunity, just like the people Paul wrote to in today's passage.

God alone is the standard of justice, goodness, and righteousness. When you choose to judge others, you allow your pride to take God's place as the one true Judge. Pride is the enemy of unity! Fight against it by seeking unity with other believers on your campus.

> Father, thank You for creating me with purpose. Take from me the desire to judge, and replace it with the ambition to love and serve.

PEACE AND THANKFULNESS

Let the peace of Christ rule in your hearts, since as members of one body you were called to peace. And be thankful. Let the message of Christ dwell among you richly as you teach and admonish one another with all wisdom through psalms, hymns, and songs from the Spirit, singing to God with gratitude in your hearts.

COLOSSIANS 3:15–16

How can we find peace? So many people struggle to define what peace is, let alone finding some amid the stresses of the day. But we don't find lasting peace through small changes or outwardly applied techniques. Peace is a result of being made alive with Christ—and thus made thankful. We can be at peace with ourselves, others, and with the future struggles we know we will still face here on this earth, because we know that He has saved us.

Ephesians 2:14 says that Jesus is our peace. Through His sacrifice, we are brought closer to God and are free to live in peace with God where there was once hostility. Because of this, we can also have the freedom to live in peace with one another.

When peace rules over our hearts, thanksgiving overflows into praise, allowing us to build each other up. Are you at peace with God and with those around you? And if so, whom are you building up today? Let's embody peace and thankfulness as we walk into the places we have been called today.

> Jesus, thank You for breaking down the barrier so I can not only live in peace with You, but also with those around me.

HONEST PROGRESS

*Therefore each of you must put off falsehood and speak truthfully
to your neighbor, for we are all members of one body.*

Ephesians 4:25

A family is created to be an intimate unit, a safe space where we can be vulnerable and open with each other. But dishonesty is the enemy of intimacy in any relationship. It's not that we lie or cover things up on purpose, out of deceit. In fact, dishonesty is usually a result of deep-rooted fear or insecurity.

When we're dishonest, it's often because we are trying to hide something out of fear of what others may think of us. But Romans 8:15 says, "The Spirit you received does not make you slaves, so that you live in fear again; rather, the Spirit you received brought about your adoption to sonship." Your adopted Father is fully committed to you, and you don't have to save face in front of Him. Families do not fear each other; they love each other in a way that drives out fear and overcomes all imperfections.

One of the biggest steps we can take toward walking intimately with each other as a family is to be vulnerable and to not let shame make us dishonest. Let's put away fear and falsehood, and let us speak with truth and vulnerability with each other, knowing that there is no room for fear in the church. After all, the perfect love of God casts out all fear!

Jesus, remove any fear that has taken root in my heart, and make me honest so I can grow together with my family.

REMAIN TEACHABLE

You then, my son, be strong in the grace that is in Christ Jesus. And the things you have heard me say in the presence of many witnesses entrust to reliable people who will also be qualified to teach others.

2 Timothy 2:1–2

Is there anyone in your life that you want to be like? Have you ever thought about how important finding a mentor—and being a mentor—might be to your Christian walk?

Paul wrote today's scripture in a letter to a younger believer named Timothy. The two were so close that Paul referred to Timothy as his son. Their relationship sets the example for mentorship with young believers. To grow strong in our faith, we are called to seek the wisdom of older teachers, and then share their teaching with others.

If we humble ourselves and allow teachers into our lives, companionship and accountability add fuel to our faith. Be humble, remain teachable, and be eager to teach. In this way, you'll contribute to the unity and growth of the body of Christ, which is together submitting to the name of Jesus. God's name is glorified as His people love, disciple, and teach each other, in order to unify the church and amplify His name. Find people today whom you can pour into, and look out for new mentors God may be placing in your path.

Lord, give me the humility to learn from those wiser than I am and the courage to lead others who come after me.

ONE HOPE

There is one body and one Spirit, just as you were called to one hope
when you were called; one Lord, one faith, one baptism; one God
and Father of all, who is over all and through all and in all.

Ephesians 4:4–6

In today's scripture, Paul urged the Ephesians to stick together, because he knew these believers would do much greater good for the kingdom of God if they linked arms and did it together—which they did. The believers in Ephesus were so influential that there was a citywide protest challenging them, because their faith was changing the city's religious views (Acts 19:23–41)! This is why Paul often knelt before God, asking for favor and strength for the Ephesian believers, because in their unity they glorified God greatly.

Unity isn't just found in the trivial things we have in common; it's established by our relationship to our Father. God unites us to share the same body, Spirit, hope, faith, baptism, and access to Him. Too often we find ourselves wanting to be set apart from the crowd, but being co-heirs with Christ is both what sets us apart and unites us as believers! When we start moving as one, championing each other on, we're a force to be reckoned with. Let's be the reflection of heaven's oneness for those who are in need of eternal hope.

Jesus, thank You for providing us with a family, just when we thought we were alone. Help us press farther and wider for You today.

UNIFIED FOR HIM

"The glory that you have given me I have given to them, that
they may be one, even as we are one, I in them and you in me,
that they may become perfectly one, so that the world may know
that you sent me and loved them even as you loved me."

JOHN 17:22–23 ESV

When he closed His prayer for the believers who would come after Him, Jesus asked that the world may come to know God through their *unity*—not proper theology or devotion to dogma, which are typically viewed as the lynchpins of growing God's kingdom. But instead of all these, Jesus emphasized unity as the key ingredient for the church's continued success.

Jesus said that we have been given what He was given, the glory of God; but Jesus did not use this glory to promote His own supreme position. Instead, He humbled Himself and served the people He came to save. In the same way, we have been given God's glory, not so that we can promote ourselves, but so that we can follow Jesus' example and serve. This is the key to unity: put the needs of others ahead of our own. So let's be willing serve our brothers and sisters in all ways—even those people we disagree with. Through our unity God's glory is reflected to the world.

God, help me serve others and serve with others whom I may disagree with. Show us how to work together to show Your glory to the world.

THE BENEFIT OF A DOUBT

"Do not judge, and you will not be judged. Do not condemn, and
you will not be condemned. Forgive, and you will be forgiven."
LUKE 6:37

In your interactions with others, are you the first to abandon the benefit of the doubt? Or do you always try to assume the best of people?

We have all been on the wrong side of judgment at some point in our lives, so we know how much it hurts when someone jumps to negative conclusions about us. But people who love to judge do more than just hurt others; they hurt themselves by assuming everyone around them is judging others just as harshly, even when that's not the case. When we judge, we push sinners and struggling believers away from the God who loves to forgive.

The right to judge is reserved for the Lord. Yet even Jesus did not come to condemn the world, but to forgive, and He did it better than any of us ever will (John 3:17). He forgave those who spat in His face and laughed at His kindness. He forgave those who did not even ask for forgiveness. And He commands that we do as He did.

Next time you are tempted to judge someone, pray for them instead. Rather than thinking less of those around you, look for ways you can show them the same love and forgiveness Jesus showed you.

> Lord, give me the strength to forgive those who hurt or offend me, even when they do not ask for forgiveness.

ENCOURAGE WITH HOPE

God did not appoint us to suffer wrath but to receive salvation through
our Lord Jesus Christ. He died for us so that, whether we are awake
or asleep, we may live together with him. Therefore encourage one
another and build each other up, just as in fact you are doing.

1 Thessalonians 5:9–11

Today's verse gives us some very good news: God didn't make us so that we'd suffer. From the very beginning He planned for us to receive salvation through Jesus Christ. This truth is our hope; Christ is coming back for us, and we will get to spend eternity with Him!

It's easy to get caught up in the "wrath" of our day-to-day lives and problems. When we focus on the storms around us rather than on Jesus, the world starts to drag us down. We can feel overwhelmed by all the pressures of this world, and we stumble in our walk with God. But God set up a safeguard for this: we look out for one another as brothers and sisters in Christ. When one of us is struggling, we can come around and help each other up.

How can we encourage each other today to stay strong? As hard as things might be, the trials and worries we face on earth will not last forever. Let's remind each other to live a life of joy because we know that when Christ comes back, we will have an eternity of worshiping and resting in His presence.

God, give me discernment to know when my brothers and sisters are struggling, and show me how to encourage them with the hope we have in Jesus' return.

214

A TRUE FRIEND

*Two are better than one, because they have a good return for
their labor: If either of them falls down, one can help the other up.
But pity anyone who falls and has no one to help them up.*

ECCLESIASTES 4:9–10

A friendship is a relationship unlike any other. It provides the
sweetness and security of having someone who just gets us, someone with whom we can be completely ourselves. A true friend
will be more than just a good hang and a trustworthy companion; they'll love us enough not to be impressed with us. They'll be
there in the best times to remind us of God's faithfulness and in
the worst times to lift us up in truth.

The beauty of the gospel is that we always have a friend, the
best Friend—Jesus! He saw us for who we were: broken and fallen
people. Yet He took on human form, lived the life we couldn't, and
died the death we deserved to give us the grace we needed. By no
means was Jesus ever impressed with us, but when we were at our
worst, He loved us enough to bring us His best gift: salvation. To
follow His example of true friendship, let's commit to being there
to lift up our friends when they fall, ready with truth and grace.

Jesus, thank You for the friendships You have put in my life.
Thank You that You are the best Friend I could have. Help
me be a friend to others as You are to me.

UNCOMFORTABLE LOVE

Anyone who claims to be in the light but hates a brother or sister is
still in the darkness. Anyone who loves their brother and sister lives
in the light, and there is nothing in them to make them stumble.

1 JOHN 2:9–10

Loving people is not always easy. It's frustrating to love people who do not treat you with the same kindness that you give them. However, we are not called to treat others like they may treat us; we're supposed to do things differently from the crowd, just like Jesus did.

Who are we to say who deserves love and who doesn't? Jesus came down to a broken world, suffered ridicule and persecution, and was betrayed and killed by the very people He came to save. He could have said that we absolutely didn't deserve His love because nothing is truer, but His love was greater! He was nailed to that cross to give us an example of perfect love.

Loving someone often means sacrificing, serving, and giving up your comfort for their good. Jesus did that in the extreme, and we can follow His example in our small ways. We get the opportunity to show His love in every conversation, every action, and every moment we have with people around us. It may seem like a challenge in the moment, but the result of our love will always bring light. Remember today: loving Jesus means loving people!

Lord, show me who You want me to love today. Give me Your love and not my own. Help me walk in Your light, and run from the darkness of hate.

DEALING WITH DISAGREEMENT

*Accept the one whose faith is weak, without
quarreling over disputable matters.*

Romans 14:1

Have you ever disagreed with another Christian? Did it leave you frustrated and confused?

Within the church, we often come across situations where people see things differently from us. Some people's opinions may actually challenge our beliefs, and some may leave us confused by their perspective. Differences can leave us aggravated, uncertain, or regretful of our reactions. When disagreements arise, often our first reaction is to try to prove that we are right. But is there a better way?

Instead of spurring on arguments, we can view times of disagreement as opportunities for mutual growth and sharpening. We can't know all the details of someone's situation or why they react in certain ways, but we can speak truth and encouragement in love. We are all on a journey toward Jesus, in different seasons of life and different places in our walks.

The purpose of community is to encourage each other to keep pressing on and keep fighting, because Jesus is worth it. As a generation, we can be people who continue to refresh others. We can set the temperature of encouragement high within the church.

> Lord, show me how to defuse the small disagreements that our Enemy uses to divide us, and fill me with compassion for others.

IN LINE WITH THE GOSPEL

When I saw that they were not acting in line with the truth of the gospel, I said to [Peter] in front of them all, "You are a Jew, yet you live like a Gentile and not like a Jew. How is it, then, that you force Gentiles to follow Jewish customs?"

GALATIANS 2:14

Paul wrote to the Galatians to raise a red flag, because they had started following a warped form of the gospel. He told them of a similar occurrence: while visiting the apostles, Paul noticed Peter (a Christian Jew) begin to distance himself from the Gentiles out of fear of strict Jewish groups. Peter's actions contradicted the truth that salvation comes through faith, not works.

Peter's fear of others' opinions led not only him to act out of "line with the truth of the gospel" but also with his fellow believers. Peter was faced with a question: *Do I truly believe that Jesus frees me from the works of the law and the expectations of others?* According to the gospel, we cannot do anything to free ourselves—only Jesus sets us right before God. If we believe that, then we don't have to act out of fear of judgment.

Paul admonished Peter because he had forgotten this fact. When we live like our former selves, in fear of judgment, it's as if we don't accept the work of God's grace in our lives. "You are all sons of God through *faith* in Christ Jesus" (Galatians 3:26 NASB). Let's choose this God-given identity and embrace this freedom.

God, help me remember and live Your gospel in its entirety. Thank You for meeting my inadequacy with Your freedom.

EQUALLY YOKED

Do not be yoked together with unbelievers. For what do righteousness and wickedness have in common? Or what fellowship can light have with darkness? What harmony is there between Christ and Belial? Or what does a believer have in common with an unbeliever? What agreement is there between the temple of God and idols? For we are the temple of the living God. As God has said: "I will live with them and walk among them, and I will be their God, and they will be my people."

2 CORINTHIANS 6:14–16

A yoke is a device that anchors two work animals together so they can pull a plow through a field. In an unequal yoking, the burden of work is not shared equally, partners get worn out, and both may get off course.

From the beginning of Scripture, God has expressed His will to make for Himself a chosen people who identify themselves as His own. At the time of Paul's writing, there were people in Corinth who identified themselves with the church, yet still maintained their practices and partnerships with idols. Because of this rebellion, Paul labeled them as unbelievers.

Paul exhorted the church of Corinth not to "be yoked together with unbelievers." This doesn't mean we have to separate ourselves from *all* unbelievers. But as God sends us into the field for ministry, try to find a partner who can pull an equal weight, so the task can be accomplished.

> God, keep my relationship with You above all others, and help me choose relationships that glorify You.

LOVE THROUGH ACTION

We love because he first loved us. Whoever claims to love God
yet hates a brother or sister is a liar. For whoever does not love
their brother and sister, whom they have seen, cannot love God,
whom they have not seen. And he has given us this command:
Anyone who loves God must also love their brother and sister.

1 JOHN 4:19–21

Actions reveal the heart, and what we choose to do reveals what is most important to us. The places we spend our time and money reveal what and who we value.

What kind of actions reveal a heart of love for God? Scripture tells us we can't love Him without loving others like He does. What would it look like to love your brothers and sisters well? Would your life be characterized by peace and harmony with others or constant tension? Would you be quick-tempered or use a sharp tone? Would you claim to love God, but still have enemies?

The good news is God gives us the power to love like He loves. We can only love because He first extended Himself to us in perfect, sacrificial love. And we love God well when we love others well! Our actions toward our brothers and sisters reveal our heart. Today, reflect on your actions and current relationships: Are you tense, kind, gentle, patient, quick-tempered? Let Jesus fill your heart again with His love, so you can truly love those God puts in your path.

God, let my actions reveal my heart of love for You.

LOVE AND OBEDIENCE

It has given me great joy to find some of your children walking in the truth, just as the Father commanded us. . . . I am not writing you a new command but one we have had from the beginning. I ask that we love one another. And this is love: that we walk in obedience to his commands. As you have heard from the beginning, his command is that you walk in love.

2 JOHN 1:4–6

The apostle John had an intimate relationship with Jesus. Every day as a disciple, he observed Jesus' interactions with those He loved and those who opposed Him. During Jesus' crucifixion, John witnessed Jesus pleading with the Father, crying out for Him to forgive the sins of those who crucified Him. Repeatedly, Christ set the example for His followers: to love God was to submit completely to His will.

John could see that Christ lived His life wholly devoted to obeying God, so in today's scripture he encouraged believers to do the same. He invited them to review His most basic command to love and obey, proclaiming their love for Christ by reflecting His selfless sacrifice in every aspect of their lives.

In order to share Christ with others, we must return again and again to reflect on the way He loves the world. Each time, ask the Spirit to guide you toward new ways of showing that same love to others. Today, still your heart and reflect on the simplest command—the "one we have had from the beginning": walk in love.

Father, let my life reflect all that Christ has done for me, encouraging others to follow after You in obedience.

ONE BANNER

In Christ Jesus you are all children of God through faith, for all of
you who were baptized into Christ have clothed yourselves with
Christ. There is neither Jew nor Gentile, neither slave nor free, nor
is there male and female, for you are all one in Christ Jesus.

GALATIANS 3:26–28

We humans tend to assign labels to ourselves: smart, athletic, creative, middle-class, poor, white, Asian, black, Protestant, Catholic—the list is endless. We divide ourselves into groups, and often we become insulated. But one label has the power to surpass all these: *Christ.*

When we add other labels to our banner, we falter. When we think Christ isn't enough for us, our behavior changes; jealousy, conflict, and strife start to creep into our actions. These behaviors happen when we fail to recognize the worth He assigned to us all. But we shouldn't let this happen! To be bought by Christ's blood means nothing should divide us; we all stand equal and beloved before our King.

This equal standing in Christ's kingdom enables us to love those completely unlike us. No background, race, or socioeconomic status should become a barrier to community in the Spirit. Today, as members of the Lord's family, let's pay close attention to the labels we assign to ourselves and to others. Instead of these words, let's raise together His banner, and love and serve one another under it.

Lord Jesus, thank You that we each have worth because You are worthy.

LISTEN AND LOVE

*This is how we know what love is: Jesus Christ laid down his life for us.
And we ought to lay down our lives for our brothers and sisters. If anyone
has material possessions and sees a brother or sister in need but has no
pity on them, how can the love of God be in that person? Dear children,
let us not love with words or speech but with actions and in truth.*

1 JOHN 3:16–18

The word *love* is difficult to define. We use the word to define our affection for trivial things, like our favorite movies, or really important things, like our significant others—this makes the word even more difficult to interpret. Thankfully, God has shown us the true meaning: it's found in Jesus' sacrifice.

The ultimate human need is to have a connection with God. Jesus saw this need and laid down His life so that He could fulfill our ultimate need. That's true love.

To love people well, we need to listen to their needs. So many in the world still need Jesus. And through Him, we can listen to others and minister to their needs by sacrificing our time and talents, just like Jesus did.

Father, help me see the needs of others, and help me love them actively so they can know You better.

A DESIRE TO SEE CHRIST CELEBRATED WHERE I LIVE

Because many around me are separated from God,
I will share the story of Jesus where I live.

I blame the combustion engine for more than it deserves, I'm sure. I come from a long line of folks who thrive on blame displacement, all the way back to the first one of my kind. It is a developed, innate compulsion. From the moment, "the woman, she gave me the fruit," was uttered, we've gotten quite good at such a thing. Me, I take issue with the combustion engine. It changed church forever.

There were simpler times—you know, *Little House on the Prairie*–type times—when a church was the centerpiece of a community, a town, a neighborhood, and you used to have to walk there. Humans have always been pretty big on efficiency, so if you were gonna have to walk to church, or take advantage of the latest technology and ride a horse, you'd pretty much just get yourself to the closest one. This resulted in a diverse cross-section of socio-economic backgrounds gathered into one place at one time every week. The disadvantaged and the privileged sat there, next to each other, on the same pew. Most folks never ventured farther than a few miles from their homes from birth till death. Commerce and life were the same thing. You and your boss, and the butcher, and the banker, and the baker, and the candlestick maker were all together hearing the same Scripture read and expounded upon within close enough proximity throughout the week to observe its efficacy on one another.

And then . . . the combustion engine.

Now we get to drive to where there are people just like us. We get to live in a neighborhood where there are people just like us, and drive into town to work and shop at places made for people just like us, and commute to a church that is made up of people just like us. It has, in the here and now, become more difficult than ever to see anything in ourselves, but ourselves.

To celebrate Jesus where we live is to rail against the distance between us all. There are so few people who are awake, and those who are awake walk around in a constant state of amazement. They walk around stunned by the beauty of us all. To be brought, by Jesus, from death to life, to be awakened to His glory and grace, is to be brought into the communion of His diverse and creative works. Jesus turns the tables on the cultural norm. I believe He is angry about it. Homogeneity is anti-creation. When we acknowledge and hold to the uniqueness of where we live, we become resistant to, and adversarial of, what is lifeless and trite. When we are moved, by the breath of the Spirit, to that space that is beyond what is boring and ordinary and common, into what is extraordinary and intended, we walk into the center of the town that we live in. And that is more powerful than any engine the will of man has bent itself to craft.

—DAVID CROWDER

AN ASTONISHING LIFE

When they saw the courage of Peter and John and realized that
they were unschooled, ordinary men, they were astonished
and they took note that these men had been with Jesus.

ACTS 4:13

Many of us believe that we need a certain skill set to tell people about Jesus. But in reality, all we need is a desire to see Jesus celebrated in our lives and in the lives of people who don't know Him yet.

This is what we see in Acts 4 with Peter and John. Full of the Holy Spirit, they spoke about Jesus to anyone who would listen. But there was nothing special about these "unschooled, ordinary men." They weren't educated preachers, but they believed passionately that Jesus died and was now alive. Their conviction inspired them to speak boldly the message of hope. They spoke this truth and were thrown in jail, but they didn't cower. They shared all the more, and something amazing happened: the cultural and religious leaders were astonished because they saw, perhaps for the first time, the confidence that comes from a personal relationship with Jesus.

Peter and John weren't qualified experts, but they were more devoted than afraid. Because Jesus is alive, let's live with a courageous confidence that astonishes those around us.

Lord, grant me courage to share Your story with those around me. Remind me that when ordinary people champion You, extraordinary things occur.

YOUR HONEST TESTIMONY

We are therefore Christ's ambassadors, as though God were
making his appeal through us. We implore you on Christ's behalf:
Be reconciled to God. God made him who had no sin to be sin for
us, so that in him we might become the righteousness of God.

2 CORINTHIANS 5:20–21

Being an ambassador of Christ means we not only tell people about what He did for us on the cross, but also what He has done for us personally. We share how He breathes life into us every day and how He has seen us through our struggles. We tell how His strength has helped us in our weaknesses and how His grace has been enough for us. This doesn't require us to act like we have it all together—because that is not true, and people will see right through it. It's more important to be honest and let people know that even though life is still hard, and we still make mistakes, Christ still loves us and continually forgives us.

When we are honest about our walk with Christ, we can share how we face suffering and heartache with hope, because we know that the trials we face in this world won't last forever; we'll eventually go home to heaven to spend an eternity of peace with Jesus.

Let's be genuine. Don't worry about covering anything up. Instead, boldly speak about what God has done for you. Sharing your testimony is the best way you can share Jesus with the world.

> God, help me share my testimony openly and without shame so that others can see You through me.

BE A LIGHT

*For this is what the Lord has commanded us: "I have made you a light
for the Gentiles, that you may bring salvation to the ends of the earth."
When the Gentiles heard this, they were glad and honored the word
of the Lord; and all who were appointed for eternal life believed.*

ACTS 13:47–48

The first time Paul and Barnabas spoke in Antioch, they spoke in
front of the Jews in the synagogue. Their message was so gripping
that the next time they spoke, almost the entire city gathered to
hear them speak—Jews and Gentiles alike. This pattern played out
time and time again as Paul and Barnabas traveled throughout
the region. Huge crowds would gather to hear them speak, and the
power of the Word of God would convict many to believe.

As He did for Paul and Barnabas, God has commissioned us
as His messengers to shine the gospel everywhere we go. The gospel is not meant to lie dormant in our lives, but to be shared so the
people around us can experience the grace and hope of Christ.
There are people in our classrooms, workplaces, and dorm rooms
waiting to be filled with the hope and love of Christ; all they need
is someone to share it with them.

> Jesus, help me take every chance to tell Your story to the
> people around me who so desperately need to hear it.

A GRACIOUS ANSWER

Be wise in the way you act toward outsiders; make the most of every opportunity. Let your conversation be always full of grace, seasoned with salt, so that you may know how to answer everyone.

COLOSSIANS 4:5–6

In response to our critics, many Christians think we should argue aggressively to communicate our perspective. Yet when Paul said our speech ought to be "seasoned with salt," he pointed to a different path. Gracious speech isn't argumentative; it means giving an answer that makes sense in the context of that person's life. Intelligent rationale is important, but grace is the greatest defense of our faith.

The call to know how to "answer everyone" seems daunting; how can you possibly understand the circumstances of everyone you meet? But Paul pointed out that graciousness is a basic element of those answers. As Christians, our actions reflect Christ. So in all things, including our speech, we should reflect God's love and grace. When deliberating on what to say to defend your faith, remember Jesus, who taught us that grace is more powerful than rhetoric.

Jesus, I want my actions to show others the love You've shown me. Give me wisdom so I can answer those who question my faith with grace and love.

A DOCTOR FOR THE SICK

Jesus answered them, "It is not the healthy who need a doctor, but the sick. I have not come to call the righteous, but sinners to repentance."

LUKE 5:31–32

When Jesus told Levi to follow Him, He knew that Levi was a tax collector—reviled by the Jews at that time. Levi, overwhelmed by Jesus' kindness, immediately responded by throwing a banquet for Jesus. As some of the religious teachers saw that Jesus was associating Himself with a tax collector, they complained; they saw tax collectors as traitors, since they collected money for their oppressors, the Romans. Jesus' response to the Pharisees' complaint was sharp: His mission was to the lost and needy, not to those who thought they didn't have a need. He came to be a doctor to "the sick."

God is not calling believers to an isolated life of holiness. Instead, we can live a life that associates with the "sick" and shares the good news with people who haven't heard of Jesus. As we observe who Jesus was, we find that He spent time with the "wrong type" of people. If we want to be like Jesus, we shouldn't be afraid to do the same.

This may be challenging and even frightening, but God is with us. Even if we find opposition from religious people, as Jesus did, let's remember that we are not simply following men, but Jesus—the Son of Man.

God, give me opportunities and boldness to share Your good news with those who have not heard.

ALL THINGS TO ALL PEOPLE

Though I am free and belong to no one, I have made myself a slave to everyone, to win as many as possible. . . . I have become all things to all people so that by all possible means I might save some.

1 CORINTHIANS 9:19, 22

Freedom in Christ allows us to relate to anyone; in fact, we all have imperfection in common. And because we know we've been saved, we can freely give this gospel to anyone we encounter.

When he was in Athens, Paul tailored his message to an audience that valued high intellect and reasoning (Acts 17). He presented the gospel this way because Greek poets agreed on the idea that humans are God's offspring, concluding that God is not made by human hands like the idols the Athenians were worshiping. Instead of secluding himself from the world, Paul saw an opportunity to infiltrate culture and share the gospel. As a result, he was able to use the gospel to relate to others and win some to Christ.

There are people all around us who might miss out on the freedom the gospel brings because we think we can't relate to them. But God enables us to adjust and relate to others, just like Paul did. Let's be flexible and look for opportunities to share the gospel of Christ with others.

> Jesus, show me how the people around me need to relate to You, and help me to point out where they are already seeking You in their lives.

CLAY JARS

For God, who said, "Let light shine out of darkness," made his light shine in our hearts to give us the light of the knowledge of God's glory displayed in the face of Christ. But we have this treasure in jars of clay to show that this all-surpassing power is from God and not from us.

2 CORINTHIANS 4:6–7

What is the purpose of a clay jar? Today, it would typically function as decoration, but to Paul it was an object of labor. Jars transported water, a valuable and often scarce resource. So when he calls us "jars of clay," we can make the connection: God shaped us to carry the life-giving knowledge of His glory. We are vessels filled with His light, and we are created to pour it back out.

The "light" mentioned in today's passage is the light that shines from a life that knows its Creator and its purpose. Rather than concerning ourselves with polished exteriors, our purpose is to carry that light and let its glory be seen through our relationship with Christ. In college it's easy to become intimidated by our surroundings and to let our desire for acceptance control our actions. In these trying times, remember that as jars of clay, we don't have to try to be something we're not. We have a function, and that's to deliver life-giving light and show where "all-surpassing power" really comes from: Jesus.

> As the potter shapes the jar, Lord, shape me to carry Your light wherever You send me.

A NEW CREATION

So from now on we regard no one from a worldly point of view. Though we once regarded Christ in this way, we do so no longer. Therefore, if anyone is in Christ, the new creation has come: The old has gone, the new is here!

2 CORINTHIANS 5:16–17

We probably all have at least one person in our lives who is more than willing to point out our flaws. They may even disregard your successes and try to define you by your imperfections. The world is quick to point out what is not good enough about us, and sometimes we join the ridicule. When we listen to these voices above Jesus', we allow our mistakes and others' opinions to become our identity.

But Jesus offers us a new identity: His creation! As Paul urged the Corinthians, we too can take advantage of the clean slate offered to us. Through the death and resurrection of Jesus, the world was reconciled to God. Our record of wrongs has been replaced with a message of redemption and hope.

When Christ was nailed to the cross, all your worst mistakes, insecurities, and greatest shortcomings were put to death. And as He was raised to new life, so are you. Today, you have the opportunity to walk as a new creation. No longer bound by your past, you are now a billboard displaying God's grace and reconciliation to a world of people in desperate need of a new identity.

> Father, I'm so thankful that when You look at me, You see Christ. Help me embrace the new identity You offer me so that my life is a constant demonstration of mercy and hope.

REASON FOR HOPE

*In your hearts revere Christ as Lord. Always be prepared to give
an answer to everyone who asks you to give the reason for the hope
that you have. But do this with gentleness and respect, keeping a
clear conscience, so that those who speak maliciously against your
good behavior in Christ may be ashamed of their slander.*

1 PETER 3:15–16

Although our world is a place of pain, fear, and suffering, Jesus
gives us a reason to hope. Because the wounds of this world run
deep, Peter told us to approach the topic of hope with "gentleness
and respect." We shouldn't discount suffering; instead, we should
tell the good news of hope of a forever with Christ with no pain,
fear, suffering, or sin—a hope available to everyone.

As we spread the gospel to the ends of the earth, people will
wonder why we do what we do, and they might even accuse us
of impure motives. As Christians, our goal is to show them the
truth of the gospel and to continue living our lives in a such way
that accusations cannot hold water. When we act with gentleness,
respect, and a clear conscience, even our enemies can recognize
that this great hope is valid.

Let's strive to keep the values we say we have in line with the
values we actually practice, so the world's criticisms will fall flat.
How can you infuse your actions with the hope you have today?

God, thank You for giving me hope. Show me where I can better align my actions with the hope I have, and give me a spirit
of gentleness and respect when telling others about You.

HOPE FOR THE WORST

Christ Jesus came into the world to save sinners—of whom I am the worst. But for that very reason I was shown mercy so that in me, the worst of sinners, Christ Jesus might display his immense patience as an example for those who would believe in him and receive eternal life.

1 TIMOTHY 1:15–16

Paul was a notorious persecutor and opponent of Christians. But after an encounter with Jesus on the road to Damascus, Paul surrendered his life completely to God. He began boldly proclaiming the gospel and was compelled to travel to the ends of the earth to share it. Paul was not afraid to tell others, even those who were hostile, what the Lord had done for him.

After years of giving his life for ministry, Paul remained full of gratitude to God for his salvation. In the eyes of many, himself included, Paul was unworthy of redemption, but Paul explains that Jesus came into the world to redeem the unredeemable.

Like Paul, you have been given life through Christ Jesus so that His perfect love, patience, and grace would be displayed to the world. Whether at school, at work, among your friends, or even in your home, you are constantly surrounded by people who are separated from God. No matter what your past looks like, whether as dramatic as Paul's or ordinary by comparison, Christ's blood has redeemed us all the same. And that unconditional redemption can give hope to those who think they are too lost to be found.

Father, prepare me to show the world that no one is so far gone that they can't be completely redeemed by Your grace.

SHARING THE CELEBRATION

All have sinned and fall short of the glory of God, and all are justified
freely by his grace through the redemption that came by Christ Jesus.
ROMANS 3:23–24

Today's verse tells us that based on our actions, none of us qualifies for God's grace; on our own, we are hopeless and separated from God. But because He loves us so incredibly much, God sent His Son to die for our sins so that we may receive eternal life through Him (John 3:16). Christ lived the perfect, sinless life that none of us could; He took on our sins and the death penalty that hung over our heads. Though we deserve death, today we celebrate the new life we have in Christ! And because we've experienced such great joy, we want to see others celebrating too.

The greatest news we'll ever hear is that we don't have to work to get to God, and our greatest joy will be sharing that news with others. How does this joy change the way you live your life? How can you make your life a celebration of redemption? And how can you invite others into this celebration?

Father, open my heart to the redemption I received through Your Son. Allow my joy to overflow into the lives of those far from You so that one day they may know and celebrate Your name.

WORKING FOR CHRIST

Whatever you do, work at it with all your heart, as working for the Lord,
not for human masters, since you know that you will receive an inheritance
from the Lord as a reward. It is the Lord Christ you are serving.

COLOSSIANS 3:23–24

When faced with a task, we often base our efforts and diligence on how we feel about the person in charge, our opinion of that task's importance, or how we are feeling that particular day. This passage completely challenges that mentality, calling us to live our lives "as working for the Lord." Imagine how much more diligent you would be at work if Jesus were a manager at your company, or how much more effort you would put into assignments if Jesus were your professor. When we walk through this life devoting our whole hearts to the work set before us, working as unto Christ, others are able to see Him celebrated through us.

What would it look like to begin every day ready to serve Jesus in all areas of our lives? How would that change us? Our work in the small things will eventually become our work in the big things. Let's resist the temptation to see our work as a reflection on ourselves—or to do it for what recognition we might gain, be it a promotion, a degree, or other recognition. Better than all those is the "inheritance from the Lord" that comes from knowing the person truly in charge: Christ. Celebrate Christ by completing everything put before you with excellence, as if working for Him.

Lord, I give You my work today. Help me honor You in every-thing I do.

WARRIORS

My dear brothers and sisters, stand firm. Let nothing move you.
Always give yourselves fully to the work of the Lord, because
you know that your labor in the Lord is not in vain.

1 CORINTHIANS 15:58

God is looking for fierce warriors to do His work—for immovable
people who fight to the end, disregard fear, commit completely,
and never give up. These are the kind of warriors we should be
for God's kingdom. In any fight, a warrior runs the risk of being
defeated, but this verse follows a declaration that death has been
swallowed in victory—the power of sin is no more! The "work
of the Lord" will last forever because Christ has already won.
Knowing and believing this should motivate us to be the fiercest,
boldest, and bravest in the fight to spread the gospel. The fight is
not in vain, because no matter what happens or how many hits we
take, God's love wins!

So let's ask ourselves: Are we giving ourselves fully to the
work of the Lord? Or are we wasting time, energy, and resources
on things that won't outlast one lifetime? Jesus has already won,
so what are you waiting for? Invest fully in His mission; you will
never regret giving everything you have for His purposes.

Lord, help me live in the wake of Your victory. Show me how
to stand firm in confidence for You.

STAND FIRM

Then they ordered them not to speak in the name of Jesus, and let them go. The apostles left the Sanhedrin, rejoicing because they had been counted worthy of suffering disgrace for the Name. Day after day, in the temple courts and from house to house, they never stopped teaching and proclaiming the good news that Jesus is the Messiah.

ACTS 5:40–42

As believers, we often face this choice: do we stand firm in our beliefs, or do we compromise under external pressures? Have you found yourself recently in a situation in which it was difficult to stand for Jesus?

Peter and the disciples faced a situation like that. After they were arrested and freed for preaching the gospel at the temple, the disciples were ordered not to preach in the name of Jesus. But the disciples simply couldn't stop preaching the gospel; their conviction and revelation of Jesus' life, death, and resurrection was so deep that nothing was going to stop them from proclaiming the good news—not even suffering or persecution.

When we stand for Jesus, there may be moments when our faith is tested by direct opposition. But in those moments, we get to represent the King of kings. What an honor! While nobody *wants* to suffer, it is during these moments, when we are suffering because of our faith, that the world sees that we belong to God—and He is more than worth it.

> Lord, when opposition and persecution come, help me stand firm for the glory of Your name.

GOD'S GREAT PURPOSES

During the night an angel of the Lord opened the doors of the
jail and brought them out. "Go, stand in the temple courts,"
he said, "and tell the people all about this new life."

ACTS 5:19–20

God works in supernatural ways to accomplish His purposes. He split the Red Sea and led the Israelites through on dry land. He brought down the walls of Jericho with the sound of trumpets and shouts. And He sent Jesus, His only Son, to earth through a young virgin. He did these things to show the world who He is and to redeem us. Nothing can stop God's purposes; His gospel will be spread—even if angels have to break believers out of prison to tell people about it.

So what should we fear? If our lives are dedicated to expanding God's kingdom, nothing will be able to stop us. This knowledge should fill our hearts with confidence! God has given us the big mission of making disciples, and He's promised to be with us every step of the way. So let's be bold in our classes, in our communities, and in our families, for if we have the mind-set of affecting people's lives for the gospel, God, the All Powerful, will be with us.

Father, let my mission today be to make Your name known by showing Your love and telling people Your story.

THE HERALD

How, then, can they call on the one they have not believed in? And
how can they believe in the one of whom they have not heard?
And how can they hear without someone preaching to them?
And how can anyone preach unless they are sent? As it is written:
"How beautiful are the feet of those who bring good news!"

ROMANS 10:14–15

Imagine an army that has finally won a long, hard battle. As the soldiers celebrate, the king sends a herald to tell everyone the great news of victory and peace. The king is then trusted and celebrated because he has saved his people from death.

Without the herald, no one would hear the good news of peace. The same is true of our faith. If we don't tell anyone what we believe, the people who don't know Jesus will never get to know Him. In today's scripture, Paul presented a series of questions that reveal the process of how God spreads the gospel. These questions show Paul's readers that they have a pivotal role to play in God's work of salvation.

God has placed you where you are for a specific reason, so invest in the people around you. Is there someone in your life who doesn't know Jesus? Tell that person the news that has changed your life, and leave the rest to God's perfect will. Whatever happens, God will use you powerfully when you trust in Him.

God, give me the courage to tell the good news of Your salvation to the lost. Let my life herald Your love to my community.

THE BUBBLE

*"I am sending you out like sheep among wolves. Therefore
be as shrewd as snakes and as innocent as doves."*

MATTHEW 10:16

You've probably heard of the "Christian bubble." That comfortable place where we're tempted to create our own little society that shields us from the rest of the world and to live our lives with little opposition from anyone around us. But here's the reality: we are surrounded by people who are separated from God, and it's on us to carry the message of salvation to them.

Jesus would burst the Christian bubble. When He sent the disciples to proclaim the gospel, He compared them to "sheep among wolves." Like sheep, we are vulnerable, but will do anything to follow our Shepherd. Because His gospel is peace, Jesus discourages aimlessly engaging in conflict. Shrewdness, like snakes, and innocence, like doves, are our strongholds in the midst of vulnerability—not separating ourselves from others.

As you share the story of Jesus with people around you, approach conversations with vulnerability so that your life is an unmistakable display of God's grace. Likewise, allow the Spirit to lead you when the world attacks you because of the gospel. Scripture promises He will give you the words to say; let His message be your defense.

> God, thank You for allowing me to play a part in Your mission of salvation. Help me fight against the need to be comfortable, and give me courage.

243

SEND ME!

Then I heard the voice of the Lord saying, "Whom shall I send?
And who will go for us?" And I said, "Here am I. Send me!"
ISAIAH 6:8

Have you ever said no to God? Maybe you felt led to pray for a stranger on a crowded street or to buy a meal for someone begging at a busy intersection, but you resisted for some reason. When we turn our faces from these people, we allow our fears to harden our hearts.

When Isaiah was called to be a prophet to the nation of Israel, he likely knew the danger and suffering that awaited him. His call was to proclaim an unpopular message to many hard-hearted people. This call promised to bring him ridicule, violence, and even death, but Isaiah showed no trace of hesitation.

Isaiah could face the incredible challenge of being God's prophet because he had seen the Lord in all His glory. At His throne, Isaiah received the grace and mercy that would forever change his life. Suffering and alienation were inevitable, but Isaiah knew there was no better place to be than in the center of God's will.

Jesus made a way for us to taste the sweetness of God's mercy, just like Isaiah did. Don't let fear prevent you from telling someone about Jesus or serving on His behalf. When we respond in faithfulness and boldness, God will do incredible things.

Father, thank You for Your faithfulness. Wipe away my fears and use me to reach people for Your kingdom.

REAL WORTH

*I consider my life worth nothing to me; my only aim is to finish
the race and complete the task the Lord Jesus has given me—
the task of testifying to the good news of God's grace.*

ACTS 20:24

Why did Paul say that his "life [is] worth nothing"? Paul was not
expressing a low view of himself; instead, he spoke to the greater
value of something else—the gospel. After three years of sharing
the gospel with the Ephesians, Paul decided to head to Jerusalem
where he knew that only "prison and hardships" awaited him
(Acts 20:23). Yet despite the persecution to come, he still aimed to
glorify God by "testifying to the good news of God's grace." Paul
valued spreading the gospel so highly that he didn't care what
would happen to him in Jerusalem.

Likewise, on our campuses or at our jobs, let's be similarly
motivated to testify of God's grace. If it comes at the cost of comfort, time, or possessions, so be it. Just like Paul, we have been
radically changed by God's grace and can say with him that our
lives are "worth nothing" in comparison to the gospel.

Lord, help me testify with my life the good news of Your grace
to those around me. Help me value You above all else so that
I can better spread Your gospel.

FOLLOW GOD'S LEAD

The eunuch asked Philip, "Tell me, please, who is the prophet talking about, himself or someone else?" Then Philip began with that very passage of Scripture and told him the good news about Jesus.

ACTS 8:34–35

The story of Philip and the eunuch perfectly captures our role in sharing the gospel with others. Philip, one of Jesus' original disciples, was told by an angel to head to the road leading from Jerusalem to Gaza. Philip obeyed, and as he went, he ran into an Ethiopian eunuch—an important political official. The man was wrestling his way through a scripture from Isaiah. Philip, recognizing that the Lord had led him to this specific place in time, took this chance to share the story of Jesus. The Ethiopian eunuch believed, and at the first sight of water, asked if he could be baptized! Philip's obedience led him to a place where God could use him to share the gospel with a man who was seeking truth.

Today, we can also be a part of somebody's miraculous journey of finding Jesus—we just need to follow God's lead without hesitation. If we direct our focus to how God wants to be glorified where we are, instead of how *we* want God to be glorified, we will see that God is the one who brings people to Himself. So let's be watchful and obedient, knowing that God orchestrates unexpected opportunities for us to share the story of Jesus with others.

Dear Father, please help me be obedient to Your voice, so I can be ready to share the story of Jesus whenever an opportunity arises.

ORDINARY PEOPLE

*I came to you in weakness with great fear and trembling. My
message and my preaching were not with wise and persuasive
words, but with a demonstration of the Spirit's power, so that your
faith might not rest on human wisdom, but on God's power.*

1 CORINTHIANS 2:3–5

Paul knew something about humanity that is strikingly obvious:
we have a tendency to complicate simple things, and we want to be
recognized for our accomplishments and abilities. But the gospel
is a simple and powerful message that we don't need to decorate,
and that we can't take credit for; we only need to speak it, and God
will do the rest.

God chooses ordinary people to do incredible things. Moses
was a shepherd with a past and a stuttering problem. David was an
adulterer and a murderer, yet he was called a man after God's own
heart. The disciples had no special prerequisite training. Paul was
a murderer of Christians. The list goes on and on.

God loves to use simple, broken people to deliver His message! Why? So there is no confusion about where our faith and
glory should rest. Take heart: there are no requirements or
accomplishments needed for you to be used by God! You need
only love Him and rest in His power.

> Jesus, help me understand that You have qualified me and
> called me. Help me be bold and rest in You.

SHARE YOUR STORY

I waited patiently for the LORD; he inclined to me and heard my cry. He drew me up from the pit of destruction . . . He put a new song in my mouth, a song of praise to our God. Many will see and fear, and put their trust in the LORD.

PSALM 40:1–3 ESV

Think about a time when God delivered you from an impossible place. Perhaps it was an important test, a crisis within a relationship, or a battle with a mental or physical illness. What was your reaction to this redemption? For David, the psalmist, thanksgiving was his heart's natural response to God's rescue.

Strikingly, David didn't keep his praise within his own heart. Rather, he verbalized his thanks in a new song, telling everyone about the rich miracle of God's redemption. In turn, the people who heard him saw the truth and turned to God.

Your story of how Jesus has changed your life is something people can't argue with, especially in our modern culture, where personal experience is often viewed as unquestionable. When you share your story, you can turn the conversation to the larger truth of the gospel.

You can thank God in ways that will impact others by thanking Him in one-on-one conversations, on social media, or within groups of friends. Praising God not only gives Him all glory, it roots your identity in Him, reminds you of His faithfulness, grows your trust, and gives you His story to share.

Lord, thank You for Your faithfulness and unfailing love in my life. Help me share Your story passionately.

SERVING THE LORD

Serve wholeheartedly, as if you were serving the Lord, not
people, because you know that the Lord will reward each one
for whatever good they do, whether they are slave or free.

EPHESIANS 6:7–8

At the end of Ephesians, Paul addressed the people on the lowest rung on the social ladder: slaves. Slavery was deeply entrenched in the social structure of Ephesus, and Paul spoke a message of empowerment to people who didn't command much authority themselves. That message was that while they couldn't choose *whom* they were serving on earth, they could choose *the way* they served their earthly masters.

The same holds true for us. Say you have a teacher you don't get along with, or a boss at work you disagree with more than you'd like to. Instead of viewing that person as *just* your boss or teacher, try to picture that you're actually working for God, not them. Wouldn't that change how you approach your work?

Although life today looks much different from the world of Ephesus, let's also serve the Lord by serving others, for when we do so we reflect Christ, who served us.

> Jesus, help me serve well and honestly, knowing that in serving people, I am reflecting You to them.

A STORY TO TELL

Peter and the other apostles replied: "We must obey God rather than human beings! The God of our ancestors raised Jesus from the dead—whom you killed by hanging him on a cross. God exalted him to his own right hand as Prince and Savior that he might bring Israel to repentance and forgive their sins."

ACTS 5:29–31

People are hungry for authentic stories. In a world where we are daily bombarded with messages and advertisements, a real, personal experience carries a lot of weight.

When you have seen the power of death conquered in your life or in the life of someone you know, you cannot help but tell others. Peter and the other apostles were ordered by the highest authorities to not speak or teach about Jesus within the city. But the apostles wouldn't listen because they had to obey God instead of people; there was more at stake than a riotous city or an angry government official. The apostles wanted Jesus to be celebrated in the hearts of those who were far away from Him, and they knew that since they had personally experienced new life in Jesus, others could as well.

If we have been with Jesus, we have a story of grace to tell. There are people around us who simply want to know that the same hope in you is available for them as well. Your story matters, so share it with others.

> Lord, may I be bold in my faith because others are desperate to hear the real stories about how You have changed lives forever.

COME AND HEAR

Come and hear, all you who fear God; let me tell you what he has done for me.
PSALM 66:16

We all have a story. We were once spiritually dead and walked in darkness, then God intervened. Now, as we walk with Him, our story of redemption is written into the eternal story of salvation in Jesus Christ.

In today's verse, the psalmist writes to those who fear God, those who live in awe, wonder, and complete reverence of Him. The psalmist wanted all to hear the magnificent things God had done for him! Praise flowed easily off his lips, because he recognized the wonder of God's working.

As God continues to direct our paths and orchestrate our lives, we have countless reasons to bless Him along with those around us. God intersects our stories with those of others as a source of encouragement and refinement. Share your story of redemption with others, and tell how God continues to work in and through your life. Reflect on how He has heard and answered your prayers, inviting others to join you in prayer and praise. Let His praise be the anthem of each of your days, for He has done great things!

Jesus, remind me daily of Your grace in my life. Show me how to use my story to encourage and uplift those around me.

THE SACRIFICE OF PRAISE

Through Jesus, therefore, let us continually offer to God a sacrifice of praise—the fruit of lips that openly profess his name. And do not forget to do good and to share with others, for with such sacrifices God is pleased.

HEBREWS 13:15–16

Under Old Testament law, sacrifices were continual, costly, and imperfect. Yet they were the only way sinful people could approach God. The rules and requirements to make sacrifices were strict, and one misstep could have dire consequences.

One sacrifice the Israelites made each year was the firstfruits offering. The people would bring the first of their harvest, the first sign of reward from their year of work, and present it at God's altar (Deuteronomy 26). This was their declaration of His supremacy and provision over all their lives.

By giving His perfect blood, untainted by sin, Jesus forever satisfied the need for this old system of sacrifice. Because He has given all, we can now give to God from a place of joy, not obligation or fear of mistakes. Instead of sacrificing physical fruits, we now sacrifice our lives. Our firstfruits are our praise, and by giving ourselves to a life of worship we declare that Jesus is worthy of it. Paul reminds us to "do good to and share with others" as part of this sacrifice. As we praise, let's share that fruit with those we meet, telling others of the One we serve.

> Jesus, You alone are worthy of my worship. Fill my mouth with Your praise.

CITY ON A HILL

"Let your light shine before others, that they may see your good deeds, and glorify your Father in heaven."

MATTHEW 5:16

Here's the challenge for all of us who have struggled with acceptance, insecurity, and self-esteem: *take the hand of Jesus and rise out of the bed of shame.* He has breathed life into you, and others need to know this life is available to them too!

When you read today's verse in context, it compares your influence as a believer to a light shining in the darkness; verse 14 likens it to a city on a hill. The city didn't just spring up on the hill by itself; it was intentionally set there for its vantage point because it was like a beacon. In the same way, Jesus made you a light of hope and truth to those in your sphere of influence.

But how do you shine your light for others? By showing those around you who Jesus is by your actions: You show His mercy when you forgive those who've hurt you. You show His grace when you offer it to someone who has wronged you. You show His love when you reject the need for reciprocation. And you show His hope when in the midst of tragedy you lift up a tear-stained face and praise His name.

Leave behind the world of insecurity that is focused on yourself, and shine out the security you have found in Him. He has set you on a hill of influence so that you can bring honor to His name!

Jesus, use me as a beacon for the people You've placed in my life.

CHOSEN TO SEE

The God of our ancestors has chosen you to know his will and to
see the Righteous One and to hear words from his mouth. You will
be his witness to all people of what you have seen and heard.

ACTS 22:14–15

On the road to Damascus, Paul experienced one of the most powerful conversions ever recorded. Today's verse comes after his famous, blinding encounter with Christ, when Paul lost his sight as Jesus swept him from a life dedicated to persecuting the church to a life of suffering for the sake of the church. Paul's sight was restored when God worked through a man named Ananias, who then spoke these prophetic words about Paul recounted in Acts.

These words echo beyond Paul to all believers. Just like Paul, our once-blind eyes have been opened, and we have been chosen to know God's will, to see Jesus, and to hear His words. Like Paul, we are destined to be a witness to the people around us. God has chosen us specifically to testify about His Son. This is His will for our lives! May we all then be encouraged by Paul to live boldly and to let our lives be a testimony to the grace, love, and mercy that saves us from blindness and lets us see amazing things.

Father, help me to know Your will, to grow in knowledge of Your Son and His Word, and to be a witness to those around me.

STAY SALTY

"You are the salt of the earth. But if the salt loses its saltiness,
how can it be made salty again? It is no longer good for anything,
except to be thrown out and trampled underfoot."

MATTHEW 5:13

Historically, salt has served two purposes: to preserve food in harsh environments and to enhance flavor. Jesus calls us "the salt of the earth," and apparently we can lose our saltiness. What does that mean?

Jesus was intentional in His words. By identifying His people this way, He gives us insight into our purpose on earth: we're called to preserve others and to enhance the flavor of the world. Our job is to use our lives to reach out to people, inviting them into eternity, and to make this dark world brighter with light-bearing deeds.

Jesus also warns that our saltiness can be lost. This may not mean having a falling-out with God—it might just be the staleness that comes from not actively seeking Him. If you feel out of step with God, look for places in your life where you may be ignoring or disobeying Him.

Losing flavor doesn't usually happen all at once; it's a gradual and subtle process. Spend time in His presence today, and ask Him to restore the flavor you once had. And go pour this seasoning onto the lives of others!

Jesus, I want to live my life according to Your purpose. Use me today. Thank You for the privilege of carrying Your flavor across the earth.

GOD'S CHILDREN

If anyone obeys his word, love for God is truly made
complete in them. This is how we know we are in him:
Whoever claims to live in him must live as Jesus did.

1 JOHN 2:5–6

On earth, it is a parent's responsibility to give children instruction, guidelines and parameters, and goals to reach for. Out of love, parents set boundaries to protect and direct their children to the best kind of life.

Our heavenly Father is the same way. Throughout Scripture, He calls us His children. He wants us to follow His instruction and His Word, not only because He loves us, but also to perfect His love in us.

Our heavenly Father, who is love, wants us to be full of the same kind of love! Today's scripture tells us to follow the perfect instructions He gave and to walk the same way Jesus walked. He set the example of obedience to the Father and selfless love for others while He was here on earth. And He gives us His Spirit to guide us as we walk.

Examine your life. Are you keeping the instructions God has given you? Are you following in the footsteps of Jesus? Live in this kind of obedience, and let His love be perfected in you.

> Lord, I want Your love to be perfected in me. Help me love others the way You did and walk in the ways that You walked.

WAKE-UP CALL

This is why it is said: "Wake up, sleeper, rise from the dead, and Christ will shine on you." Be very careful, then, how you live—not as unwise but as wise, making the most of every opportunity, because the days are evil. Therefore do not be foolish, but understand what the Lord's will is.

EPHESIANS 5:14–17

When your alarm goes off, it can be a struggle to obey its call to wake up. But when there is something wonderful ahead of you that day, it's easy to spring out of bed. Paul used the metaphor of sleep to explain that it's time to wake up and start living with the wisdom that comes from celebrating our salvation.

Within our normal routines, it's easy for our spiritual lives to become lethargic as our hearts, minds, thoughts, and desires begin to revolve around ourselves instead of God. But God has so much more for us. He has brought us from the sleep of death into His light of life. In the knowledge of Christ's gift, we should live wisely, not being self-centered, but consistently seeking the will of God and His glory.

The specifics of God's will for your life are unique and perfectly fitted to your gifts, but the heart of His mission is universal to all believers—to share the good news with those who do not know Jesus. So wake up joyfully and shine your light on others, sharing the grace that has given you life.

God, thank You for the freedom to share Your gift of saving grace with others. Help me wake up and faithfully seek Your will.

A CHOSEN PEOPLE

But you are a chosen people, a royal priesthood, a holy nation,
God's special possession, that you may declare the praises of him
who called you out of darkness into his wonderful light. Once
you were not a people, but now you are the people of God.

1 PETER 2:9–10

Every day, we struggle to choose who or what defines us. Society perpetually throws labels at us, trying to get anything to stick, but God explicitly tells us who we are in Him.

You are holy, chosen, considered royalty, and special to God. You have significance and worth as a son or daughter and heir of the Most High, because He reached beyond darkness and called you to Him. His call is intentional; you are hand-selected and chosen. It is immediate; you are now a priesthood, no longer bound by religious law and sacrifice, but living in freedom. It is eternal; you are a nation, established to rule and reign forever with Jesus. And it is purposeful, that you may declare that our God makes the outcast family and the guilty redeemed. He did it with you, and He can do it with others.

Chances are, people around you are wondering who they are. They could be one step, one conversation, one interaction away from light and life in Jesus, from knowing their place as His beloved and chosen. Will you declare the truth to their hungry souls?

> Jesus, You have brought us back into Your light. May we shine boldly, intentionally, and wholly for You.

SHINE IN THE DARKNESS

"Arise, shine, for your light has come, and the glory of the LORD rises upon
you. See, darkness covers the earth and thick darkness is over the peoples,
but the LORD rises upon you and his glory appears over you. Nations
will come to your light, and kings to the brightness of your dawn."

ISAIAH 60:1–3

If you've ever been in a physical state of complete darkness, you know how terrible it can be. You stumble around aimlessly and, most likely, end up hurting yourself or breaking something. The darkness discussed in today's verse is much worse, and it describes the state of many people in the world. It leaves its victims trapped in sin and on a path to spiritual death and separation from God. And worse, they often don't even realize it, because they've never seen the light.

But when we were still walking in darkness, God sent Christ to die for our sins. We now live in the light because of Christ, but there are still so many trapped in darkness. For these lost ones, your salvation can act as a light. When they see that your words and actions are different, they are drawn to the light of Christ in you. You don't have to show them how perfect you are; you just have to point them to Christ, the One shining through your imperfections. So don't keep your faith a secret. Share it with those around you, for it's the hope that the world is searching for.

Lord, give me a desire to share Your glory, starting with those You have placed close to me. Let them learn of Your beauty as they see You work through me.

PREPARED FOR WAR

Dear friends, I urge you, as foreigners and exiles, to abstain from sinful desires, which wage war against your soul.

1 PETER 2:11

Do you struggle with being overly competitive? How about telling a little white lie? Or maybe you constantly compare yourself to others and wish your life was more like theirs. If you indulge in these behaviors, you're not alone. We are living in an active war zone surrounded by temptation. While our actions, words, and motivations are meant to be beautiful reflections of God's heart, we are continually pulled away.

Peter wrote letters to encourage the church during times of difficult circumstances and to prepare them for times of intensified persecution. In today's scripture, Peter used the image of a battle—a "war against your soul"—to remind us that the church needs to prepare to fight persecution. When he challenged Christians to live exemplary lives even in times of trial, Peter knew that the world would be watching the church's reaction to persecution.

Our lives are not our own; they belong to God. Keep this in mind as you take steps in preparing to fight against temptation. Surround yourself with a group of Christian friends, read Scripture on a regular basis, and spend time alone in prayer to build a defense against the sinful desires that wage war on your soul. God is with you in the battle!

Father, be my strength, sword, and shield in the battle I face daily. Help me live a life that glorifies You.

PERSPECTIVE

Whatever is true, whatever is noble, whatever is right, whatever is pure,
whatever is lovely, whatever is admirable—if anything is excellent or
praiseworthy—think about such things. Whatever you have learned
or received or heard from me, or seen in me—put it into practice.
PHILIPPIANS 4:8–9

You may not always be able to change your circumstances, but you are always able to change your perspective.

As Paul closed his letter to the Philippian church, he encouraged his readers to focus their perspective on godly things. This challenge from Paul is remarkable because of the circumstances under which he wrote. He wrote this letter from prison, potentially facing death for the gospel. His situation seemed dire, but he didn't give up or complain. Rather, he sought to glorify God with every breath. No matter what circumstance he found himself in, Paul always knew that God's truth, not his situation, determined his perspective.

When we experience circumstances that test our faith, we often pray desperately for deliverance. But sometimes God wants us to go through tough situations to bring Him glory and to make us more like His Son. Circumstances are temporary, but our perspective can always be eternal. What perspective will you choose to have today?

> Father, I give You my mind today. I ask that You would change my perspective despite my circumstances, and help me be a light to others around me.

LIVES OF PRAYER AND THANKS

I urge, then, first of all, that petitions, prayers, intercession and thanksgiving be made for all people—for kings and all those in authority, that we may live peaceful and quiet lives in all godliness and holiness. This is good, and pleases God our Savior, who wants all people to be saved and to come to a knowledge of the truth.

1 TIMOTHY 2:1–4

Scripture urges us to pray for our secular leaders and those in our government. We pray for their ultimate salvation, and that God will be glorified no matter what decisions they make. When we do this, we remind ourselves that God, not humanity, is ultimately in control. With this knowledge we are able to live at peace, trusting that His plans are always good and will always prevail.

In addition to praying for our leaders, today's verse urges us to be thankful. When we express thanks for our blessings, all our stress, worry, and anxiety melt away, because we remember how much God has given us and that He will provide again.

Lives full of trust and gratitude will look different to the world. People will notice and want this life of rejoicing. Thanksgiving opens doors to share all God has done for us. He loves us all, and wants all of us to enter into a relationship with Him. With a thankful heart, remember your leaders in prayer today.

> God, teach me to pray continuously for those in my life. Help me to have a thankful heart, so I can live a peaceful and grateful life that points others to You.

AN ANGUISHED HEART

*I have great sorrow and unceasing anguish in my heart. For I could
wish that I myself were cursed and cut off from Christ for the sake
of my people, those of my own race, the people of Israel. Theirs is
the adoption to sonship; theirs the divine glory, the covenants, the
receiving of the law, the temple worship and the promises.*

ROMANS 9:2–4

In today's passage, Paul spoke passionately to followers of Christ
about the gospel and how important it was to him. Paul even
wished to be separated from Christ, if it meant his people could
experience a relationship with Christ Himself. He would've traded
anything to bring them into Christ's light.

This is the kind of sacrificial love Jesus displayed in His death
for us. How much would you have to love someone to feel that
kind of "unceasing anguish"? How overwhelmed by the truth of
God's sacrificial love would you have to be? Today, let us ask Jesus
to move us so deeply that our hearts grieve for those who don't
know His life. Let's ask Him to make our hearts burn for their
welfare, and for them to experience the adoption, the glory, and
the promises of our great God.

God, thank You for sending Your Son to lay down His life, so I
can pick mine back up. I pray that as I grow closer to You, I will
develop a heart that breaks for anyone who doesn't know You.

THE SERVICE OF SUFFERING

What has happened to me has actually served to advance the gospel.
As a result, it has become clear throughout the whole palace guard
and to everyone else that I am in chains for Christ. And because of
my chains, most of the brothers and sisters have become confident in
the Lord and dare all the more to proclaim the gospel without fear.

PHILIPPIANS 1:12–14

Paul loved the church in Philippi, and they loved him. When they heard he'd been thrown in prison, they were deeply concerned for their friend. They even sent Epaphroditus to visit him in prison and bring him gifts to lighten his burden (Philippians 4). Although they wanted to comfort Paul, Paul wrote to comfort them. He wrote about a joy that does not depend on external circumstances, but rests in the truth that Jesus is alive, reigning and ruling for our good and His glory.

A message of hope spoken out of a seemingly hopeless situation is like a bright light bursting through a dark, broken world. That is why Paul's reaction here is so powerful. Though people sought to break him and keep him in chains, he could see that God was using this situation to reach the "whole palace guard and . . . everyone else."

Jesus gives us the power to preach a message of hope in the midst of any circumstances. The next time you are placed in a seemingly hopeless position, look for the ways God can be glorified. In the darkness, you can shine His light so much brighter.

Jesus, I put all my hope in You. I love You and I trust You.

COMPELLED

Yet when I preach the gospel, I cannot boast, since I am compelled to preach.
Woe to me if I do not preach the gospel! If I preach voluntarily, I have a
reward; if not voluntarily, I am simply discharging the trust committed to me.
1 CORINTHIANS 9:16–17

The weight of the gospel redirects our lives. Sharing the living hope of Jesus with others is not just something we get to do; it's what we are commissioned to do as believers.

Paul was an ordinary man like any of us, but he understood the extraordinary calling on his life. Even in as simple a gesture as writing a letter, Paul used his platform to remind the Corinthians of the weight of the gospel. As he chose to trust God with his life, God trusted Paul to spread the good news far and wide and offer it freely. We as believers are trusted to do the same.

Though you may not have a pulpit to stand in today, you do have a platform right where you are. Whether it's in a dorm room, in a cubicle, or on your cul-de-sac, speak about the One you've put your trust in. Just like Paul, none of us has it all together, but that's no reason to withhold the gospel. Someone today needs to know the message you're carrying: no matter what you're walking through, Jesus can use your life to extend His eternal gift to the world.

> Jesus, You've placed me right where I am supposed to be. Help me not be afraid, but instead give me confidence to share Your gospel.

KEEP SPREADING THE WORD

"I must proclaim the good news of the kingdom of God to the other towns also, because that is why I was sent."

LUKE 4:43

After being rejected in Nazareth, His hometown, Jesus found Himself with an extremely successful ministry in Capernaum. He drove out demons, healed the sick, and taught the Word with authority—people were drawn to His message. But when the time came for Him to continue His ministry in other towns, the people of Capernaum desperately clung to Him and tried to prevent Him from leaving. They wondered why He couldn't stay, but Jesus knew He had a bigger purpose: to go out and preach the good news to those who still needed to hear.

It's easy to stay stationary when God has done incredible things around us. We want to sit in His glory, basking in the success of our local ministry. That may be a beautiful thing. But we can't forget that the kingdom of God is not restricted to one place; it needs to expand beyond the walls of our ministry. While our circumstances and relationships may seem great where we are, our mission is to continue sharing the good news with those who haven't heard yet. God has given you a story to tell. How can you tell it to those who haven't heard it before? God is calling us to go beyond what's comfortable and reach all people for His glory.

> Lord, I pray that I have the courage to go out and spread the good news of all You have done.

DON'T HOLD BACK

My brothers and sisters, if one of you should wander from the
truth and someone should bring that person back, remember
this: Whoever turns a sinner from the error of their way will
save them from death and cover over a multitude of sins.

JAMES 5:19–20

Have you ever reasoned your way out of sharing Jesus with someone? It's a common struggle for Christ-followers. There are many reasons we withhold ourselves from spreading the gospel; some of us keep waiting for an easier scenario that may never come.

What would you do if a friend, or even a stranger, were in physical danger? Overcome by impulse, you probably wouldn't overthink your response; you'd look for any opportunity to save them, regardless of how uncomfortable it made either of you feel. You'd operate with a heart of compassion and urgency, not passive obligation.

We can look at talking about Jesus the same way. We have the life-saving cure to the sin that causes spiritual death. We have the opportunity to guide those drowning in the weight of their sins to the path to redemption. Keep that in mind. Evangelizing is not an awkward obligation; it is bringing others from death to life! Today, ask God to open your eyes to life-and-death situations, and pray for wisdom and boldness.

Lord, help me always remember what's at stake. Please work through me to lead the lost back to You.

FREED TO BE FREE

It is for freedom that Christ has set us free. Stand firm, then, and do not let yourselves be burdened again by a yoke of slavery.

GALATIANS 5:1

Did you know that you are the subject of a rags-to-riches story? You were a slave, but now you are an adopted child of the King. You were struggling with limited resources, but now you are free. Why would you ever choose to go back to the place you've been freed from? In an unmerited exchange, Jesus removed and carried your "yoke of slavery" to sin so that He could adopt you as a child of God and place upon your head a crown of sonship: freedom.

Your identity now as a child of God is *freed*. Yet Paul warned us to not take on our old burden: service out of obligation, heavy expectations, and untenable standards. God has lifted them. You are free now to be a child—free to love, believe, and dream again, and free to be with the One who loves you. The Enemy will try to yoke you with the pressures of the law and try to quench the joys of freedom, pulling you back into slavery—to live to please the world again instead of God. Shake off those shackles, and stand firm in the truth of who Jesus made you to be. You are His child, and you are free. Rejoice in His love, and remember who you are!

> Jesus, thank You for the freedom I have as Your child. Help me live continually in it.

GOOD FRUIT

Who is wise and understanding among you? Let them show it by their
good life, by deeds done in the humility that comes from wisdom.

JAMES 3:13

Can a tree become a tree if its seed never sprouts?

If you put apple seeds into the ground, others would only know it was an apple tree when apples started growing on the branches. Likewise, if the seed of Jesus is planted in us, people will know by our fruit, our good "deeds done in . . . humility," and the kind of people we are. In Him, our roots grow deep in wisdom, and our trunk is strengthened in humility. Your actions nourish people and point them back to Jesus. When they eat your good fruit, the seeds of Jesus grow in their hearts too.

If you claim to know Jesus, are you living your life in a way so that people can see your fruit? Not just your words, but your actions? People are hungry for wisdom, and they will seek endless solutions for their hunger in things that are not Christ. But these things leave them empty, and they keep on searching. If only they knew that the good fruit of Jesus would stop the hunger and bring real wisdom! How can you humbly share your fruit with others today?

Jesus, help me grow and bear good fruit, and help me show others the glory of Your love.

DIVINE WEAPONS

For though we live in the world, we do not wage war as the world does.
The weapons we fight with are not the weapons of the world. On the
contrary, they have divine power to demolish strongholds. We demolish
arguments and every pretension that sets itself up against the knowledge
of God, and we take captive every thought to make it obedient to Christ.

2 Corinthians 10:3–5

Today's verse accurately describes living in this world as a war. Chaos surrounds us, and violence prevails over kindness. In its celebration of selfishness, our culture has almost pushed Christ completely out of its way of thinking. How do we spread Christ's message in the face of such an onslaught?

Paul tells us we have weapons for this war—divine weapons to "demolish strongholds." In our own lives, Jesus helps us throw down strongholds of sin, so we can live a pure and blameless life as a testimony to those around us. This passage tells us to aggressively take every loose thought or desire and channel it into obedience to Christ. We live in a way different from the way the world operates. When the world responds with violence, we offer kindness. When the world explodes into chaos, we become a sanctuary of peace. When the world holds grudges, we forgive without hesitation.

We have been forgiven; our sin has been atoned for because Jesus has restored our relationship with God. So let's live for God and show the world how He has changed our lives.

> Jesus, help me wage war Your way, living a life that brings honor to You.

CHILD OF LIGHT

For you were once darkness, but now you are light in the Lord. Live
as children of light (for the fruit of the light consists in all goodness,
righteousness and truth) and find out what pleases the Lord.

EPHESIANS 5:8–10

What does it look like to walk as a child of the light? What makes it different from the darkness? Is it joy? Fun? Gratitude? Compassion? Take a minute and think about the things Paul described in today's verse: all that is good and right and true. How do those things display themselves in your day-to-day life as a child of the light?

God calls us to live lives of holiness, inviting others into the joy in which we live. This means we daily choose to focus on Jesus as the lens through which we see our world, to submit ourselves to His plan and to look for ways to serve Him. Rather than allowing despair in, we rest in our unfading hope.

Think about one friend who doesn't know Jesus. Does your life sing of the grace and hope of Jesus in a way that they notice? Ask God to show you how to live in the light, and He will (James 1:5–6). Engage in meaningful conversations and intentional relationships with others, encouraging them to know Christ and to experience a life saturated with all that is good, instead of the faded options the world offers. As we seek and obey Jesus with joy, we walk in the light as children of God.

Lord, give me the discernment to see who You call me to share Your message with and help me joyfully obey.

VICTORIOUS GOD

So Christ, having been offered once to bear the sins of many, will appear a second time, not to deal with sin but to save those who are eagerly waiting for him.
HEBREWS 9:28 ESV

God's story is one of redemption. Beginning in Eden, moving through Egypt into the promised land, lasting through exile, and culminating on the cross and in the empty tomb, it will be brought to a close with thunderous triumph one day. Jesus will come to us once again, and all of God's people will praise and enjoy His glory. Just as an army roars in triumph as their king claims victory, so we will shout when Christ our King comes for us.

This picture of Jesus' final victory intersects our lives the same way it did for Paul. Throughout his ministry—where he proclaimed the life promised in Jesus—Paul looked back at the history of grace, anxiously longing for the people to join him in making God's victory known. Friends, this kingdom is wide open! Make no mistake: we carry the responsibility to herald the good news of Jesus. When we share the gospel, let's remember God's victory—for Jesus, our King, is coming again!

> Jesus, give me faith and power to carry the message of Your grace to those around me.

ALIGNMENT

*Do not be conformed to this world, but be transformed by the
renewal of your mind, that by testing you may discern what is
the will of God, what is good and acceptable and perfect.*

Romans 12:2 esv

When you live in a certain area long enough, your life begins to reflect the city you live in, the people who surround you, and the leaders influencing culture. This same principle is also true in our walks as believers. Even though we understand this world is not our permanent home, our close alignment with the world changes us into who people say we should be rather than who our Father says we are. Our boldness for Christ is toned down, and suddenly we look up and find we are like everyone else.

Our walk throughout life is determined by the thoughts we nurture. As Paul wrote in Romans, we are to "be transformed by the renewal of [our] mind." How do we renew our minds? By realigning our lives with Jesus and studying His Word. When the world tells us to accumulate, we remember Jesus said it's more blessed to give than receive. When the world tells us success is measured in elevating ourselves, we think of Jesus, who humbled Himself for the sake of others. Whenever culture rises to tell you how to live, look to Jesus. Remember who He is and who you are in Him, and realign your life to Him.

Father, set my mind on You rather than on the world. Take my mind and heart and make them Yours.

SIGHT RESTORED

Jesus stopped and ordered the man to be brought to him. When he came near, Jesus asked him, "What do you want me to do for you?" "Lord, I want to see," he replied. Jesus said to him, "Receive your sight; your faith has healed you." Immediately he received his sight and followed Jesus, praising God. When all the people saw it, they also praised God.

Luke 18:40–43

When the blind beggar heard that Jesus was passing through, he knew this was his one opportunity to meet the Lord. Those around him told him to be silent, but the man who was once begging for money was now crying out to Jesus, begging for mercy. It's an amazing story, but so is his response to being healed. The beggar did not return to the side of the road in silence. He instantly began to follow Jesus and glorify God. Because of this, those who had been silencing him before were now giving praise to the Father.

Believe it or not, we have a lot more in common with the blind man in Luke 18 than most people think. At some point in our lives, our eyes were completely veiled to the glory of God, and we walked in darkness. But God has met us right where we are. He has recovered our sight, and our immediate response must be to follow Him. Instead of returning to our normal routine, let's walk with God and be a billboard for grace and mercy to those around us.

God, thank You for Your grace in my life. I am grateful that You choose to turn my broken story into a story of redemption.

WE WON'T BE QUIET

They called them and charged them not to speak or teach at all in the name of Jesus. But Peter and John answered them, "Whether it is right in the sight of God to listen to you rather than to God, you must judge, for we cannot but speak of what we have seen and heard."

ACTS 4:18–20 ESV

The religious leaders of the Sanhedrin were disturbed. People were turning toward Jesus in droves because of the witness of the apostles and the miraculous healings. In an attempt to neutralize this situation, they threw the apostles in jail, brought them to court, and ordered them to be silent. But the apostles replied essentially, "We can't!" Even in the face of threats and prison, they could not be quiet.

Telling others about Jesus may not be the most popular choice; in fact, it may come at great cost sometimes. But just like Peter and John, we cannot let adversity silence us. When we recognize all that Jesus has done in and for us, telling others should be our first reaction to His grace.

Be encouraged by the testimony of the apostles in Acts. Let their lives be an example of the overflow of passion that gives us courage to proclaim God's story. When we share our stories with this kind of urgency, we remind people of the very present greatness of a God who wants to heal them.

> Lord, may my life be one that celebrates You in everything I do. Help me experience You in such a way that I cannot help but proclaim Your majesty.

UNDESERVED GRACE

But God demonstrates his own love for us in this:
While we were still sinners, Christ died for us.
ROMANS 5:8

Imagine that you deserted your best friend, and then, when something went wrong and you needed them the most, they were still there for you, holding no grudge and loving you just the same.

This is the power of undeserved grace and exactly the kind of love that Jesus has for us. We did nothing to deserve it, but He gave it to us anyway. Even when we reject Him, He keeps coming back for us. We have received such constant grace from Him that we must now know that it is available to *anyone* who calls on Him.

Let's reflect on the meaning of the word *undeserved*, and not pass judgment based on what our eyes tell us about somebody; we all need His grace equally. We share the gospel freely with those around us, because we all come from the same place. Even for those far away from God's mercy, Christ reaches out His hand and calls them—and us—to Himself.

> Jesus, thank You for loving me even when I was far away from You. Please help me see others the way You see them, so that I can share Your love and mercy with them.

IDENTITY CRISIS

"He must become greater; I must become less."
JOHN 3:30

John the Baptist was a celebrity. Emerging from the wilderness in a camel-hair robe and with locust crumbs in his beard, John proclaimed the kingdom of God with the fire and authority of a prophet. Entire villages went to the river to listen to his teachings and be baptized for the repentance of their sins. His reputation gathered quite a following, catching the attention of the priests and Jesus Himself. Despite the popularity John may have enjoyed, he understood that he was the messenger, not the message. The Savior of the world had arrived, and John's goal was to make Jesus known above everyone else, including himself.

In a culture prone to overemphasizing the importance of the individual, it is no wonder we struggle to obey Christ's call to deny ourselves. Yet when Christ calls us to follow Him, we must be prepared to leave personal glory, and even our identity, behind. With everything in your life, make God the focus and the priority. Every time your mind wanders to ways to "increase" yourself—whether it's your reputation, image, social standing, or anything else—stop and remember John the Baptist's words. How can we reverse the urge, and let God increase as we decrease? As He increases, we get the pleasure of living a life of meaning beyond our imagining.

Father, forgive the pride in my life. Humble me, and show me where I must let You increase in my life today.

SANCTIFYING WORD

"My prayer is not that you take them out of the world but that you protect them from the evil one. They are not of the world, even as I am not of it. Sanctify them by the truth; your word is truth."

JOHN 17:15–17

Today's verses are part of the prayer Jesus prayed at the Last Supper for Himself, the disciples, and all believers. Jesus said that following Him wouldn't be easy, but He also promised to sanctify and preserve us. Jesus isn't just a teacher; He's also an intimate and caring friend.

Sanctification isn't a one-time thing. It's a process—it purifies us, sets us apart as holy for God's use, and makes us more like Him. Jesus didn't expect us to sanctify ourselves. He knew that sanctification is God's active work in and through us. When He says, "Sanctify them by the truth; your word is truth," He points us toward God's Word—the Bible. His Word works in us when we read, understand, and apply it. Throughout His prayer, Jesus mentions that because His disciples have obeyed His Word, they are not of this world; instead, their thoughts and hearts are set upon the world to come.

To stand the test of time, let's also dive into the Word and let it change us. When we have His truth in our lives we can stand firmly against the evil one while we do our work in this world.

Lord, help me rest in You and relinquish my life to the sanctifying work of Your Word.

THE WORK-OUT

Continue to work out your salvation with fear and trembling, for it is God who works in you to will and to act in order to fulfill his good purpose. Do everything without grumbling or arguing, so that you may become blameless and pure, "children of God without fault in a warped and crooked generation." Then you will shine among them like stars in the sky as you hold firmly to the word of life.

PHILIPPIANS 2:12–16

"Fear and trembling" and "work out your salvation"—these phrases tend to paint a rather severe picture in our minds. If Jesus has saved us and done all the work of our salvation, what is there left for us to work out? Why should we fear and tremble? Know this, once you're saved, you're saved completely—all through Jesus' grace, not your own work. That's great cause for rejoicing. But do you then go on autopilot and cruise from then on? Not hardly! You "work out" your salvation, as in exercising it. You build your decision-making muscles by making active, obedient choices to live a pure life that's reflective of Him and astonishing to the rest of the world.

So when you work out your salvation with "fear and trembling," you make choices out of deep respect and reverence for the seriousness and depth of Christ's sacrifice. We do have a part to play. Let's exercise salvation, which God gave us, and choose to live like Him every day.

> Lord, thank You for the humbling gift of salvation. Show me how to exercise it in obedience and shine Your light to others.

WORTH THE WAIT

The grace of God . . . teaches us to say "No" to ungodliness and worldly passions, and to live self-controlled, upright and godly lives in this present age, while we wait for the blessed hope—the appearing of the glory of our great God and Savior, Jesus Christ.

TITUS 2:11–13

Waiting is not often valued in our culture. We want our food fast, our Internet speedy, and the world at our fingertips. But this culture of hurry is in sharp contrast to what Jesus wants for us.

From an eternal perspective, our entire lives could be considered a period of waiting. The great news is we've already gotten a taste of what we're waiting for: a forever spent worshiping God in His presence. We wait for an eternity that's better than life, and knowing that drives us to live as God calls us to on earth.

When we forget this hope, not grasping the fullness of Jesus, we turn to immediate gratification: drugs to escape, alcohol to forget, sex to fulfill. This fulfillment is temporary and actually ends up taking from us. But the lifestyle Jesus calls us to offers eternal, permanent fulfillment beyond what we thought could fit in our lives. Every time we say no to "ungodliness and worldly passions," we say yes to Jesus—and He lasts forever.

Let His grace teach you to say no to the things that aren't of Him. Tune your heart to the heart of God, and receive the blessed hope of Jesus, which lasts for all time. It's worth the wait.

Jesus, You are more than enough. Help me look to You for my self-control and turn me away from ungodliness.

GO AND TELL

The man from whom the demons had gone out begged to go
with him, but Jesus sent him away, saying, "Return home and
tell how much God has done for you." So the man went away
and told all over town how much Jesus had done for him.

LUKE 8:38–39

When Jesus came to the region of the Gerasenes, which was across the lake from Galilee, He encountered a naked, homeless, demon-possessed man. His demon possession was so strong that the local authorities couldn't even contain him. But when the demons that possessed the man saw Jesus, they recognized His power and begged Jesus not to torture them. In a miraculous turn of events, Jesus commanded the demons out of the man, healing him from the oppression he had endured for years. The man's reaction? He went and told everyone all over town how much Jesus had done for him.

Most of us have probably not experienced healing from demon possession, but we all have experienced Jesus' life-giving salvation. And God is calling us to share what He has done. What has God freed you from? What new insight has He shown you? How is your life different now that you know Him? Don't let fear hold you back from telling others what God has done in your life; your story can point people to finding healing and life in Christ too!

> Father, give me the courage to tell others what You are doing
> in my life so they are blessed through Your work in me.

CHOSEN INSTRUMENTS

"Lord," Ananias answered, "I have heard many reports about this man and
all the harm he has done to your holy people in Jerusalem. And he has come
here with authority from the chief priests to arrest all who call on your name."
But the Lord said to Ananias, "Go! This man is my chosen instrument to
proclaim my name to the Gentiles and their kings and to the people of Israel."

ACTS 9:13–16

Saul was an enemy of God. He famously opposed the name of
Jesus, threw many saints in prison, persecuted the believers in the
synagogues, and even put men to death for their faith in Jesus
Christ. But the Lord told Ananias in this scripture that Saul was
His "chosen instrument."

Can you feel Ananias's suspicion? Saul was the worst of the
worst and posed an immediate threat to the lives of his friends.
But God let him in on His amazing plan: What better person to
show God's transforming power than the worst of them all?

God, in His endless creativity, chooses broken people to glorify Him. The next time you come upon a seemingly hopeless
case (or if you feel hopeless yourself), remember that fact. And
pray that God would turn that hopelessness on its head and into
something miraculous. Jesus transformed Saul into a new man.
He was no longer Saul the Pharisee, but Paul the missionary to
the Gentiles—and missionary to us! Our great God brings eternal
good out of hopeless cases.

Lord, we rejoice that no one is too far gone for Your transforming power!

NO OFFENSE

Do not cause anyone to stumble, whether Jews, Greeks or the church of God—even as I try to please everyone in every way. For I am not seeking my own good but the good of many, so that they may be saved.

1 CORINTHIANS 10:32–33

Members of the Corinthian church were zealous, to say the least. In fact, they were so concerned with knowing the truth that they would drag disagreeing Christians into the streets of the city and openly quarrel with them! Instead of commending their pursuit of truth, Paul shocked them, telling them that demonstrating the love of God is more important than proving you are right. Paul sets the example, not by exposing falsehood, but through patience and an inoffensive approach.

Many Christians still think that if people are offended by our words, it must mean we are speaking truth—that the offense others are feeling must be the work of the Holy Spirit exposing some hidden sin. Some romanticize and elevate confrontation, preferring strong words and accusations over gentleness, patience, and temperance. Yet this is not the attitude Paul condoned. The world cannot find Jesus if the church presents itself as being against them—this will only breed dissention and hate. It's not our job to defend truth, for truth protects itself; rather, it's our duty as Christ's church to show the love of God to all people.

Jesus, help me be gentle, patient, and kind with those around me, showing Your love first and then declaring Your truth.

START NOW

They must exercise self-control and be faithful in everything they do.
1 TIMOTHY 3:11 NLT

Have you ever wanted something with your whole being? Maybe it was getting into a certain school or making a team. Chances are you didn't just sit around waiting for that dream to become a reality; you probably took active, thoughtful steps to get what you wanted. Why? You realized what you do today impacts tomorrow.

In this letter to Timothy, Paul laid out necessary characteristics of church leaders. They were to be respectful, faithful in everything, exercising self-control, and not slandering others, just to name a few. This is a weighty call, and answering it starts now while you are young.

The body of Christ is called to be a living example of Him, a daily reflection of the life He lived. But living that kind of life doesn't just come overnight. The decisions you make today shape your future character and person. Now is the time to start cultivating the kind of Christ-honoring behavior that you are called to. If you seek to be more like Him now, you will find yourself better prepared for the future work He has called you to. Make the decision to honor Him with your character, actions, and decisions today, so you will be fit to serve Him in every day to come.

Lord, give me a teachable heart. Show me what actions to take today as You prepare me for tomorrow.

FREE PEOPLE

Live as free people, but do not use your freedom as a cover-up
for evil; live as God's slaves. Show proper respect to everyone,
love the family of believers, fear God, honor the emperor.

1 PETER 2:16–17

How do we share the story of Jesus? It's tough to know where to begin. It can be painful and frustrating to see our friends, co-workers, classmates, or family live without Him or even openly reject Him. You may have been belittled or questioned because of your faith. Or you may feel stuck trying to figure out how to lead and love people who hold on to wrong ideas about God.

Today's verses show us the way God has called us to react in these situations: doing good and showing respect and love. His love and redemption has freed us from fear, pride, insecurity, and need for approval—and from sin. Yet, we aren't freed for ourselves, but to be the vessels God uses to display the truth that will free others.

Many people have turned against Jesus because they've felt condemned or attacked by people who claim His name. How does your example combat these painful misconceptions? Jesus came to set us free and did so by loving, serving, and redeeming us. Do we live like it? Do our words match up with our actions? Are we abounding in good works that point to Him? Hurt people can hurt people, but free people will free people. Let your freedom proclaim Him today, with love, respect, and good works.

> Lord, let me recognize the freedom You give me, and use it
> to bring others into Your kingdom.

WORDS FROM THE SPIRIT

Pray also for me, that whenever I speak, words may be given me so that I will fearlessly make known the mystery of the gospel, for which I am an ambassador in chains. Pray that I may declare it fearlessly, as I should.

EPHESIANS 6:19–20

Words matter. But when the pressure's on, we often don't know where to find them.

Paul understood the weight of his message and the power of words in his mission. His plea to the church in Ephesus was one of humility, acknowledging that his words meant nothing without the Spirit of God behind them. God's gospel is one that must be proclaimed boldly, and the places where Paul took it required him to risk his very life in sharing it. That's why he pleaded for prayer that the Spirit would inspire him with words more fearless than he could come up with on his own.

Our pastors, missionaries, and even our own selves require this same kind of prayer and encouragement. It's important that our words are chained not to opinions or feelings, but to the Sprit of God and the power of the Word. Let us then pray this same prayer over our leaders and our lives, asking for the wisdom, words, and courage to declare the mystery of the gospel fearlessly, as we should.

> God, please give me the gift of the right words at the right time, and give my pastors and leaders words to proclaim the mystery of Your gospel too.

PROCLAIM GLAD TIDINGS

I have proclaimed glad tidings of righteousness in the great
congregation; behold, I will not restrain my lips, O LORD, You
know. I have not hidden Your righteousness within my heart;
I have spoken of Your faithfulness and Your salvation.

PSALM 40:9–10 NASB

Today's Scripture can be particularly challenging for those of us who are quiet about our faith. We may believe that lifestyles or actions will manifest our faith adequately, but the result is that the word *Jesus* hardly leaves our lips. Without speaking the name of Jesus, praying becomes difficult, the Bible starts to seem like no more than a textbook to be memorized, and church turns into something as laborious as studying Hebrew grammar. And relating to fellow believers, though it's our calling, can become the most difficult of tasks.

Like the disciples, the men who saw Jesus work and talked with Him every day, we ask each other, "Who is this? Even the wind and the waves obey him!" (Mark 4:41). The answer is clear: Jesus is the Savior, though maybe we have become so familiarized with Him that we forget what that means for others. So open your mouth today and talk about Jesus. Whether it's with someone from church, a family member, or a friend—with someone safe or someone new—don't restrain your lips. The more you talk about His lovingkindness, the more infectious it will be.

God, help me rejoice with creation, and bring joyful words
to my lips.

OPENED EYES

A second time they summoned the man who had been blind.
"Give glory to God by telling the truth," they said. "We know this
man is a sinner." He replied, "Whether he is a sinner or not, I
don't know. One thing I do know. I was blind but now I see!"

John 9:24–25

There had to be some rational explanation. Could Jesus have given this man sight after a lifetime of blindness? The Pharisees' hypocrisy and pride blinded them from believing Jesus could heal, and they attempted to prove the miracle was a hoax.

But they failed. Instead of changing his story to avoid their threats, the man pointed the Pharisees back to Jesus with a simplicity even they couldn't deny: "I was blind but now I see!" These religious leaders were frustrated. Jesus threatened their power, and they couldn't explain how or why He did what He did.

Yet Jesus was on a greater mission. He told His disciples that this man's blindness was meant to display God's work in his life. Similarly, God has designed every detail of your life to display His miracles to the world—even the ones that seem like burdens.

The miracles God works through us may leave those around us stumped, like the Pharisees. The beginning of your miracle story is this: you were born spiritually blind, but God has opened your eyes to the beauty and truth of the gospel. Now that you see, you can put His death-defeating power on display each day.

God, thank You for opening my eyes. Help me use the miracle story You've given me as a hope for those around me.

LOSING YOUR LIFE

"Whoever finds their life will lose it, and whoever
loses their life for my sake will find it."
MATTHEW 10:39

Losing your life seems counterproductive if the goal is to find life, doesn't it? We want to have control over "our lives"—we are the ones living them, so why can't we own them? But, as paradoxical as it may seem, this scripture contains a profound truth about God's grace.

Before we knew Christ, we were clinging to a life that was separate from God. We held on to the things of this world with a white-knuckle grip. Yet God had something better for us: new life in Jesus, and the power of the Holy Spirit. To take hold of it, we had to let go of the "life" we thought we had, and open our hands to receive new life. Jesus' sacrifice is the reason we have life; we owe everything to Him, and our lives are not our own. We lose our lives and find something much better.

Are you struggling to find and create a dream life for yourself? If so, it's time to let that go. Let's loosen our grip on our own lives for His sake, acknowledging that Jesus has a much better idea of what "life" should be like. He is calling the shots, and we trust Him to put the right things in our hands.

> Father, as I walk through life, help me remember who really has ownership over my life. Help me trust in You and Your guidance as I follow Your lead.

GOD'S WORD IS NOT CHAINED

Remember Jesus Christ, raised from the dead, descended from David.
This is my gospel, for which I am suffering even to the point of being
chained like a criminal. But God's word is not chained. Therefore
I endure everything for the sake of the elect, that they too may
obtain the salvation that is in Christ Jesus, with eternal glory.

2 TIMOTHY 2:8–10

Paul wrote these verses as a farewell letter to Timothy while he was chained in a dark, cold Roman prison cell shortly before he was killed. He knew that his death was imminent. Even so, Paul proclaimed the message of Jesus Christ from right where he sat in chains because, as he said, "God's word is not chained."

You may think you can't share the message of Jesus because of your current place in life. Maybe your circumstances are not ideal, but the message of Jesus is not limited by your situation. God's Word always accomplishes what He desires! Though we may feel weak or underprepared, God's Word is never useless and never constricted by our circumstances. It goes far beyond just us, and can reach people with a power that comes from the Spirit, not the presentation we make.

Remember the life-giving, death-defeating power of His message and boldly proclaim it to those who need life!

Jesus, thank You for Your message that is stronger than me. Make me a source of hope and light, regardless of my circumstances.

LITTLE CHILDREN

Then people brought little children to Jesus for him to place his hand on them and pray for them. But the disciples rebuked them. Jesus said, "Let the little children come to me, and do not hinder them, for the kingdom of heaven belongs to such as these."

MATTHEW 19:13–14

In Jesus' time, children were of little value to society: they had no rights, didn't contribute to the household income, and were completely dependent on others for their sustenance. So why did Jesus say the kingdom belonged to them? The kingdom of heaven belongs to children because it doesn't operate by human standards. Admittance into the kingdom isn't determined by social status, race, gender, or background, but by a dependent, childlike faith.

Like the disciples, we sometimes act as bouncers for God's kingdom, but it's not up to us to decide who can have access to Jesus. Our role is to simply *let* people come to Jesus. God is the one who determines the sincerity of someone's faith, not us! So when the unfit, the outcast, and the not-good-enoughs approach the doors of our church, let us welcome them! Jesus has swung the doors of the kingdom open wide so that those who approach God with a sincere faith can find Him.

> Lord, I want to believe in You with that simple, childlike faith. Teach me to seek You with innocence and unabashed hope and to welcome others into Your light.

WITNESSES

"You are my witnesses," declares the LORD, "and my servant whom I have chosen, so that you may know and believe me and understand that I am he. Before me no god was formed, nor will there be one after me. I, even I, am the LORD, and apart from me there is no savior."

ISAIAH 43:10–11

A witness is someone who has seen an event take place and can testify it occurred. So why is God calling the Israelites His witnesses here? Earlier in this chapter, we read of God's promise to bring Israel back from her Babylonian exile. They would "pass through the waters" and not be swept away, "walk through the fire" and not be burned (v. 2). God would gather the Israelites out of the four corners of the earth and lead them home in more glory than their escape from Egypt. Their return would be famous, and all earth would know that no other god could save but Israel's.

There's one problem in all of this: return from exile was unheard of at that time. But history does not limit God's power. God told the Israelites, "See, I'm going to do this, and you will be witnesses that I alone am God, and salvation is found only in Me."

We too are witnesses of God's power to save. In Jesus, He brought us out of death, an eternal exile away from Him, and into life. We are witnesses to the power of the gospel—our story of redemption is solid evidence of His grace!

Jesus, thank You for releasing me from eternal exile from Your presence. Help me to be your witness to the world.

THE LORD RESCUES

The kings of Assyria have destroyed all these nations. And they have
thrown the gods of these nations into the fire and burned them. . . .
Now, O LORD our God, rescue us from his power; then all the
kingdoms of the earth will know that you alone, O LORD, are God.
2 KINGS 19:17–19 NLT

Do you ever wake up and feel overwhelmed by everything going on in the world? It doesn't take more than a couple of minutes watching the news to realize just how broken our world is.

The world has always been a chaotic place. King Hezekiah spoke the words in today's scripture after hearing dire news of an attack planned on Jerusalem by one of the most powerful armies of his day. His prayer expressed the burden he felt for his country and for his people. But, more importantly, he expressed hope and trust that God would save them. In the midst of destructive threats on the people of Israel and on Hezekiah's life, this king knew that the Lord was the only One who could save them.

The same is true today. No matter how burdened and hopeless you feel, the same God who rescued Hezekiah is your God. He is always there, always ready to listen and to be a source of hope. Lean into Him today, knowing that He has already rescued us from the darkness of this world. Declare His rescuing power to the people in need of hope around you!

> Lord, thank You for being my hope. Reach down and heal this hurting world as I wait for eternity with You.

TRUTH DRIVES PERSPECTIVE

Rejoice in the Lord always. I will say it again: Rejoice! Let
your gentleness be evident to all. The Lord is near.
PHILIPPIANS 4:4–5

The truth we accept determines our perspective. The perspective we hold drives our actions. And our actions reflect our faith.

So we start with the truth that in Jesus, we are made new, we have been bought by His blood, and we are involved in a bigger God story than we could ever imagine. But how does this perspective show up in our actions? We can proclaim that His gospel is a reality, but in moments of hardship, we often find ourselves paralyzed by a fear that cripples our joy. All the while, God—all-knowing and all-powerful—holds the future in His hands and wants us to enjoy and rest in His gift of life.

In a moment our emotions may sway, but we know the truth of the Lord is the same yesterday, today, and tomorrow. We can count on His steadfastness and rejoice in it. Paul said that this kind of trust and rejoicing is reasonable! When we allow this to be our truth, our perspective is rooted in God's faithfulness and our actions reflect His unconditional compassion, forgiveness, and love. Rejoice today in God's unchanging truths and promises!

Father, thank You that no matter what happens, my rejoicing is rooted in an understanding of Your truth. Thank You for redeeming me!

BUILT UP TO BUILD

*Christ himself gave the apostles, the prophets, the evangelists, the
pastors and teachers, to equip his people for works of service, so that
the body of Christ may be built up until we all reach unity in the faith
and in the knowledge of the Son of God and become mature.*

EPHESIANS 4:11–13

Who are these apostles, prophets, evangelists, pastors, and teachers God has given us, His body? You may think about those who
are highly visible leaders in your church, leveraging their influence for the glory of God. They are there, yes, to build you up, but
as you mature, *you* become one who builds up the church. Have
you ever taken the time to consider what your role in the church
might be, globally and locally? Are you maturing into one of the
roles on the list above? How are your God-given passions preparing you for "works of service"?

God has given every individual in His kingdom skills and
passions that make us special parts of His body. Allow yourself to
be fully built up and mentored in these. Then, as you grow, you'll
give back to the body (even your mentors!) as the church becomes
equipped, unified, and full of the knowledge of Jesus.

The Lord has distinctly crafted you to convey His amazing
power to the world. What better use of your passion and time than
growing in and serving the body that glorifies the Lord?

> Father, let me learn, live, and lead in such a way that brings
> You amazing praise!

RICH GENEROSITY

We want you to know about the grace that God has given the Macedonian churches. In the midst of a very severe trial, their overflowing joy and their extreme poverty welled up in rich generosity. For I testify that they gave as much as they were able, and even beyond their ability. . . . And they exceeded our expectations: They gave themselves first of all to the Lord, and then by the will of God also to us.

2 CORINTHIANS 8:1–5

College students face many challenges each semester: stress, finances, grades, relationships, work, and more. With hectic schedules and minimal income, giving our time or money may seem like one burden too many. But for the Macedonians, it was the opposite.

Paul praised the Macedonian churches because they saw financial giving as a privilege, not an obligation or a stretch. Paul never revealed the monetary amount of their giving; he simply said they gave as much as they could and beyond. Obviously, he was more impressed with their selflessness and the posture of their hearts than whatever amount they gave. And, even more amazing, all this happened during a "very severe trial."

With everything we must face as young people, many of us feel we have no time or money to spare, but Jesus asks us to be generous. He promises to provide everything we need, and He never fails. Trusting Him frees us to eagerly give Him and others our finances and time.

> God, You have been richly generous to me. Show me where I can give and give generously.

NO DIFFERENCE

As Scripture says, "Anyone who believes in him will never be put to shame." For there is no difference between Jew and Gentile—the same Lord is Lord of all and richly blesses all who call on him, for, "Everyone who calls on the name of the Lord will be saved."

ROMANS 10:11–13

Salvation is a scandalous offer. Love, forgiveness, deliverance, righteousness, and healing—open to all, no strings attached. God is not exclusive or impossible to please. He is a God of love and of justice. He does not demand perfect church attendance, a family heritage of purity, financial security, or a spotless track record of holiness. What He does demand is belief—belief that Jesus is Lord, crucified and risen, and that His righteousness is given to anyone and everyone who believes.

Some religious people might be aggravated that Jesus doesn't care if you're a Jew or Gentile, or how "moral" you are. "Everyone" includes *everyone*: the rich, poor, slave, free, foreigners, locals, women, men, priests, and prostitutes. The riches of Christ are given freely to *all* who call—including you—regardless of merit.

Be encouraged: you are no better or worse than your neighbor. Every human is in desperate need of God, so share the truth boldly. No one is out of reach—and some have never heard. Will you share Christ's offer with someone today?

> Jesus, thank You for the riches of Your salvation. Use me so that many more can believe.

TRUE WISDOM

Since in the wisdom of God the world through its wisdom did not know him, God was pleased through the foolishness of what was preached to save those who believe. Jews demand signs and Greeks look for wisdom, but we preach Christ crucified: a stumbling block to Jews and foolishness to Gentiles, but to those whom God has called, both Jews and Greeks, Christ the power of God and the wisdom of God.

1 Corinthians 1:21–24

The kingdom of God is upside down. God uses the unexpected, what we may think is useless or foolish, for His glory. Jesus is God's prime example: He came as a helpless baby in a manger, not a victorious prince in a palace, and died on a cross. His divine wisdom disarms any preconceived notion we may have that our actions or wisdom could get us any closer to salvation.

How does this change our lives? Today's verse teaches that Christ crucified is the *power* and the *wisdom* of God. His resurrection is the marvelous display of God's power. His life displays the wisdom of God in choosing such a humble story. And He is *your* wisdom. Going forward, we don't have to try to figure out God or life on our own.

If you desire His wisdom in your life, seek Him first. Learn about Him; spend time with Him; search His Word. There we find the treasures of His wisdom.

God, thank You for making Your wisdom available to me! Help me rest in You and Your wisdom every day of my life.

LAMB OF GOD

The next day John saw Jesus coming toward him and said, "Look,
the Lamb of God, who takes away the sin of the world!"

JOHN 1:29

As a yearly remembrance of the Passover, Jewish tradition required each family to sacrifice a year-old male lamb that was free from defect. Once the lamb was inspected and found to be without flaw, it was slaughtered to remove the sins of the family for that year. This annual ritual served as a divine foreshadowing of the ultimate sacrifice to come.

In a collision of love and justice, the final sacrifice for sin was offered: Jesus Christ, the perfect Lamb of God. He was inspected by the Father and found to be without defect. His innocent blood, shed on a cross, removed the sin of the world—not just for one year, but for all time!

Look to Jesus—though He was slaughtered, He overcame death and is alive. When you approach God, you are not being inspected according to what you have done, but according to the sacrifice of the perfect Lamb of God. Jesus is enough for every person, problem, and sin. As you accept this revolutionary news in your life, share it with others: His sacrifice is enough to set us free and take away the sins of the world!

Jesus, I am so grateful for Your sacrifice. Help me point others to this miraculous news.

WILLINGNESS TO SHINE THE GOSPEL TO ALL PEOPLE

Because God is seeking worshipers of all peoples, I will spread His fame among the nations, fully participating in His global purposes and engaging poverty and injustice in Jesus' name.

Generally when we talk about the gospel, we mention the beginning and end, but skip the middle part of Jesus' story. We don't know what to do with it. It's as if His miracles, sermons, and parables are literary sideshows along the way to the cross and the empty tomb. For some, they serve as mere confirmations of ancient prophecies. But Jesus' gospel is much more than a "ticket to heaven." He was inaugurating a new kingdom, a new order of society, a new way of life. The gospel—the story of how God reconciles creation through Jesus' life, death, resurrection, and coming again—is for everyone, and it's for right here and now.

It's not hard to see why Jesus caused such a stir in His hometown, the surrounding Judean country, and Jerusalem. He associated with prostitutes, touched lepers, dined with tax collectors, and healed on the wrong day of the week. His disciples—and closest friends—were a ragtag group of Galilean fishermen and peasants. In the eyes of some He was a misfit—an unorthodox preacher who claimed that the good news of God's redemption embraces people from every social stratum: from Jewish Pharisees to Roman centurions to kings, aliens, vagabonds, and all those on the social fringes. In Jesus' eyes, no one was excluded. And by offering freedom, forgiveness, and healing to them, He showed us that engaging injustice, poverty, and inequality is as much the gospel as proclaiming His birth, death, and resurrection

To follow Jesus is to defy the hierarchy we live in. It is to get our hands dirty, bruised, and cut as we step into the lives of the people around us and engage in the real challenges they're facing today. So when we see injustice, we stand for the oppressed; when we run into the marginalized, we invite them into our home; when we see the naked, we take the clothes off our back and give them away. In everything we do we live the gospel, inviting everyone—as we ourselves were once invited—into God's incredible story of grace.

SPIRIT OF POWER

God gave us a spirit not of fear but of power and love and self-control.
2 TIMOTHY 1:7–8 ESV

The fifth prayer of the 268 Declaration is bold, terrifying, and exhilarating to pray. Leaving behind our own desires, we give all to Christ and ask Him to use us in His mission (Philippians 3:13–14). If praying these words scares you, take courage from Paul.

Paul wrote his second letter to Timothy while awaiting execution. In the letter, Paul encouraged Timothy to be confident in God's provision and not to fear persecution. Suffering is inevitable in following Jesus—He suffered, and so must we—but God gives us power to stand up while we're wading through it. When an obstacle seems impossible to overcome, take heart that Jesus has overcome the world and has good plans for His people (Matthew 28:20; Romans 8:28). The Spirit in us destroys our fear, and replaces it with perfect love and boldness.

Be encouraged: God will equip you with everything you need to accomplish what He has for you. Giving everything for the sake of the gospel is a radical, dangerous lifestyle. But God does not call us to exist in quiet mediocrity; He invites and equips us to live with a higher purpose, sharing the news of life with everyone who will believe.

Lord God, I choose You and Your mission. Equip me and give me confidence in Your perfect sovereignty.

PURE GOSPEL

What I received I passed on to you as of first importance: that Christ
died for our sins according to the Scriptures, that he was buried,
that he was raised on the third day according to the Scriptures,
and that he appeared to Cephas, and then to the Twelve.

1 CORINTHIANS 15:3–5

In today's verse, we see that Paul considered the spread of the gospel the most important part of his life. Notice the words Paul used: what he "received," meaning he did not create the gospel; and he "passed [it] on," meaning he did not alter the gospel.

The message Paul delivered is simple and straightforward: the story of the life, death, and resurrection of Jesus Christ. Christians are often tempted to try to change the gospel to make it more appealing. But when they do that, they weaken the gospel's message. That's why Paul reminds us that no matter what we do, the gospel should be what dictates our message—and not the other way around.

We've all been given passions and gifts to spread Jesus' fame in the world. There are many needs we can meet and causes we can champion that'll let us to use those gifts for God's glory. Yet, just like Paul, our first priority should be spreading the gospel in everything we do. So as you pursue your Christian walk and unite your passions with causes in this world, never lose sight of what's most important: the full story of Jesus Christ—the gospel.

> Lord, wherever I go, may spreading Your fame be my deepest passion.

NO PRESSURE

"But you will receive power when the Holy Spirit comes on
you; and you will be my witnesses in Jerusalem, and in all
Judea and Samaria, and to the ends of the earth."

ACTS 1:8

Many of us feel enormous pressure to be a "good Christians" and to share Jesus with others. But sometimes we need to take a step back and realize that God hasn't abandoned us to fulfill this mission alone; He has equipped us through the Holy Spirit.

Note the phrase "Holy Spirit comes on you." Naturally, nothing inside us moves us to share the gospel, but the power of Jesus inside of us compels us to share. What a powerful thing to realize that the pressure is not on us to *do*, but we are instead called to *surrender* to the Holy Spirit—and He'll help us out!

With the gift of the Holy Spirit comes the promise that God will call us outside of our comfort zones. Jesus declares that we will be His witnesses in Jerusalem (for His audience, their homes) and in Samaria (a foreign place for His followers). But remember: He calls us not out of our own strength, but out of His strength. That takes the pressure off us—what freedom!

> Lord, what a gift You have given me: Your Holy Spirit! Whenever I feel incapable or afraid, help me remember that You are my strength.

A GOD WHO WELCOMES ALL

*Then Peter began to speak: "I now realize how true it is
that God does not show favoritism but accepts from every
nation the one who fears him and does what is right."*

ACTS 10:34–35

Romans and Jews did not get along, and the thought that a Roman
would partake in the gospel, particularly in the Holy Spirit, was
unheard of. So when Peter encountered Cornelius, a religious and
devout Roman, he was shocked by what he saw. The Lord didn't
just guide Peter to Cornelius's house to share the gospel—He
straight-up *interrupted* Peter's message as He poured the Holy
Spirit onto Cornelius and his entire household. This is when Peter
realized that the Lord does not play favorites, but welcomes anyone who sincerely fears and follows Him.

God's mercy doesn't operate under human standards. His
kindness doesn't draw lines, casting out people by their race,
background, or societal status. Instead, the gospel shows us that
God will always accept those who fear and honestly seek Him.

Do we as Christians sometimes play favorites when it comes
to sharing the gospel? This passage reminds us that we should seek
all who are lost, not just those we feel comfortable sharing our
faith with. God doesn't show favoritism, and neither should we.

> Lord, help me to be unreserved with Your good news and
> sensitive to Your love for all people.

POURED OUT

But you, keep your head in all situations, endure hardship, do the work of an evangelist, discharge all the duties of your ministry. For I am already being poured out like a drink offering, and the time for my departure is near. I have fought the good fight, I have finished the race, I have kept the faith.

2 TIMOTHY 4:5–7

If you are in Christ, every aspect of your life is ministry; relationships, family, work, and activity all exist to proclaim God's authority, power, and worth. The road is long, and the journey will take our all—but one day, we will look back and see the results of our work. God will be praised, and we will be overjoyed.

In today's scripture, Paul said that his ministry—his life's work—was to give himself completely to others, pouring out his life over the lives of those around him so they could be saved. As he pursued Christ, no cost was too great to fulfill his duties.

Is your pursuit of Jesus characterized by such passion? Are you doing things today that will cause you to one day look back and say with Paul, "I fought the good fight, finished the race and kept the faith"? As you make your decisions today, whether in hardship or in "all situations," consider your ministry. Yes, your life is a ministry, and one that requires pouring yourself out over and over again. Pause to ask God for strength, and remember that we are promised the crown of righteousness from the Author of life when we pour out our lives for those Christ loves and calls.

> Jesus, give me the strength to fulfill my ministry, encouraged by the certainty of Your final victory.

THE WATCHMAN

"Son of man, I have made you a watchman for the people of Israel;
so hear the word I speak and give them warning from me."
 EZEKIEL 3:17

The work we have been tasked with is not small or inconsequential; it takes constant care to make sure it gets done. Like a watchman who watches over his city, we are also called to watch over those around us—and warn them if they're in danger of spending eternity apart from God.

Don't let the responsibility of your call leave you overwhelmed or paralyzed. Though your calling may be tough, God designed your path to lead to this very place. And just as Jesus prepared Ezekiel, He'll prepare you too.

When he started his mission, Ezekiel did some specific things we can glean from: he feasted on the Word; he listened to the Spirit and followed His direction; and he sat among his hurting, lost people, to feel their need for the Lord. He felt the weight of the responsibility the Lord gave him, and had to rebuke the people of their evil actions while also telling them about God's redemption.

When it came to delivering God's message, Ezekiel never gave up. Though it can be daunting to deliver hard truths, we also get to deliver good news! So don't give up: be the messenger that God has called you to be.

Jesus, open my heart to the people I sit with day after day. Give me a heart of compassion, and help me tell them about the gift that has changed my life forever.

THE PRESENT TASK

Then he said to his disciples, "The harvest is plentiful, but the workers are few. Ask the Lord of the harvest, therefore, to send out workers into his harvest field."

MATTHEW 9:37–38

From natives on a desert island to business executives on Wall Street, people who don't know Jesus are everywhere. When we think of the sheer volume of unbelievers, it's hard to believe our lives can make a dent in that number, and that can paralyze us from talking about our faith even with the person next door.

Thankfully the first step in reaching "the harvest" doesn't begin with a plan, vision, or strategy. It simply starts with prayer—an authentic conversation with the Lord that aligns our hearts with His purposes. Prayer moves us to trust and obey: if God calls us to give, we give; if He calls us to go, we go; and if He presents us with an opportunity to share His name to the neighbor next door, we do it with boldness. Today's verse advises us to begin with prayer, asking Jesus to send us as workers to the field. Then we move in obedience, following Him wherever He leads us to share His name and fame.

> Father, help me engage people who do not know You. I trust in You, and I want to obey You with my life.

INTO ALL THE WORLD

He said to them, "Go into all the world and preach the gospel to all creation."
MARK 16:15

Jesus' call to "go into all the world" conjures images of visiting distant countries and exotic cultures—it can make us wonder if we should quit school and travel the world for Jesus. While some people are called to that life, not all of us were made to be missionaries in other countries. But we are all called to share Christ's message with the people in our lives. He has crafted us for just this time, in just this place. All we need to do is say yes and go.

Even if we stay in one place, we shouldn't live sedentary lives. There's always something to be done in your corner of creation—always someone to tell. Jesus is the answer to every human's longings, but some people don't know His name. We are blessed with the knowledge of Christ and a relationship with Him, so it is our responsibility, actually our privilege, to share Jesus wherever we go. None of us knows how much time we have on earth, or how long we'll be where we are. You might only have a limited amount of time to share with those in your current sphere. That's why this command is so urgent—but don't let it overwhelm you. Trust Christ to give you the words to say, the courage to say them, and the discernment to know who needs them.

> God, please help me share Your gospel enthusiastically. Your good news is so contagious that I cannot keep what I know to myself.

FAITH TO TALK ABOUT

*I thank my God through Jesus Christ for all of you, because
your faith is being reported all over the world.*
ROMANS 1:8

The Roman Christians had the kind of faith that was talked about all around the world. This God-given faith in the risen King drew people in, spread the message, and caused Paul to break out in joyful thanksgiving in today's verse.

The Roman church faced intense persecution, but the believers still rejoiced in proclaiming God's goodness and salvation. No earthly circumstances could deter their faith. And our faith can still speak just as loudly and reach just as widely as the Romans' faith did. When we trust God with our lives, He provides faith that will change hearts and change the world.

God says that a mustard seed–sized faith can literally move a mountain. Do you trust all that He has promised? By solely depending on God's provision for our lives, we open ourselves to all He can and will do through us. When we faithfully follow God, He will faithfully lead us in every step as we spread His name all over the world!

Dear God, I pray that my faith in You speaks loudly through my life. Through my dependence on You, may people be drawn in to know You more.

PROMISE-BASED CONFIDENCE

Among the gods there is none like you, Lord; no deeds can compare
with yours. All the nations you have made will come and worship
before you, Lord; they will bring glory to your name. For you
are great and do marvelous deeds; you alone are God.

PSALM 86:8–10

David saw God work in his life in marvelous ways, and he knew that the Lord alone was God. Sandwiched between David's awe is the extraordinary promise in today's passage—that all the nations *will* come and worship and they *will* bring glory to God's name. This is a guarantee. Until that time, we get to tell others of how great our God is and all that He has done for us. We become proclaimers, awestruck and amazed that the God of all creation personally knows us and that He has saved us. We are alive in Jesus.

God is deeply passionate about reaching "all the nations" for His glory. He invites us to join Him, that we may declare to the world how God has changed our lives. Our best testament is our own personal experience of God.

If all nations will come and worship Jesus, how are we bringing people with us as we march toward that day? Who are we engaging with and sharing with about how God has changed us? No one is like our God; therefore, we proclaim His name.

> Jesus, because of Your promises, allow us to confidently spread Your fame to all people and all nations.

REMEMBER THE NEEDY

Whoever oppresses the poor shows contempt for their Maker,
but whoever is kind to the needy honors God.

PROVERBS 14:31

God spoke, and out of nothing, the wonders of the heavens and earth danced gloriously into existence. From the dust of this earth, the most precious of all creation was made: humanity. In a declaration of identity, the Godhead announced, "Let us make mankind in our image" (Genesis 1:26). So God formed a human body from the dust of the ground and breathed into Adam the breath of life.

All humans, without trying, are the very reflection of their Maker. The rich and the poor alike are a mirror of the beauty and creativity of God. If you oppress, neglect, or mistreat the poor, you dishonor and insult God, their Maker. However, if you are kind to them, you honor and obey God.

Honor the poor. Take care of their needs. Look past the problems and the need and see the prized creation of the God of heaven staring back at you. Love them, and you love God's chosen. Honor them, and you honor God's image.

Jesus, let me look at the needy and see You, that I may honor You as I honor them.

A BEAUTIFUL LIFE

Love must be sincere. Hate what is evil; cling to what is good. Be devoted to one another in love. Honor one another above yourselves. Never be lacking in zeal, but keep your spiritual fervor, serving the Lord. Be joyful in hope, patient in affliction, faithful in prayer. Share with the Lord's people who are in need. Practice hospitality.

ROMANS 12:9–13

This passage shows us the beauty of a life modeled after Jesus. Human edicts and false religious practices have made Christianity look more like a checklist than a lifestyle. Unbiblical religious practices and attitudes have always pushed people far away from the foot of the cross. But the kind of life Paul described here is full of what people crave—love, goodness, devotion, honor, joy, hope, and hospitality.

Scripture shows us that God is concerned with how we treat others because it reveals our heart's condition and our character. And God calls us to be like Him, because being like Him enhances the quality of our lives.

If you want to follow Jesus, look at the words above and ask yourself, "Does my life look like this? How does the way I treat others reveal who I am?" This scripture and the life of Jesus show us that our lives matter when we give everything to serve others and to know Him.

Jesus, show me how to follow Your example. You lived on this earth, not to condemn or judge, but to show what it looks like love others. Let me be more like You every day.

KEEP MINISTERING

They preached the gospel in that city and won a large number of disciples.
Then they returned to Lystra, Iconium and Antioch, strengthening the
disciples and encouraging them to remain true to the faith. "We must
go through many hardships to enter the kingdom of God," they said.

ACTS 14:21–23

Remember when you said *the* prayer? The moment you put your faith in Jesus and entered into relationship with Him? Maybe it happened at a church gathering, a camp, or maybe even your own home. That moment was huge, but that was just the start of your journey. As believers we always aim to grow deeper in our relationship with Jesus, but even more, we continually minister the gospel, not just to unbelievers, but to believers as well.

In Acts we see that Paul and Barnabas were around the same people over and over again. They didn't keep moving from one place to another without checking in with those they had already ministered to. Imagine if Paul and Barnabas had just shared the good news, planted the church, and then left. Wouldn't those early believers feel discouraged in their faith? That's why we continually need to minister to each other, even after the moment of conversion. Let's go beyond the initial moment of faith and keep strengthening our brothers and sisters.

> Lord, help me minister to those around me, knowing that the ministry of the gospel is for a lifetime, not just a short moment.

THE NEXT GENERATION

*Since my youth, God, you have taught me, and to this day I
declare your marvelous deeds. Even when I am old and gray,
do not forsake me, my God, till I declare your power to the next
generation, your mighty acts to all who are to come.*

PSALM 71:17–18

Life is a journey—and with Jesus, it is a journey forward, deeper
into relationship with Him. As He directs our steps, we have
infinite reasons to declare the miraculous things He has done.
And as long as we live, we will leave a legacy of the power and joy
that comes from a relationship with Christ and show the truth of
God's promises for the next generation.

The psalmist describes the importance of passing on God's
truth and power to future generations. As young leaders, our
hearts and minds must be set on investing in our peers and rais-
ing up the next generation to fervently follow Christ.

Because of His faithfulness and provision, our eagerness
to further His name should increase as we walk through life
with Him.

Today, reflect on God's marvelous deeds throughout
history—both in books and in your own life. Then, fueled by
remembrance, seek out opportunities to speak of His power to the
next generation.

> Father, I'm thankful that You use people like me to carry the
> Your gospel through generations. Use the wisdom and tal-
> ents You've entrusted to me to shine the gospel to all people.

COMPASSION

Continue to remember those in prison as if you were together with them in prison, and those who are mistreated as if you yourselves were suffering.

HEBREWS 13:3

The Christian community that received the letter of Hebrews experienced hardship early in their faith. They were persecuted, publicly shamed, and had their property confiscated. But in the midst of these hardships, they stood side by side with their brothers and sisters in prison, joyfully facing persecution because they knew they had a lasting inheritance in Christ (Hebrews 10:32–34). Now, in today's verse, they are being reminded to do that once again: to show compassion for the church, not simply through felt emotion, but through emotion put into action.

Living behind metal bars is not something many of us have experienced, but we know that there are many brothers and sisters who are in prison for their faith. Sometimes we are so far removed from their suffering that it can be easy to forget them, but we must remember them as if we were in prison and suffering persecution together. Take a second and put yourself in their shoes; God is calling us to remember them, not just with our prayers, but with our actions. Will you act in compassion for them today?

> God, please give strength to those who are in prison, suffering for Your name. Show me how I can help care and minister to them.

HUMAN AUTHORITY

Submit yourselves for the Lord's sake to every human authority: whether to the emperor, as the supreme authority, or to governors, who are sent by him to punish those who do wrong and to commend those who do right. For it is God's will that by doing good you should silence the ignorant talk of foolish people.

1 PETER 2:13–15

Ignorance is loud. It often drowns out righteous voices, but ignorance is nothing more than a fading echo compared to a righteous and obedient life. As merely sojourners in the world, it's difficult to know how we should respond to the world's rules, but today's passage points out that our obedience to Christ also means obedience to authority. Why? Because God works through authority just as He does through our lives.

Although this world encourages individualism and selfishness, Scripture reveals the power of submission and obedience. When we obey, we aren't proclaiming the glory of any system; we're proclaiming God's glory. Peter mentioned how the suffering we endure while in obedience is an image of Christ's obedience. Although this doesn't mean we are to obey authority even when we know we're disobeying God, Peter's words mean that we shouldn't view ourselves as warriors against worldly systems, but rather as ambassadors for God's message. In times when our cities, schools, and government seem to be against us, recall how Christ endured suffering despite His perfection, and endure.

Lord, ease my anger over injustice toward myself, and guide me in knowing when to stand for others and Your truth.

SELFLESS SERVICE

One Sabbath, when Jesus went to eat in the house of a prominent Pharisee, he was being carefully watched. There in front of him was a man suffering from abnormal swelling of his body. Jesus asked the Pharisees and experts in the law, "Is it lawful to heal on the Sabbath or not?" But they remained silent. So taking hold of the man, he healed him and sent him on his way. Then he asked them, "If one of you has a child or an ox that falls into a well on the Sabbath day, will you not immediately pull it out?" And they had nothing to say.

LUKE 14:1–6

The Sabbath is a day of rest, to be spent in worship and reverence of God. It was made for our benefit—to redirect us to God's heart in a world that constantly demands our work. The Pharisees, however, used the Sabbath as an excuse to remain indifferent toward those in need. In contrast to the Pharisees' hypocrisy, Jesus offered His power to bring healing and rest.

Most of us think we're like Jesus, mindful of the needs right in front of us. But how many times have we missed out on opportunities to help someone who is suffering because we were focused on ourselves?

The Pharisees were known for their legalism, and in their pride, they made excuses to ignore a person in need. Similarly, we tend to be quick to help in situations that have some sort of benefit in store for us, but turn away from difficulty. Yet Jesus urges us to set our own interests aside and do whatever it takes to demonstrate and preach the gospel among all people—whatever the cost.

Lord, give me opportunities to serve others selflessly.

SPEAK UP

Speak up for those who cannot speak for themselves, for the rights of all who are destitute. Speak up and judge fairly; defend the rights of the poor and needy.

PROVERBS 31:8–9

Did you know that Jesus speaks to God about you?

Genesis says that God created humankind in His image. Since we have the fingerprints of the Almighty stamped into our DNA, we are infinitely valuable to Him and carry His glory. When we were unable to speak for ourselves, Jesus was the one who spoke on our behalf to God, and He continues to do so. This is a heartwarming feeling and also a beautiful example for us.

The world is dealing with so much pain, suffering, bondage, and despair, yet God wants to use us to fight for others who cannot fight for themselves. There are people, created in His image, who have never heard the hope we cling to. We have an amazing opportunity to speak to God and to others on behalf of those who do not know Him, or who are trapped in situations where they cannot speak for themselves. We can do this in a number of ways, but it always starts with speaking to God on their behalf through prayer.

Pray today for the lost, destitute, poor, and needy. Don't let the silent cries of those who need eternal hope and earthly care go unnoticed.

Father, help me today to see people the way You see them and to fight in hope that they may know Your name.

LET IT BE KNOWN

In that day you will say: "Give praise to the LORD, proclaim his name; make known among the nations what he has done, and proclaim that his name is exalted. Sing to the LORD, for he has done glorious things; let this be known to all the world."

ISAIAH 12:4–5

Think back and remember: what has your faith journey been like so far?

Every step is a line in your story. Through the trials and the joys, we are called to give praise to the Lord, to proclaim who God is and what He's done, to remember what hard times we have had and how the Lord walked with us through them for His glory and our good.

When we remember the joys and blessings God has bestowed, we can see how much He loves to give good gifts. We remember so we will not lose sight of the Lord's faithfulness, and so we will not turn our eyes back to ourselves. Ultimately, we remember and proclaim!

Today, no matter your circumstances, you have a story: a wonderful story of how a loving God died for you, rose again, and loves you unconditionally and eternally. "Let this be known to all the world . . ."

> Lord, give me the stillness to remember Your goodness with each step of my journey. I rejoice in where You have brought me today. Let me be bold to share Your message with others so they will exalt You too.

SAYING YES

But if I say, "I will not mention his word or speak anymore in his name," his word is in my heart like a fire, a fire shut up in my bones. I am weary of holding it in; indeed, I cannot.

JEREMIAH 20:9

When God speaks, one of two reactions follows: either a joyful *yes* or a heart-sinking *no*. God is looking for followers who will say yes to trusting Him and carrying His message to the world.

When Jeremiah was too young to even speak, God called him to be a prophet. But Jeremiah wasn't asked to be a regular prophet; he was to prophesy about God's coming judgment because the people had turned away from Him. Jeremiah's calling got him beaten and mocked by his own people and eventually landed him in jail. There, Jeremiah realized the absolute power of God's Word; trying to bury it inside him was like trying to contain fire! Although his message caused controversy, making him want to quit his calling, Jeremiah knew that the people needed to hear God's Word.

Sometimes we don't want to do what God asks us to do. His requests often put us in awkward situations with our friends, make us vulnerable, and require a lot from us. But in the end, God is asking us to obey and carry His message to others, so they can know Him. Today, when He asks you to speak, will you obey?

> Lord, though I do not know what the question is, I want to say yes to what You ask from me. Give me the strength to proclaim Your truths faithfully.

HE HELPS FOR US

Blessed are those whose help is the God of Jacob,
whose hope is in the LORD their God.

PSALM 146:5

We have a God who fights for us. The Creator of the mountains, the waves, and the universe goes to battle for you each day. He fights for the oppressed, provides for those in need, frees those in bondage, gives sight to the blind, and watches over the wanderer. We are blessed because of who He is and who we are in Him. He created us for an intimate relationship, and He is incredibly faithful in His love.

We have nothing to fear—because of Him. Persecution, suffering, and whatever comes cannot paralyze you because the God who created everything backs you. The most powerful Being in existence is our Helper, and He equips us for great things! This absence of fear frees us to go wholeheartedly after what God is passionate about. As His hands and feet, we get the opportunity to feed the hungry, take care of the widows and the fatherless, and lift up those who are in need. Is there something you want to do for Him, but you're afraid you won't have the resources? Don't worry—the God of Jacob is working through you, and He will help you.

Jesus, thank You for being a God of love. Give me opportunities to fight for freedom and justice along with You.

GIVE FREELY

*If anyone has material possessions and sees a brother or sister in need
but has no pity on them, how can the love of God be in that person? Dear
children, let us not love with words or speech but with actions and in truth.*

1 JOHN 3:17–18

There is no limit to Jesus' generosity. And because we've put our trust in Him, He makes us a generous people.

What does generosity look like for you? Is it related to money or food or possessions or time? How does a generous person respond to a need? Today's passage clarifies: "with actions and in truth." Not just with a prayer (though prayer is essential), and not merely with good intentions. It is with action, with the truth of God's love behind you.

What's holding you back from living a generous life? Are you consumed by fear that you might run out of the things God has given to you, or do you feel like you have nothing to give to begin with? Regardless of what you think you're capable of, remind your heart that there are new mercies today and that you've been given what you need by the One you need. Let this be the overflow that spreads love with action—from material goods to the gospel—to those around you.

> Jesus, thank You that You don't withhold any good thing from me, but You generously give me everything I need. Help me to see people who are in need of Your generosity today.

FROM OBLIGATION TO ACTION

*Learn to do right; seek justice, Defend the oppressed. Take up
the cause of the fatherless; plead the case of the widow.*

Isaiah 1:17

Earlier in Isaiah, God expressed His disdain for the practices
of Judah and Jerusalem. Even though they completed all of the
religious festivals, sacrifices, and prayer times required, God saw
they weren't living for Him outside of their self-righteous requirements. He told the people their practices meant nothing to Him if
they didn't result in justice for others.

We may not hold the same sacrifices and festivals today, but
we encounter the same attitudes as the people in Isaiah's day when
we allow our faith actions to become a routine instead of a way of
life. Church can turn into a box to check off on Sundays, and even
Bible studies can turn into a scheduled obligation.

God wants all of us, beyond the time we squeeze Him into
our calendars. When God is our life and not just our religion, we
yearn to seek Him and live in His image twenty-four hours a day,
seven days a week. How does this show in our lives? In burning to
love and help His children, as Isaiah prophesied in today's passage.

So instead of seeing where He fits in our lives, let's try to see
where we fit in His eternal plan for justice.

Dear God, Your ways are too good for just Sunday. Help me
seek You always and serve in Your name.

FAR FROM FORGIVENESS

Therefore I want you to know that God's salvation has
been sent to the Gentiles, and they will listen!
ACTS 28:28

While we may not like to admit it, we can all think of someone who seems like too great a challenge for Jesus. In our eyes, there are some people we consider too far removed to receive God's grace.

When the apostle Paul obeyed God's call to proclaim the gospel to the Gentiles, many Jews criticized him for it. The Jews had suffered slavery, captivity, and death at the hands of the Gentiles, and yet God was choosing to include them in His kingdom? How could this be? The Gentiles were the nations and tribes outside of traditional Jewish heritage. Throughout history, these nations often oppressed and persecuted the Israelites. Yet Paul proclaimed the promises and blessing of salvation to the Gentiles. In this radical message, the heart of God is displayed. In the sacrifice of Christ for the sins of all humanity, God extended love to all, even those who hated Him.

Christ made it possible for the enemies of God to receive forgiveness. Christ endured ridicule, torture, and death for those who hated and persecuted Him, so we are called to share Christ with those who mock and mistreat us. Now that God has forgiven you, invite even those you consider unworthy into relationship with Christ, so they too can experience grace and forgiveness.

Father, forgive me of my partiality. Open my eyes to let me see people as You see them: broken, lonely, and in need of Your love.

EMPTY YOURSELF

"If you do away with the yoke of oppression, with the pointing finger and malicious talk, and if you spend yourselves in behalf of the hungry and satisfy the needs of the oppressed, then your light will rise in the darkness, and your night will become like the noonday. The LORD will guide you always; he will satisfy your needs in a sun-scorched land and will strengthen your frame. You will be like a well-watered garden, like a spring whose waters never fail."

ISAIAH 58:9–11

Before the galaxies came to be, God knew you. He formed your frame and gave you the breath of life, the profusion of His passion. Yet your intricate design was not fashioned to accumulate, but to empty. God made you to be a blessing, so in spending yourself for others, the world would be touched with His love.

You are invited to release all that you have—your time, money, strength, and heart—to feed the hungry and satisfy the needs of the oppressed. In the hollow of your emptied spirit, He will continue to fill you. As you are full of Him, God will draw others to His light.

So pour out every drop of your being without a care about tomorrow. God will replenish you with even more to give. Spend yourself for the hungry, and God will feed your spirit. Satisfy the needs of the oppressed, and God will satisfy your every need. Spend your all, and just wait; His light will radiate from you.

> Jesus, thank You that, though Your command is to empty, You promise to fill. In faith, all that I am, I release to You.

HEART INTENTIONS

"Be careful not to practice your righteousness in front of others to be seen by them. If you do, you will have no reward from your Father in heaven. So when you give to the needy, do not announce it with trumpets, as the hypocrites do in the synagogues and on the streets, to be honored by others. Truly I tell you, they have received their reward in full. But when you give to the needy, do not let your left hand know what your right hand is doing, so that your giving may be in secret. Then your Father, who sees what is done in secret, will reward you."

MATTHEW 6:1–4

Throughout history, people have reasoned that if we could impress God by doing good deeds, then we could get things from Him. But when Jesus came, He preached a different message. He reminded us that God cares about more than our actions; He cares about our *intentions*.

First Samuel 16:7 says, "People look at the outward appearance, but the LORD looks at the heart." God wants us to obey Him because we love Him and want to glorify Him, not just because we want to impress others or gain something from Him. Jesus tells us that He would rather have our hearts devoted to His glory, with lives reflecting His generosity and grace, than to have our hearts focused on lifeless adherence to a set of legalistic rules.

So before we give to those in need, let us first give the intentions of our hearts to God. And let us ask ourselves, are we giving to impress others or to glorify God?

Jesus, I give You my heart today. Help me to give with the right motivation.

WALKING WITH GOD

*He has shown you, O mortal, what is good. And what does the Lord require
of you? To act justly and to love mercy and to walk humbly with your God.*

MICAH 6:8

Only the path of walking humbly with God will lead to something that endures past our lifetimes. No matter how grand, all other paths we walk without the Lord by our side will return to dust. The command in today's verse might intimidate us as we wonder if we're walking humbly with God. Yet the good news is that the Lord promises to be with us as we are conformed to Jesus' image through His Word. As the gospel works in us, our hearts are awakened to the presence of God and to those who cross our path every day.

Living in the reality of the gospel means that we live as Jesus lives. All His ways are just; ours must be too. He sits on the great mercy seat; we must also show mercy to those in need. He has died for the enemies of His kingdom, redeeming them by His Spirit; we are to deal in unmistakable generosity, even through our own sacrifice, toward those around us.

Jesus is calling us to walk with Him and work for a kingdom that will never fade. As His presence goes with you, let His Word compel you to act justly, love mercy, and walk humbly with God.

Lord, establish my work today as I walk humbly with You.

RELATIONSHIP RESTORED

All this is from God, who reconciled us to himself through Christ and gave us the ministry of reconciliation: that God was reconciling the world to himself in Christ, not counting people's sins against them. And he has committed to us the message of reconciliation.

2 Corinthians 5:18–19

There is little that grieves the heart more than a broken relationship. At the root of many broken relationships is the feeling we've been wronged, which compels us to feel entitled to wait for an apology that may never come.

Paul had a strained relationship with the church at Corinth. After he rebuked some individuals for immoral behavior and idolatry, a divisive group formed within the church and challenged the apostle's authority. The distress within the church was so great that it attracted a group of rival preachers, who further damaged Paul's reputation and ministry. Deeply hurt, Paul implored the church to repent of its petty quarreling and return to the gospel. By causing division and strife within the church, the Corinthians had rejected their new identity as Christ's ambassadors and instead became active opponents of God's work.

Christ has restored us to relationship with God so we can live the hope we have in Jesus. Today, look for ways to forgive those who have wronged you and always be first to initiate and encourage reconciliation.

Father, I was once Your enemy, but You changed my heart. Teach me to forgive and restore.

OVERCOME EVIL WITH GOOD

Do not take revenge, my dear friends, but leave room for God's wrath, for it is written: "It is mine to avenge; I will repay," says the Lord. On the contrary: "If your enemy is hungry, feed him; if he is thirsty, give him something to drink. In doing this, you will heap burning coals on his head." Do not be overcome by evil, but overcome evil with good.

ROMANS 12:19–21

It doesn't take much more than a quick glance through the top TV ratings to realize our culture loves a good revenge story and to see people getting their comeuppance. We crave revenge on the people who have hurt us, stolen from us, wronged us, lied to us, taken advantage of us, or cheated us. We want the people who inflicted or allowed the pain to hurt like we have hurt.

But Jesus has another plan for us. He doesn't stop at telling us not to avenge our pain, and He doesn't tell us to just forget it and move on; He calls us to provide, care for, pray for, and serve our enemies!

Jesus longs to fill our hearts with His goodness. The more we serve, forgive, and love like Him, the less room we will have in our hearts for anger and bitterness. This is the way to abundant life. Only with Jesus are we able to forgive, realizing He first forgave us. So instead of indulging in revenge fantasies, let's leave it to God and be defined by Christ's revolutionary forgiveness.

Jesus, help me forgive my enemies and those who have wronged me. I no longer want to carry bitterness in my heart.

TRANSFORMED HEARTS

Circumcise your hearts, therefore, and do not be stiff-necked any longer. For the LORD your God is God of gods and Lord of lords, the great God, mighty and awesome, who shows no partiality and accepts no bribes. He defends the cause of the fatherless and the widow, and loves the foreigner residing among you.

DEUTERONOMY 10:16–19

Our Lord created the galaxies and knows the stars by name. He reigns over all things. Still, He knows each of us more intimately than we know ourselves and desires to walk with us daily. He tells the sun when to set and rise, yet He defends the oppressed, seeks justice for the fatherless, and pleads the widow's cause.

While the people in the Old Testament were only concerned with physical circumcision, God desired more than external conformity; today's passage tells us that He requires an internal transformation. This is the circumcision of the heart that He commands in Deuteronomy. God wants us to cut out whatever is in our hearts that keeps us from whole-hearted devotion to loving, knowing, and following Him above all else. When our hearts are completely focused on Him, our lives conform to His will.

God sought you when you had nothing to offer Him but your brokenness. In response, seek justice and offer freedom through the gospel to those who can offer you nothing in return.

> Lord, ignite the desire in me to engage poverty and injustice, and give me the ability to love people impartially so that they might experience You and bring You praise.

THE ANSWER

Rejoice with those who rejoice; mourn with those who mourn. Live in harmony with one another. Do not be proud, but be willing to associate with people of low position. Do not be conceited.

Romans 12:15–16

Jesus at work in our lives marks us with countercultural qualities. The world tells us to be proud and self-serving, but our faith tells us to mingle with people who don't have much power. Culture tells us we get what we deserve, but we don't deserve the grace of God—yet it is still given to us freely. Culture tells us to look like we're on top of things at all costs, but today's verse tells us to stay humble—and to be attentive to those around us as they both rejoice and weep. This is the beauty of the gospel, and one of the many reasons we celebrate and worship God; and this same grace is freely offered to all who simply believe.

Today, remember that we are all equal under the grace of God, and the impact this has on our stories. Allow this to push you into an attitude of humility. Look for people, near and far, who are searching for answers, who are suffering, who are rejoicing, and respond to them in love. Seek harmony, and have the boldness to share Jesus with everyone. Together we can spread His love by abandoning pride and running relentlessly after a lost, broken world.

God, thank You for Your grace. Help me to keep a right attitude about my place in the world, and show me where I can minister to others today.

TRUE FASTING

"Is not this the kind of fasting I have chosen: to loose the chains of injustice and untie the cords of the yoke, to set the oppressed free and break every yoke? Is it not to share your food with the hungry and to provide the poor wanderer with shelter—when you see the naked, to clothe them, and not to turn away from your own flesh and blood? Then your light will break forth like the dawn, and your healing will quickly appear; then your righteousness will go before you, and the glory of the LORD will be your rear guard."

ISAIAH 58:6–8

The first and greatest commandment, to love the Lord your God with all of your heart, is also the hardest for us to follow. We are often guilty of the same sin that God rebuked Israel for through Isaiah: even in our fasting and religious activity, we often don't honor God in our hearts

When fasting, the Israelites sought their own pleasure and security, all the while neglecting the needs of those around them. True fasting means setting your heart on God and His will; this compels us to show God's love for His people.

The brokenness of Isaiah's time is still prevalent today; knowing this, we must still practice "fasting." God tells us through Isaiah what His heart desires. Let's seek to loose the chains of injustice, to plead the cause of the oppressed, and to provide for the poor. Let our fasting be giving up our selfishness in order to share His love with those around us.

> Father, please set my heart fully on You. I want to live out Your love in the midst of the brokenness of this world.

TO DIE IS GAIN

For me, to live is Christ and to die is gain.
PHILIPPIANS 1:21

Paul confessed an inner struggle to the Philippian church. He explained that to him, it was better for him to die than to live, because his deepest desire was to be in heaven with Jesus. But he also said that he understood he had a responsibility to spread the gospel, and he knew living longer gave him more time to do so. He considered this responsibility a privilege, so he chose to sacrifice his desire to be in heaven with Jesus, so he could have more time to spread the gospel on earth.

When we die, we will stand face-to-face with Jesus and experience the fullness of His presence. That's why we can say "to die is gain." We don't know when God will call us home to be with Him, but when He does, we won't be able to invite others into eternity anymore.

Like Paul, we can look forward to joy in heaven with Jesus. Let's fix our eyes on that future, and make seeing Jesus the deepest desire of our hearts. Yet we only have a limited time to share Him with others. So with heaven as our focus, let's live our lives urgently sharing the gospel, so that others can experience Him for eternity too.

God, fix my eyes on heaven. Be the one desire of my heart. Help me live a life that points others to You.

A SAVIOR TO THE LOST

"The Son of Man came to seek and to save the lost."
LUKE 19:10

Throughout the Gospels, Jesus is compared to a shepherd—one who will diligently search for and joyfully bring home a single sheep that has strayed from the rest. In the midst of humanity, our Savior's mission was to find and save everyone, including you. When you decided to follow Jesus, His mission became your purpose: sharing the gospel to restore other straying sheep.

Make it your goal to seek out and bring home the lost by participating in God's plans and proclaiming Christ's love. Identify and invest in "the one"—a specific person in your life whom God leads you to love, encourage, and tell about Jesus. How can you minister to that person? How can you respond to their needs? How can you pray for them? Take time to actively seek them, as Jesus would a lost sheep. Trust their future to Him, knowing that there is great rejoicing in heaven when one person decides to come home, and God can use you—through Christ—to make that happen.

> Lord, align my heart with Your plans for this world. Reveal to me the people in my life who are far from You and use me to bring them home.

THE ENDS OF THE EARTH

[The Lord] says: "It is too small a thing for you to be my servant to restore the tribes of Jacob and bring back those of Israel I have kept. I will also make you a light for the Gentiles, that my salvation may reach to the ends of the earth."

ISAIAH 49:6

For thousands of years, the people of Israel were God's chosen people—the only people on earth who carried the presence and blessing of God with them. When Jesus came, He swung open the gates to His kingdom, making Himself the way for all to enter. He declared God's grace and love was not just for the Jews; it was for everyone. The same is true now. God sees far beyond His church to the billions of people who do not have a clue who He is.

If we do not remind ourselves of the almighty power of God, we can easily confine the power of salvation to just ourselves or the people around us. So let's not forget: God's vision of salvation extends to the farthest recesses of the world, and He has invited us to help turn that vision into reality. Who will you invite into His family today?

> Jesus, open my eyes to the ends of the earth that desperately need to know You. Give me an uninhibited desire to join Your global mission and spread Your name among the nations.

HEAVEN ON EARTH

"This, then, is how you should pray: 'Our Father in heaven, hallowed be your name, your kingdom come, your will be done, on earth as it is in heaven.'"
MATTHEW 6:9–10

Just as Jesus teaches His disciples to pray in Matthew 6, we also learn to pray by setting His name above any other and asking for His will to be done—that the gospel shine in every corner of the world. Jesus tells us to start our prayers by asking God to bring heaven to earth. In heaven, injustice, pain, poverty, and sin will be gone forever, as we worship in the fullness of God's presence and perfect love. In praying this prayer, we ask Him to bring heaven's qualities to earth through His presence in us!

How can you bring heaven to earth today? What aspects of this broken world also break your heart and make you long for Jesus' healing and reconciliation? Pray that His will be done, and ask Him what you can do to make that happen. This task isn't specific to just one season you're in, or even to a specific group of people. Jesus wants the hearts of all people, on earth as it is in heaven. Surrender your heart and life to His will today, so He can bring heaven to earth through you.

> Jesus, You desire to save all people. I pray that my heart would align with Yours daily.

GOSPEL POWER

"This gospel of the kingdom will be preached in the whole world as a testimony to all nations, and then the end will come."

MATTHEW 24:14

When Jesus' disciples asked Him for the signs of His second coming, Jesus responded that false teachings and suffering would come, especially for His disciples. It's easy to imagine the fear and uncertainty that began creep into the disciples' thoughts. Jesus reminded His disciples that although it may seem that evil will triumph, the gospel is more influential than any false teaching and more powerful than any evil to come.

The gospel has the power and tenacity to pierce through the hardest hearts and to break down the most fortified walls. Even more amazing, it has the power to save the entire world! Do we even have a glimpse of the scope of influence and power the gospel has on this earth?

However we understand the gospel's power, let us relentlessly share it with others. As individuals, we might not be able to touch all nations, but we can definitely point every single person within our small spheres of influence to Jesus.

Lord, I ask You to remind me just how powerful Your gospel is. Thank You for my testimony and that I get to share it.

ANOINTED

The Spirit of the Sovereign LORD is on me, because the LORD has anointed me to proclaim good news to the poor. He has sent me to bind up the brokenhearted, to proclaim freedom for the captives and release from darkness for the prisoners.

ISAIAH 61:1

In today's verse, we find a kingly inauguration! Jesus, the long-awaited fulfillment of this Old Testament prophecy, astounded many who watched Him with eager expectation—those who had been bound under slavery of sin and were in desperate need of a divine Savior's hope.

Before we met Jesus, we were slaves to sin; we were under the lock of the Law we couldn't keep and without any hope of escape. Liberated from death's cold, iron chain, we should be the loudest of messengers! Through Jesus' work on our behalf, we are empowered and sent by the Holy Spirit to continue the mission that Christ Himself started.

How many of your days are characterized by the comfort and encouragement of today's passage? You are anointed through the Holy Spirit of God; nothing can stand in your way. His purposes of freedom will stand, and we, His church, are here to proclaim the liberty of the good news. Declare it well.

> Jesus, as You have liberated me from death, reach those lost around me through my proclamation of the gospel.

ETERNAL SECURITY

Command those who are rich in this present world not to be arrogant nor to put their hope in wealth, which is so uncertain, but to put their hope in God, who richly provides us with everything for our enjoyment.

1 TIMOTHY 6:17

In our culture, we are bombarded by the idea that our professions, our success, and our achievements will lead us to a fulfilling life. So we hold on to these things, believing that in them we can have the control and joy that we crave.

God actually proclaims the exact opposite. He says, "You may work and earn, but I am the Provider. You may have financial security, but I am the one who gives life and eternal security." Just as money is as uncertain as the days you will be alive, so is the fleeting joy that comes from the accumulation of things.

God's words challenge what we often hear, but they enrich the soul. Our joy begins when we take on the character of Jesus. He tells us to drop our hold on wealth, so we can grip Him and hold true riches. He calls us to be rich in generosity and good deeds—to share, so He can give us unparalleled gifts to enjoy. Relinquish your hold on what you think keeps you stable, and hold tight to Jesus. He will hold you secure for all eternity.

> Jesus, today, help me take hold of life that is truly life. Set my heart on You as my perfect Provider. You have given me everything, so let me be open-handed with others.

341

GIVE TO GIVE MORE

Each of you should give what you have decided in your heart to give,
not reluctantly or under compulsion, for God loves a cheerful giver.

2 CORINTHIANS 9:7

Have you ever opened gifts alone on Christmas or your birthday? If you have, you probably wished someone were there to share your excitement. When you are given something incredible, you want to talk about it and express thanks. The joy of receiving is only complete when the gift is shared.

This example is a reflection of God's design. Through Jesus, God shared with us the most generous gifts of all: Himself and His unlimited resources. He is a generous God, and He made us to share His incredible gifts with others. As with earthly gifts, we experience the joy of sharing when we reflect His generosity.

But this joy doesn't stop with us. Fearless generosity often brings an abundant harvest. When we give to glorify God, He not only gives us joy. He gives us more of Himself so His work keeps advancing. Our never-ending God fills us completely and constantly as we work for Him, so in everything we do, He will be glorified.

Do you view God's blessings as an opportunity to share with others, or do you have a stranglehold on the resources He's given you? Trust His promised provision today, and share what you have with joy!

> Jesus, thank You for giving Your life as the most generous gift of all. Let it be my joy to give for Your kingdom, so all people can see You.

THE LEAST OF THESE

"Then the righteous will answer him, 'Lord, when did we see you
hungry and feed you, or thirsty and give you something to drink?
When did we see you a stranger and invite you in, or needing clothes
and clothe you? When did we see you sick or in prison and go to visit
you?' The King will reply, 'Truly I tell you, whatever you did for one
of the least of these brothers and sisters of mine, you did for me.'"

MATTHEW 25:37–40

In this passage, Jesus' words are simple, but filled with incredible depth. And it is a hard truth to shake when we consider just how many times each day we pass up the "least of these": the homeless man begging for change, the classmate whose pleas for friendship are disguised as irritating insecurity, and the girl at church who spent years in an abusive relationship but suffers in silence. These people are all not only members of Christ's family, they're also representatives of Christ Himself.

How much more would we respond to and treasure others if we saw them as Jesus Himself? What's more, ask yourself who "the least of these" are to you personally. Who are those people you tend to ignore? It is just as important to feed, clothe, and welcome those in need as it is to love those who ask nothing of you.

Father, forgive me for rejecting You through the "least of these." Grant me the grace to see You in every member of Your family.

343

THROUGH HIS POWER

"But when they arrest you, do not worry about what to say or how to say it. At that time you will be given what to say, for it will not be you speaking, but the Spirit of your Father speaking through you."

MATTHEW 10:19–20

When Jesus sent out the twelve apostles, He referred to them as "sheep in the midst of wolves" (v. 16). He promised they would be hated by all, for His name's sake. He told them they'd be flogged, rejected, and arrested because of the message they preached. So why would they even go? Because Jesus sent them.

When you devote your life to preaching the gospel, you will be rejected. If we were to rely on our own strength and ability, we would fail miserably at the calling set before us. But Jesus tells us to stand firm in the midst of persecution and promises to give us the strength to do so. He encouraged the apostles not to be anxious, because the Spirit would speak in their defense. God promises persecution, but His greater promise is provision.

God will speak through you, even when you don't have the words to say. Worry and fear have no power to keep us from proclaiming His name! So speak boldly when proclaiming the gospel. Take risks. Pray for wisdom and humility, yet believe that the power of God is available to you through the Spirit.

> Father, I'm so thankful that I don't have to rely on my own abilities or strength. Give me the courage to step out in faith when proclaiming the gospel, knowing You will give me the words to speak.

344

THE IMAGE OF GOD

Then God said, "Let us make mankind in our image, in our likeness, so that they may rule over the fish in the sea and the birds in the sky, over the livestock and all the wild animals, and over all the creatures that move along the ground." So God created mankind in his own image, in the image of God he created them; male and female he created them.

GENESIS 1:26–27

When God created humanity, He blessed us with a special distinction that exalts us above all creation. This inherent value is given to every human, no matter where they come from or what they do. Humankind is the only creation described as being made in the image of God.

Humanity reflects some of God's characteristics, such as the ability to love and execute justice. God made us, as image-bearers, to bring Him glory through relationship with Him and reflection of His infinite goodness. We point others to the glory that only God holds.

When sin came into the world, humankind's perfect relationship with God was severed. But God did not leave us to wander purposeless to death and destruction. Through Him, we are restored to relationship and can again reflect His image through the power of the Spirit.

How can you shine God's image today? Through the way you choose to love? Through sacrifice? Through creativity? Generosity? Kindness? When we make much of Him, our lives join in His eternal glory and bring that goodness into focus for all to see.

God, help me reflect You in this world, and show others Your love and redemption in Jesus Christ.

GOD SAVES, WE SPEAK

It has always been my ambition to preach the gospel where Christ was not known, so that I would not be building on someone else's foundation. Rather, as it is written: "Those who were not told about him will see, and those who have not heard will understand."

ROMANS 15:20–21

Paul did not have a blueprint for how to grow the church rapidly, but he knew two very important things: he knew people needed to hear the gospel of Jesus, and he knew the Scriptures promised that those who had neither seen nor heard would believe. In light of what he knew, there was only one life that made sense—a life dedicated to preaching the gospel where Jesus was not known. He followed the Spirit into dangerous and dark regions, and he let the gospel ring out as he taught boldly.

God doesn't ask us to save people. We are not equipped to do that. He just asks us to spread His fame as a natural by-product of what we believe. When we do so, He will do what He has already promised to do: bring people to life in Him.

Without the people of Jesus spreading the gospel of Jesus, billions of people around the world will go their whole lives without getting the chance to experience the glory and love of their Creator. Feel the urgency of this call to spread His life to the nations, and make it your ambition!

> Thank You, Jesus, for sending people to speak Your gospel in my life. Give me the desire and the ability to do the same for the people who desperately need to know You.

CALLED ALL THE TIME

For two whole years Paul stayed there in his own rented house and welcomed
all who came to see him. He proclaimed the kingdom of God and taught
about the Lord Jesus Christ—with all boldness and without hindrance!

ACTS 28:30–31

How many people in your life, if any, would you give up everything for? Would you sell all you own and leave everything behind if someone asked you to? It sounds irrational, but this is exactly what it means to follow Christ. As a believer, we must be willing to go anywhere, at any time, at whatever cost to spread the name of Jesus everywhere.

While Paul waited for his case to be heard before Caesar, he did not forget the call God had placed on his life. He rented a house and built relationships with others. He welcomed all people who came to him and acted on every opportunity to tell others about Jesus.

Paul proclaimed the gospel fearlessly, and the message of salvation spread without delay or obstruction. God is inviting each of us to do the same. Let's willingly lay down our lives, give up everything we have, and follow Him where we are right now—today. Whether we feel like we're waiting or like we're moving, we can do His will at any time.

> Lord, I know You don't need me, but I'm thankful that You choose to use me in order to advance Your Kingdom. Give me the eagerness of Paul to confidently do whatever it takes for people to hear the message of Jesus.

AUTHENTICITY TRUMPS FLATTERY

Those who consider themselves religious and yet do not keep a tight rein on their tongues deceive themselves, and their religion is worthless. Religion that God our Father accepts as pure and faultless is this: to look after orphans and widows in their distress and to keep oneself from being polluted by the world.

JAMES 1:26–27

Words can be an effective smokescreen when we have something to hide. We know what to say in the right moments and we find ways to pack away our flaws so that only our achievements are seen. We use words to create a mask to cover up our fears, doubts, and insecurities. We may speak about following Jesus, but the path of our footsteps can show otherwise. When words trump actions, we not only deceive others, we deceive ourselves. This way of life is not the way of Jesus.

Our authentic story speaks louder than polished words, and our actions toward the "nobody" speak louder than our actions toward the "somebody." Religion is not passed-down tradition and hollow language. God's idea of religion is grabbing the hand of the broken person beside you, no matter who it belongs to, and leading them to life in Jesus. Whose hand will you reach for today?

> Father, I pray that I will always declare Your goodness and that my relationship with You would never be based on empty words. Each word counts, and I want all of them to align with You.

SPRING OF LIFE

Jesus answered, "Everyone who drinks this water will be thirsty again, but whoever drinks the water I give them will never thirst. Indeed, the water I give them will become in them a spring of water welling up to eternal life."

JOHN 4:13–14

When you're exhausted and faced with difficulty, what is your motivation for carrying the gospel to those around you? When everything suggests focusing inward, how do you continue to love those nearby?

In the book of John, we read that Jesus was exhausted from His travels. He sat down at a well, and up walked a Samaritan woman. This was a problem because by societal standards, Jesus was not supposed to interact with her. But the gospel is not bound by society, and Jesus was willing to minister to her. Although Jesus was weary, He knew that what He could offer was far better than what she currently had; He knew she needed the water of eternal life. Jesus chose to love this woman, and her life was forever changed. And since the gospel is exponential in power, not only did she find life, but many people from her village did as well!

Even when we are weary, grabbing a moment to rest, we keep an eye out for opportunities, trusting in God to give us strength. Because those around us need what Jesus has—true life. Everything else leaves us empty. Look around you and carry living water to those nearby; nothing could be more energizing.

Jesus, we all need new life in You. Thank You for eternal water and for giving us the motivation to carry on.

PICK UP THE CROSS

*"If anyone comes to me and does not hate father and mother,
wife and children, brothers and sisters—yes, even their own
life—such a person cannot be my disciple. And whoever does
not carry their cross and follow me cannot be my disciple."*

LUKE 14:26–27

Without cost, there is no value. You will only pay a price for a car that reflects its value. In the same way, a cross is a demonstration of value, and the extent that you value God is illustrated by the cross you bear.

The cross you carry is just a small shadow of the cross that was carried for you. You see, this same Man who demands everything *from* you has already given everything *for* you. Though a King worthy of honor, Jesus gave up His throne to die, becoming of no value because of the value He placed on you.

Your life was ransomed, and now your life is asked of you. Jesus wants you to be His disciple, but He will not settle for part of your heart—He wants all of it. So lay down your all in exchange for the cross; the cost will never outweigh the freedom found in surrender.

Jesus, let me see Your infinite value so I am compelled to pick up my cross and follow You.

LISTEN, THEN DO

Do not merely listen to the word, and so deceive yourselves. Do what it says.

JAMES 1:22

In today's passage, James encourages us to continue in the freedom in which we've been instructed so we can receive God's blessing. God wants us to take action on His Word and walk in His ways because His ways are the best for us. God-sized transformation requires God's help, but we have to say yes in order for Him to do it.

The great news is that the One who called us and began a good work in us will finish it. James said His Word lives in us, daily instructing and teaching us what to do. As easy as it may be to stay sedentary or to return to our old ways, God is calling us to so much more—to turn listening into action. In fact, if we hold on to the idea that listening is enough and doing can wait, we "deceive ourselves" into accepting something much less than what God has for us. We have the opportunity to shine His light to the world! How can you begin to discover and do what His Word says?

> Father, there's so much fighting for my attention in my life. Set my mind on Your Word, and give me the grace to do what it says. Awaken me to experience the freedom that is found in following You.

FAITH WITHOUT WORKS

What good is it, my brothers and sisters, if someone claims to have faith but has no deeds? Can such faith save them? Suppose a brother or a sister is without clothes and daily food. If one of you says to them, "Go in peace; keep warm and well fed," but does nothing about their physical needs, what good is it? In the same way, faith by itself, if it is not accompanied by action, is dead.

JAMES 2:14–17

Salvation is a high point in our new life for Jesus. But what comes after that? What do we *do* with the faith we have? Some may suggest the greatest good we can do for others is to tell them the good news that Jesus defeated death and has given life to the world. Yet Jesus gave us life so we would do more than just talk.

Later in the chapter, James showed how Old Testament figures acted in accordance to their faith; their actions brought life to both them and the people around them. So let's take our faith off the shelf. If we are all talk or thought and no action, James said, our faith is "dead." How can you, today, turn your faith into action? Ask God to reveal to you opportunities to provide for someone today.

> Jesus, help me understand that salvation is not only for my sake, but for everyone around me. Help me to be an agent of life in the world, not only in my words, but also in my actions.

THE COMPLETION OF JOY

That which was from the beginning, which we have heard, which we have seen with our eyes, which we have looked at and our hands have touched—this we proclaim concerning the Word of life. The life appeared; we have seen it and testify to it, and we proclaim to you the eternal life, which was with the Father and has appeared to us. We proclaim to you what we have seen and heard, so that you also may have fellowship with us. And our fellowship is with the Father and with his Son, Jesus Christ. We write this to make our joy complete.

1 JOHN 1:1–4

Throughout his letters, John talks about "the Word," but he's not talking about a book or a word in the dictionary. He's talking about Jesus! In this letter, John was sharing his Jesus stories with a new generation because John was one of the few people left who had seen, heard, and touched Him.

There's something powerful about our Jesus stories—real stories from real-life experiences of Jesus rescuing us, bringing us from darkness to light and from death to life. These stories don't just impact the people we share them with; they affect us as well. Joy dies when we hold it inside. But when we share it with others, joy spreads like wildfire—and it multiplies in our hearts! So today, share the joy of what Jesus has done for you with those around you, experiencing inwardly and expressing outwardly the fullness of joy God has for you.

> Jesus, thank You for giving me a story to tell. Help me tell it! I love You, and I trust You.

THE ULTIMATE REWARD

By faith Moses, when he had grown up, refused to be known as the son of Pharaoh's daughter. He chose to be mistreated along with the people of God rather than to enjoy the fleeting pleasures of sin. He regarded disgrace for the sake of Christ as of greater value than the treasures of Egypt, because he was looking ahead to his reward.

HEBREWS 11:24–26

Life seems to be full of options with many different rewards. Much of what we choose to do with our lives shapes a deeper identity, revealing where our treasure truly lies. When we choose Christ, our identity and direction are strengthened by faith and the confidence in our reward ahead.

Moses held to his conviction of a greater reward. Like all the heroes of the faith in Hebrews 11, he was never given the full picture of what that reward would be like. However, he trusted God and knew that everything in front of him was temporary—nothing compared to the treasure of choosing God and His plan for his life.

We can rest in knowing that when we take up an identity that is centered on Christ, we will receive our reward in full. Even though we may face difficulty, like all the faithful men and women in Hebrews 11, we can overcome through faith. Look ahead to Jesus, for He is our greatest reward, the treasure that surpasses anything this world can offer.

> Father, give me faith to believe that Your plan for me is greater than anything I could think or choose for myself.

NEVER TOO FAR

When Jonah's warning reached the king of Nineveh, he
rose from his throne, took off his royal robes, covered
himself with sackcloth and sat down in the dust.

JONAH 3:6

Have you ever believed you were too far gone for God to save you? Or perhaps you have a family member or friend who has been walking in sin for years and continues to reject God. It's easy to lose hope in these circumstances. But it's never too hard for God.

Scripture tells us the city of Nineveh was teeming with so much wickedness that Jonah didn't want to even set foot there. If God wanted to destroy it, He had plenty of reasons. Instead, He instructed Jonah to bring the city a message of redemption. With only forty days standing between Nineveh and the wrath of God, Jonah finally delivered the message to the king. God gave the Ninevites the opportunity to repent of their sinfulness and live a life devoted to Him, they obeyed, and the Lord forgave.

Like Jonah, we are now entrusted us with the message of Jesus. Remain steadfast in your demonstration of the gospel to those around you. Be obedient in prayer, and never lose hope. It's never too late, and no one is ever too far gone for God's rescue.

God, thank You for Your great compassion toward the undeserving—all of us. Create in me the willingness to shine the gospel at whatever cost.

THE PROMISE OF REPENTANCE

The Lord is not slow in keeping his promise, as some understand
slowness. Instead he is patient with you, not wanting anyone
to perish, but everyone to come to repentance.

2 PETER 3:9

When God makes promises, He'll keep every single one. He's proven His promise-keeping commitment through the coming of Jesus, and we live confidently in the promise of eternity with Him.

God keeps no records of wrongdoing and extends His kindness to us time and time again. As we repent of sin, God breaks its stronghold on us. Repenting is not just an apology; it's acknowledging the sin in our hearts and turning away from it. Today's verse confirms that God's desire is to make everyone on earth whole and healed by meeting our repentance with the forgiveness and grace of Jesus.

If it seems as if God is being slow with His promise of the return of Jesus—that the world will be made new and we will be with Him—it's not because He is unnecessarily putting it off. He is waiting out of mercy, because He wants all people to be saved. Could He be waiting for us, too, to give the good news of repentance and redemption to as many as possible?

> Jesus, thank You for rescuing me from my sin and for Your patience with humankind. Move my heart to join Yours in longing for everyone's salvation.

CANCELLED DEBT

"Give generously to them and do so without a grudging heart; then because of this the LORD your God will bless you in all your work and in everything you put your hand to. There will always be poor people in the land. Therefore I command you to be openhanded toward your fellow Israelites who are poor and needy in your land."

DEUTERONOMY 15:10–11

Every seven years, God instructed His people to practice a sabbatical year. It was a time when all slaves were set free, all debts were cancelled, and all the needs of the poor were supplied. This practice was a reflection of God's abundant grace and generosity, and a foreshadowing of the most generous debt cancellation in history: through Jesus.

God opened His hand and gave His beloved Son as a divine substitution for the punishment humanity deserved. In this one act, Jesus set humankind free from slavery to sin, released us from the debt we could never pay, rescued us from the pit of poverty, and adorned us with every blessing. Jesus Christ is the revelation of the limitless riches of God's heart of generosity.

Consider the practices of the sabbatical year and the grace lavished on you in Christ Jesus. Have you truly received this gift? If you have, open your hand and give from your abundance. Through it, God will draw the lost to Himself that they too may receive the free riches of His grace.

Jesus, thank You for Your generosity. My hands are open. Show me where I can give.

THE GOOD SAMARITAN

"But a Samaritan, as he traveled, came where the [injured] man
was; and when he saw him, he took pity on him. He went to him and
bandaged his wounds, pouring on oil and wine. Then he put the man
on his own donkey, brought him to an inn and took care of him."

LUKE 10:33–34

During His time on earth, Jesus often used storytelling to teach people about God. His teaching often contradicted the predominant and pride-filled religiosity of Jewish leaders. This story of the good Samaritan is one of Jesus' best-known stories, and it illustrates how we should love and show mercy to others.

To fully understand this story, we need to understand the culture in which it was told. In biblical times, Samaritans were a racially mixed society that worshiped Yahweh, but did not adhere to all the tenants of traditional Judaism. The Jews considered Samaritans the lowest and most unclean of people, and they treated all Samaritans with disdain. So the concept this story offered would have seemed entirely contradictory to them. In Jewish culture, there was no such thing as a good Samaritan.

This, however, is the beauty of the story. Jesus shows us that loving and caring for others is the way to live. He put treatment of others far above observance of religious practices. Jesus came for everyone, and our responsibility is to demonstrate that perfect love and mercy to every person we meet.

Jesus, please give me the desire to proclaim the message of Your saving grace everywhere I go.

FREEDOM TO GIVE

*John answered, "Anyone who has two shirts should share with the one
who has none, and anyone who has food should do the same."*

LUKE 3:11

It's easy to believe our culture's lie that money is life. We can get
so focused on our bank account balance that we become enslaved
to it, no matter how high or low it is. Jesus calls us to a lifestyle of
freedom and generosity, knowing that our hands are easiest to fill
when they are open.

Look at what you have. You may feel like you're broke and
worn out, but regardless of your financial standing, you are rich
in your standing with God. This means you will always have more
than enough! Earthly blessings remind us of His provision, but
they do not last forever.

God might be asking you to give yourself to Him in some
way right now, but you don't hear Him because you're too focused
on the fading things around you—what you have or don't have.
What is God calling you to invest in? Today, look at the things
around you as blessings from God, not as things you have earned
and deserve to keep. Prepare you heart for God's gentle request to
let them go to follow Him. Your generosity may be His means of
providing for another's need.

> Jesus, help us to hold lightly to the things we love, the things
> we value, so that we can run after You with everything we
> are. Shape us into generous servants who give all for Your
> holy name.

LOVE YOUR ENEMIES

"But I tell you, love your enemies and pray for those who persecute you, that you may be children of your Father in heaven. He causes his sun to rise on the evil and the good, and sends rain on the righteous and the unrighteous."

MATTHEW 5:44–45

Loving people who love us back is easy. This is the way much of life goes: giving and receiving based on what is fair and equal. We love our friends and family, but keep our minds and hearts far from people who may hurt us.

Yet Jesus calls us to a way that is not as easy. The way of the Father is marked by grace and mercy toward those who least deserve them. So when we love and pray for those who are against us, we are acting like His children, imitating our Father's actions.

We often don't have to look far to find people who want to hurt us. How can we pray for and serve them even when it seems they don't deserve it? We remember that we once also received grace through Christ even when we were still sinners and enemies of God's perfection. Let's remember that truth as we try to see people the way He sees us, loving them unconditionally and trusting the Father to do what we can't do in their lives.

> Father, give me the grace and courage to love and pray for those who may not do the same for me. I confess that I'm not able to do this in my own power. By Your Spirit, soften my heart toward them.

GLORY IN SUFFERING

Dear friends, do not be surprised at the fiery ordeal that has come on you to test you, as though something strange were happening to you. But rejoice inasmuch as you participate in the sufferings of Christ, so that you may be overjoyed when his glory is revealed.

1 PETER 4:12–13

Suffering is not abnormal in the lives of believers, but we don't have to simply tolerate it until it passes. God is on the move, and He has great plans for our trials. In fact, Scripture tells us our trials should even be considered a gift.

When we suffer, we are given the opportunity to become more like Christ by experiencing what He did. Struggles are a painful pruning process that we often just want to come to an end. But if we are solely focused on regaining our comfort, we can miss the fruit that will come after the pruning. Suffering teaches us to lean on Him for all comfort and provision.

By drawing near to Christ in suffering, a longing grows within us for Him. As our desire for God's glory and presence increases, our desire for things other than Him fades. And this gives us strength to carry on.

Whether or not you are suffering today, it's important to understand how believers can take joy in suffering. Christ's glory eclipses our suffering, bringing incredible joy in every aspect of our trials.

> God, help me draw near to You in my pain. You are my joy, and I am glad to know that my suffering means I get more of You.

361

THE WEIGHT OF WORRY

"But seek first his kingdom and his righteousness, and
all these things will be given to you as well."

MATTHEW 6:33

Worry weighs us down. The reasons are endless; from money to relationships to where we will go in our lives, simply thinking about these things can make life stressful and unenjoyable. This is not the way God meant it to be.

God commands us not to worry. He has taken care of the flowers of the fields and the birds of the air, so we can trust that He will take care of us, His prized creation (Matthew 6:26–30). Instead of being weighed down by the worries of life, God calls us to seek Him above all.

In Matthew 13:44, Jesus said, "The kingdom of God is like a treasure hidden in a field. When a man found it, he hid it again, and then in his joy went and sold all he had and bought that field." That's what Matthew meant by "seek first his kingdom" in today's verse. His kingdom is worth giving everything for, and as we give our all, God gives us everything we really need.

Knowing God's promises gives us the faith and the strength not to worry. God has promised us everything in Christ, so exchange your worries and fears for His peace and treasure. He will supply and exceed your needs.

> Father, give me the faith to trust You with everything I think I need today. I believe that Your thoughts and ways are higher than mine, and Your plan is greater than I can imagine.

KINGDOM AND CALLING

Then I saw another angel flying in midair, and he had the eternal
gospel to proclaim to those who live on the earth—to every nation,
tribe, language and people. He said in a loud voice, "Fear God and give
him glory, because the hour of his judgment has come. Worship him
who made the heavens, the earth, the sea and the springs of water."

Revelation 14:6–7

As Christianity spread throughout the Roman Empire, oppression and persecution of believers increased greatly. Through images of horrible beasts and widespread destruction, John encouraged the churches he wrote to in Revelation to persevere in the faith and proclaim the gospel to all people during those trying times. Despite how frightening these visions were, the promise of the triumphant return of Christ in His glory outweighed them all. His return would be both beautiful and terrifying, a dividing line between the faithful and the rebellious. To those who followed Christ in obedience, His return meant the fulfillment of hope, an eternity spent in the presence of a loving Father. But to those who did not place their faith in Christ as Lord and Savior, judgment and eternal separation from God remained.

We cannot be distracted from our urgent mission to share Christ with the world. Answer the call by testifying to the hope you have in Jesus, and let your life be a witness to the immeasurable worth of a relationship with Him.

Father, use me to build Your kingdom. Empower me to share Your plan for salvation with everyone I meet.

RENEWING PRAISE

I will praise you, Lord, among the nations; I will sing of you among the peoples. For great is your love, reaching to the heavens; your faithfulness reaches to the skies. Be exalted, O God, above the heavens; let your glory be over all the earth.

PSALM 57:9–11

Praise glorifies God while also spreading His name. It affirms His character to us, and proclaims His goodness to the world.

But what is our motivation to praise Him? As we grow in our knowledge of God, we learn about His steadfast love and faithfulness. That leads to an overflowing of praise. This is why David was able to write this psalm of praise to God, even as he hid for his life in a cave. David's suffering led to worship because he found comfort in God's character and plan.

Worshiping God puts your admiration for Him on display. The words and actions that result from an overflowing love spread God's fame, reaching nonbelievers as they observe the joy you have received. Allow your praise and admiration for Christ to shine every day so you can fully participate in God's story. Let Christ's love in you seep out into the world, reaching those who don't know Him.

> Lord, help me grow in my knowledge of You, marveling at Your endless reach and capabilities. Use that knowledge to bring forth genuine praise that can be displayed for those who don't yet know You.

SEEK, CALL, TURN

Seek the LORD while he may be found; call on him while he is near. Let the wicked forsake their ways and the unrighteous their thoughts. Let them turn to the LORD, and he will have mercy on them, and to our God, for he will freely pardon.

ISAIAH 55:6–7

God is not a distant, emotionless, supreme being; He is a Father who cares for His people and can be found by those who seek Him. In fact, not only can He be found, but He is *near*! A personal God in relationship with His people would have been a radical view for the nations of Isaiah's time, and it is still radical and relevant today.

God still wants us to turn toward Him. But what does this seeking, calling, and turning look like? We are instructed to forsake wicked ways and unrighteous thoughts. These aren't prerequisites; these are examples of what actively seeking and calling on God should look like. People are changed by the relationships they are in, and when you're in relationship with God, you will be changed by Him to look more like Him. Therefore, seek this life-changing relationship with God who cares for us as our perfectly loving Father.

> Lord, help me seek and call on You daily. Remove from me all unrighteousness as You train me to be Your child and to be in relationship with You.

GOD'S PROVISION

We are hard pressed on every side, but not crushed; perplexed, but not in despair; persecuted, but not abandoned; struck down, but not destroyed. We always carry around in our body the death of Jesus, so that the life of Jesus may also be revealed in our body.

2 CORINTHIANS 4:8–10

Paul and his companions were constantly persecuted for talking about Jesus. To this day, sharing the gospel is often met with persecution, but God's plans persevere even when we feel like we can't. Earthly suffering produces Christlike strength in us as we learn to trust Him in difficulty.

God works in the contradictions of this world, providing joy in our suffering and affirming His power through our weakness. When all we see is trial and tribulation, God sees hope and freedom. Though we are hard-pressed in our faith, we can rest in the belief that our suffering works for His purposes and our good.

Remember these provisions as you face pressure and persecution when you share the gospel to those who don't believe. The power of Christ is manifested when His death brings new life, and telling others about His power is the most important conversation you can have. Proclaim the defeat of death on the cross to bring life to new believers, and hold fast to the promises of God, remembering that in our weakness His power is made perfect.

> Father, produce in me a desire to share the gospel despite pain and suffering. Use my weakness to display Your power as I persevere.

SING TO THE LORD

Sing to the LORD a new song; sing to the LORD, all the earth. Sing to the LORD, praise his name; proclaim his salvation day after day. Declare his glory among the nations, his marvelous deeds among all peoples.

PSALM 96:1–3

The story of Jesus is good news for all people. David recognized the weight of salvation, and he was so moved by God's grace that he couldn't restrain himself from telling everybody about it. In the same way, we should recognize the weight of salvation in our lives and remember that there are still people who haven't heard it yet. The world is full of people unaware that there is a Savior calling their name, offering eternal life. How can we sing to the Lord so that all will hear?

David starts by singing a "new song." God is doing a fresh, amazing work every day. If we keep our eyes attuned to His work in our lives and in this world, we see more to praise Him for and more to share. David then tells us to "praise his name." Though His list of marvelous works is long, let's keep ascribing to Him, out loud, all the amazing things He is. Then, David instructs us to do this "day after day." It's a continual lifestyle—not just a Sunday practice. Finally, we're told to take this song throughout the world. If we adopt an attitude of willingness to serve God's purposes and plans, God can use us in unimaginable ways to reach others with the gospel.

> God, give me a heart for the lost of the world today. Let others be drawn to You by my song.

PURSUE JUSTICE

How long will you defend the unjust and show partiality to the wicked? Defend the weak and the fatherless; uphold the cause of the poor and the oppressed.

PSALM 82:2–3

Worship and justice go hand in hand. Can we truly worship God without seeking justice in His name?

Throughout the Scriptures, God delivers His people from injustice, and He calls us to imitate Him in this work in today's scripture. Before He gives this command, God implies that we've been standing aside for too long. As His people, we cannot be passive to the world around us when we are called to step into our responsibility. We've been living in complacent satisfaction, but He wants us to move from observers to participators in His grace and love.

To imitate God in giving justice means to treat or represent others with fairness or appreciation. This starts with simply seeing the "weak and the fatherless"—those who cannot defend themselves. Who are those around you in need? Who is being taken advantage of, or has no one to help them?

Not only does our pursuit of justice bring healing to this world, but it also brings us closer to God. When our hearts are leaning toward what moves and breaks His heart, we experience deeper intimacy with God.

God, open my heart to the issues of justice in this world. May my worship of You move me closer to Your heart and mission.

PRAY FOR THE NATIONS

Devote yourselves to prayer, being watchful and thankful. And pray for us, too, that God may open a door for our message, so that we may proclaim the mystery of Christ, for which I am in chains. Pray that I may proclaim it clearly, as I should.

COLOSSIANS 4:2–4

Imagine being in prison. You've lost your freedom and many human comforts. Do you wallow in self-pity? Isolate yourself? Count the days to liberty? Paul, the author of Colossians, chose not to take those routes. Rather, he invested in the prisoners around him, choosing to remain faithful to his call, just as his ancestors were commanded to do many years earlier (Jeremiah 29:4–7).

Paul was willing to do anything to share the gospel: suffer pain, be imprisoned and beaten, and eventually lose his life. Even in our modern world, many Christians undergo adversities similar to Paul's for the sake of the gospel. For those who live in safety, it is easy to forget the plight of our fellow brothers and sisters.

We are called to pray every day for the gospel to be spread among the nations. Pray for your fellow Christians undergoing persecution. Research unreached nations and pray that the gospel is spread within them. Find ways to help and support God's work in those areas. Then thank God for His provision for His people, and be inspired by your fellow Christians to spread the gospel in your own environment.

> Lord, be close to those suffering for Your gospel. Give them joy in the darkness, and let them plant a harvest for You.

BLESSED TO GIVE

In everything I did, I showed you that by this kind of hard work
we must help the weak, remembering the words the Lord Jesus
himself said: "It is more blessed to give than to receive."

ACTS 20:35

We live in a world where excess usually denotes success, and amassing material possessions is admired. But for the follower of Christ, the standard of success is much different: it is not defined by what our hands retain, but by what they release.

At the conclusion of Paul's farewell address to the elders in Ephesus, he sought to remind them that he worked not only to provide for himself, but also for others. For Paul, embodying the Lord's call to give required not only action, but also the sacrifice of hard work.

Today, let's challenge ourselves to believe that a blessed life is found not in what we can accumulate, but in what we can give to others. We should still be responsible with our possessions and money, but with everything we buy and every paycheck we earn, we should keep others in mind. In everything we do, let us be a blessing to those around us, showing them God's mercy through our generosity.

> Father, show me where and how You want me to work hard to help the weak. Redefine my concept of success to center around giving, not accumulating.

YOUR TREASURE

"Fear not, little flock, for it is your Father's good pleasure to give you the kingdom. Sell your possessions, and give to the needy. Provide yourselves with moneybags that do not grow old, with a treasure in the heavens that does not fail, where no thief approaches and no moth destroys. For where your treasure is, there your heart will be also."

LUKE 12:32–34 ESV

Take a minute to evaluate what you worship. Relationships? Grades? Status symbols? Yourself? It's painfully easy to worship things other than Jesus. But materialism is dangerous: it can easily enslave your heart.

We dwell on what we value, and we are bound to what we dwell on. When we treasure success, achievement, money, or recognition, we quickly find ourselves in bondage to these idols. But we don't have to live like this, because Jesus calls us to give up our material treasures for an eternal one: Himself.

Just as materialism is heart bondage, so poverty and injustice are physical bondage. When we generously give to the needy for the good of God's kingdom, we take part in God's purpose for the world: to free creation from the bondage of evil through the love of Christ. In this process, we also free our own hearts to treasure God.

Release the love of things and make Jesus your treasure. He will use your freed heart for good and engage you in His global purposes. Adventure awaits. Will you go?

Jesus, I hand over my earthly loves. You are my treasure!

371

JESUS IS FOR ALL

"For God did not send his Son into the world to condemn
the world, but to save the world through him."
JOHN 3:17

The verse immediately preceding this one, John 3:16, may be the first piece of Scripture you committed to your heart. It says that because God loves us so deeply, He sent His Son to die so all people may have a way to life. Today's verse confirms that He did not send His Son to tell us all how bad we are and how much we deserve hell; He sent Jesus to reconcile us, even when we had no desire to be near Him.

Our own biases about others often distract us from telling them about the life Jesus offers, but Jesus did not come to condemn the world, even the people we think deserve it. He did not pick only the righteous or deserving, because none of us are—on our own. Every single person in this world is dearly loved by Jesus and in desperate need of His love, grace, and mercy.

Labeling others as unworthy of the gospel is a form of judgment. When we place a label on others according to our own prejudice, we exclude them from the story of Jesus. Is there anyone you'd rather avoid at church? Can you think of a group of people that you can't imagine in your church family? If so, go to God in prayer. How can you learn to see everyone as Jesus does—a dearly loved child in need of an eternal Savior?

> Jesus, please give me a heart for the salvation of the world.
> Help me see the people You created as You see them.

HOPE IN SUFFERING

Therefore, since Christ suffered in his body, arm yourselves also with the same attitude, because whoever suffers in the body is done with sin. As a result, they do not live the rest of their earthly lives for evil human desires, but rather for the will of God.

1 PETER 4:1–2

No one likes discomfort. Though we may understand on the surface the idea of "no pain, no gain," our first instinct is often to numb or avoid pain. This instinct to dispel discomfort often distracts us from making much of Jesus. Suffering comes in many forms: from persecution by old friends who are not supportive of a Christ-centered life, to ridicule from popular society. Fighting injustice, speaking against lies, loving others, and seeking to end poverty all require much effort and often personal discomfort— but they give so much gain.

When we are willing to endure such suffering to amplify Jesus, we show that the purpose of our lives is to glorify the Father. When we suffer for Him, we suffer with purpose: to join with Christ and free ourselves from the sins that hold us captive.

Because Christ came to earth, suffered, and defeated sin, we have the power to put to death our selfish desires and accept suffering that comes as we live for God's will and for His gain.

Are you suffering right now for the sake of Christ? Take heart and know that He is with you and will lead you in His will.

Lord, I lay down my desires. Help me follow You through suffering and make Your will more important than my comfort.

373

DEATH DEFEATED

Then Jesus came to them and said, "All authority in heaven and on earth has been given to me. Therefore go and make disciples of all nations, baptizing them in the name of the Father and of the Son and of the Holy Spirit, and teaching them to obey everything I have commanded you. And surely I am with you always, to the very end of the age."

MATTHEW 28:18–20

There can be no doubt that Jesus' authority is the main theme of Matthew's closing. From the beginning of his account, Matthew presents Jesus as having all authority: He fulfills the prophecies, presents the Law, heals the sick, forgives sin, calms the sea, feeds thousands, and walks on water. Peter even called Him the Messiah! Indeed, Jesus had shown He had authority over all things. Death had to swallow Jesus for His ultimate authority to be confirmed. Matthew leads his readers through example after example of Jesus' power in his life, but all this power would come to nothing if He could not defeat death. But here we see Jesus is the victor over death. He has all authority in heaven and earth, and because He defeated death, He is master of all things.

It is because of this authority that we follow and hope in Christ. No other man has proven authority over life and death, except Jesus. Because He lives, we have hope for life too. Let us rest in Jesus' authority, for He's promised us life in Him.

> Thank You, Jesus, for proving Yourself master of all things by defeating death. Lead me to rejoice daily and declare this good news to all people.

FULFILLING WORSHIP

Those who cling to worthless idols turn away from God's love for them.
But I, with shouts of grateful praise, will sacrifice to you. What I have
vowed I will make good. I will say, "Salvation comes from the LORD."
JONAH 2:8–9

Everyone on this earth is a worshiper. If we don't worship Jesus Christ, we will worship an idol masking itself as worthy of our hearts' affections—a shade of what is truly valuable and life-giving. Worship of anything lesser than Jesus has life-threatening consequences, and it will always leave the worshiper emptier than before.

Scripture gives us another option. By pursuing our greatest joy in Jesus, we are gifted with the most fulfilling thing imaginable: God Himself! There is no lasting satisfaction or life found in any other thing.

All worship requires giving and sacrifice. In your pursuit of joy, do you weigh the cost of bowing before anything other than God? In the end, worshiping Jesus will be the only form of worship to give us something in return—joy leading to eternal life with Him. He is worth sacrificing our worthless idols to find this life as we worship Him.

> Jesus, You are eternally worthy of all worship. Show me the lesser objects in my life that rob You of the worship only You deserve.

THE BLESSING FULFILLED

May God be gracious to us and bless us and make his face to shine on us—so
that your ways may be known on earth, your salvation among all nations. . . .
May God bless us still, so that all the ends of the earth will fear him!

PSALM 67:1–2, 7

Blessings are all around us, but what is their purpose?

When God chose to enter into relationship with Abraham, He promised to bless Abraham by protecting and providing for him. In addition, God promised to use Abraham's descendants to bless all the people of the earth. In this covenant relationship, Abraham served and worshiped God wherever he lived, using God's blessings as a witness to both his family and neighbors. Although generations of his family would waver between faithfulness and rebellion, one of Abraham's descendants would finally come to fulfill God's promises. Through the willing sacrifice of His own life, this descendant of Abraham would provide every nation of the world the opportunity to enter into saving relationship with God. His name was Jesus.

Through faith in Jesus, God has blessed us with the opportunity to be involved in His plan of redemption. No matter your circumstances, earnestly thank God for all that He has done and will continue to do in your life. Let your blessings bear witness to the love God has for each of us.

> Father, forgive my selfishness. Let the blessings You have given me be an opportunity to glorify You and invite others into genuine relationship with You.

INTENDED FOR GOOD

But Joseph said to them, "Don't be afraid. Am I in the place of
God? You intended to harm me, but God intended it for good to
accomplish what is now being done, the saving of many lives."
GENESIS 50:19–20

The evil one strategically plans his attacks to steal, kill, and destroy. He draws his bow, launches arrows, and tries to bring people to their knees. Joseph was shot with the arrow of rejection that came from his brothers, the arrow of false accusation from his Egyptian master, and the arrow of abandonment from his peers. But God is not blind to these schemes. He reveals His power and sovereignty by transforming them into glory—for the ultimate good of one and many.

Be encouraged; there is always more to the picture than you can see. God saw Joseph through his trials, knowing that his faithfulness through heartache and despair would give way for him to become a key figure in the freedom that was in store for the Israelites. Have courage amid the pain of a broken heart, gushing wounds, or deep anguish. God sees you, and He sees redemption. He sees beauty coming from your ashes, and not one, but thousands of flowers shooting up from desolate ground. Trust in God; you are not forgotten, and He is working all things out for your eternal good.

Jesus, give me hope to believe the good You're bringing.

A NEW SONG

And they sang a new song, saying: "You are worthy to take the scroll and to open its
seals, because you were slain, and with your blood you purchased for God persons
from every tribe and language and people and nation. You have made them to
be a kingdom and priests to serve our God, and they will reign on the earth."

REVELATION 5:9–10

"And they sang a new song." In Israel's history these words were used to announce a song that commemorated a great victory. Yet the victories Israel attained were always short-lived, making their songs of victory also fleeting. But the song in this passage is not short-lived, for its verses celebrate the final victory of the King. To add to the jubilation, the reference to the book with seals is an allusion to Isaiah 29:11–12, when Israel's sins had brought destruction, making the Israelites unable to know their God. Just as a blind man is unable to read a book, so were the Israelites blinded from seeing and understanding God. But now, through Christ's victory, those who were blind have received sight and are now able to open and read the book.

In the same way, we can rejoice, for we know that Jesus is the hope we have longed for. He has come and has made us co-heirs, royalty in His kingdom, no longer bound to sin, and rescued from death. Let us rejoice! For Christ, who is worthy, has given us sight and made us partakers in His everlasting victory!

> Thank You, God, for being my hope and rescuing me from blindness. Thank You for being the victor, for now I truly can sing a new song.

CONTRIBUTING WRITERS

Passion is deeply grateful for our team of contributing writers, who worked diligently to craft this rich and thoughtful offering to their peers and the church. You truly are the Jesus generation, and God is using you to change the climate of faith around the globe. We are for you. We are behind you. And we love you!

Makenzie Albracht | Amarillo, TX

Emily Albright | Macon, GA

Nicole Allison | Kennesaw, GA

Sara Arizi | New Orleans, LA

Michael Atmar | Houston, TX

Grayson Bingham | McKinney, TX

Noelle Boiano | Flowery Branch, GA

Stephanie Brand | Bowling Green, KY

Cam Buchanan | Hayward, CA

Walker Burns | North Richland Hills, TX

Sidney Carmichael | Margaree Valley, Nova Scotia

Holly Carpenter | Dallas, TX

Kasey Channita | North Bend, WA

Charissa Cox | Miamisburg, OH

Michael Craig | Atlanta, GA

Kaitlyn Crawford | Atlanta, GA

McKenzie Cunningham | Atlanta, GA

Taylor Cunningham | Atlanta, GA

Jake Daghe | Speedway, IN

Josh Dunn | Waco, TX

Josh Ellis | Kennesaw, GA

Andrew English | Flowery Branch, GA

Trey Etter | Shelby, NC

Matt Filer | Marietta, GA

Sean Foley | Marietta, GA

Duncan Fugitt | Edmond, OK

Anna Geary | Oklahoma City, OK

Charlie Grizzle | Birmingham, AL

Karlye Hayes | Douglasville, GA

Ashley Higgins | Olathe, KS

Dustin Hsu | Alpharetta, GA

Adam Hunkler | Fort Wayne, IN

Eric Hunkler | Fort Wayne, IN

Timothy Ibru | Lagos, Nigeria

Emily Ingram | Austin, TX

Jeffrey Johnson | Riverside, CA

Cheyenne Joyce | Tallahassee, FL

Heather Kurtz | Marietta, GA

Megan Legband | Dallas, TX

Todd Linder | Atlanta, GA

Shane McGraw | Naperville, IL

Taylor McMurrin | Orlando, FL

Logan Merkle | McKinney, TX

Maria Miranda | Sevilla, Spain

Conner Monda | Loganville, GA

Steven Murray | Hiram, GA

Kristen O'Neill | Suwanee, GA

Blake Odgers | Covington, GA

Sabrina Park | Atlanta, GA

Beth Phillips | Glen Ellyn, IL

Davis Powell | Columbia, SC

Jeremiah Ravindranath | Baltimore, MD

Christian Rich | Louisville, KY

Jordan Richerson | Sisters, OR

Mary Beth Rickard | Lexington, KY

Libby Rogers | Huntsville, TX

Abby Shover | Quincy, IL

Maisie Slomkowski | Woodstock, GA

Elijah Tanner | Keller, TX

Emily Thomas | Mt. Airy, GA

Mark Thompson | Juliette, GA

Abigail Timbol | Douglasville, GA

Maria Van Den Akker | Pune, IN

Ashley Waters | Silsbee, TX

Abigail Williams | Blue Ridge, GA

Jonny Williams | San Pedro Sula, Honduras

Jordan Woodsen | Hoschton, GA

Yana Yaroshevich | Sacramento, CA

SCRIPTURE INDEX